WISDOM AND SPIRIT

An Investigation of
1 Corinthians 1.18-3.20
Against the Background of
Jewish Sapiential Traditions
in the Greco-Roman Period

James A. Davis

**UNIVERSITY
PRESS OF
AMERICA**

LANHAM • NEW YORK • LONDON

ISBN (Perfect): 0-8191-4211-5
ISBN   (Cloth): 0-8191-4210-7

θεῷ πᾶσα τιμὴ καὶ δόξα

iv

PREFACE AND ACKNOWLEDGEMENTS

This book came into existence originally as a doctoral thesis completed at Nottingham University in 1982. It is presented here very much as it appeared then with, however, several minor alterations and additions. I hope these changes will reflect the fact that I continue to be interested in the manifestation of wisdom at Corinth, and continue to profit from the reactions of others to my work and my own interaction with theirs. In connection with this, the reader should be alert to the fact that much of the scholarly dialogue of this work is carried on, as it inevitably is, within the notes.

The acquistion of wisdom, as I have been reminded so often during the course of my work, is never simply a result of one's own efforts. It is a pleasure, therefore, for me to gratefully acknowledge those persons and organizations whose aid and assistance has contributed to the completion of this book. First, I should like to recognize Professor James D.G. Dunn, whose wise counsel guided my thesis work from start to finish. His gracious encouragement carried it along, and his penetrating and perceptive criticisms saved it from many errors. To him I am, and shall always remain, most profoundly grateful. To be enabled financially to undertake research is, in itself, a distinct privelege, and for it I am indebted to the Rotary Foundation and the Tyndale Fellowship whose generous grants made my experience happily possible. In the task of turning a thesis into a book I would be remiss if I did not ackowledge the patient and competent secretarial assistance of June Powers and the support of Trinity Episcopal School for Ministry. Above all, however, come my thanks to my father who dedicated so much of his life to the support and encouragement of his son; to my mother who continues to do so to this day; to my wife, Ruth, whose love, patience, assurance, and willing help have consistently sustained her husband throughout his endeavors; and, pre-eminently, to Him in whom and from whom is all wisdom, knowledge, and understanding.

Easter, 1984   James A. Davis

TABLE OF CONTENTS

INTRODUCTION

In an important and influential article published
in 1964 under the title, "Christianity at Corinth",
C.K. Barrett attempted to sketch out something of the
nature and content of the Corinthian beliefs that form
the underlying contextual background behind Paul's
first letter to that church.[1] Significantly, at least
for our purposes, Barrett begins his assessment by indicating that an analysis of the concepts of σοφία and
γνῶσις should occupy a central position in any attempt
to define the character of Corinthian Christianity.

> "No problem arising out of Christianity at
> Corinth has been more discussed during re-
> cent years than that which is suggested by
> these words. In what sense were they used
> at Corinth? What theological presupposi-
> tions and theological systems lie behind
> them? How far was Paul himself prepared to
> use this terminology and adopt the systems
> and presuppositions involved".[2]

Such questions assuredly manage to sharpen the issues, but they are far more easily asked than answered.
Even a casual review of the existing literature produced since the appearance of Barrett's essay is sufficient to uncover the fact that questions about σοφία
and γνῶσις have continued to occupy a leading position
at the forefront of research concerned with Corinthian
Christianity right up to the present. Accordingly,
these same difficult but crucial questions about the
dimensions and contours of the Corinthians' wisdom and
knowledge have provided an impetus for the present investigation as well.

Scholarship focusing upon these issues has almost
always proceeded in the course of its analysis upon the
basis of an assumption that material deriving from the
Corinthians becomes visible as careful attention is
paid to the ironical and polemical statements made
throughout 1 Corinthians, and especially in 1 Co 1-4.[3]
For in this way a number of words and phrases may be
discovered that are either clearly the focus of Pauline
criticism, or are uncharacteristic of Paul's own mode
of expression. Such terminology, it is generally
agreed, forms the best evidence that can be obtained
with regards to the Corinthians' own positions.[4]

However, this material has been subjected to a
number of interpretations as it has been placed against
different religio-historical backgrounds in an attempt

to draw together the various bits of evidence and ar-
rive at a clear and unified conception of the Corinthian σοφία.[5]   Some, for example, have regarded the evidence and the respect for wisdom at Corinth as pro-
ducts of an over-admiration among the members of the
community for the ideas, and especially the eloquence
associated with Hellenistic philosophy and rhetoric.[6]
Serious consideration of this suggestion, however, has
persuaded most that the proposal does not do complete
justice to the totality and variety of the terminology
that appears to have been in use at Corinth.

     A concerted attempt has been made recently, there-
fore, to revive the argument that contends that the
Corinthian terminology and the predilection for wisdom
at Corinth are most adequately understood as expressions of a more or less fully developed Gnosticism.[7]
Such a hypothesis certainly attempts at least to treat
the evidence comprehensively, but it also seriously
begs the historical and chronological questions associated with the postulation of a relatively mature form
of 'pre-Christian Gnosticism'.[8]   Indeed, as R. McL.
Wilson has indicated, to proceed on the basis of this
assumption,

> "to interpret the teaching of Paul's oppo-
> nents by a wholesale introduction of ideas
> from the second century (gnostic) systems
> is to run the risk of seriously distorting
> the whole picture".[9]

The amount of distortion that can be imported in this
way has been shown up quite clearly by Birger Pearson
and Richard Horsley in separate studies of the
πνευματικός and ψυχικός terminology of 1 Co 2.[10] Pearson's work in particular points out plainly, by means
of a comparative analysis, just how far the evidence in
regards to the Corinthians' views stands apart from the
use of parallel terminology and phraseology in later
gnostic literature. We concur, therefore, with him
that to speak of 'Gnosticism at Corinth' is to define
the term so broadly in relation to its later development as to render the word of little value in specify-
ing the particular significance and meaning which the
Corinthians may have accorded to their terminology at
the time that it was being used by them.[11]
     In the course of criticism concerning the validity
and usefulness of the gnostic hypothesis, however, a
third alternative background has been put forward.
This proposal, associated especially with the works of

4

Pearson and Horsley, has sought to draw attention to the pertinent parallel material to be found within Hellenistic Jewish wisdom literature. The researches of these two scholars have served to show that the gnostic hypothesis is most convincing when it utilizes evidence and material drawn from these pre-Christian sapiential sources. Furthermore, their studies have persuasively demonstrated that there is both a considerable breadth and depth of parallel terminology to be found within the wisdom sources.[12]

In this thesis, therefore, an endeavor will be made to carry forward the promising work begun by Horsley and Pearson in two ways. First of all, by broadening the scope of our inquiry, we shall try to determine whether or not affinities exist between the Hellenistic Jewish wisdom literature utilized in the studies of Horsley and Pearson, and Palestinian Jewish sapiential thought as represented in the Book of Sirach and the principal documents from Qumran. Second, by enlarging the focus of investigation once more, an attempt will be made to test the hypothesis that the whole of 1 Co 1.18-3.20, and not just certain parts of it, may be convincingly, coherently, and consistently interpreted over against the background of early post-Biblical Jewish wisdom.

5

CHAPTER ONE

WISDOM AND SPIRIT IN THE BOOK OF SIRACH

1.1 Introduction

Writing from Jerusalem in or around 180 BCE,[1] Joshua ben Sira ben Eleazar[2] composed a book intended to provide its readers with instruction in understanding, knowledge, and wisdom.[3] In and of itself, the aim of ben Sira's work was neither new nor highly original within the historical context of Jewish wisdom.[4] What distinguishes him from his sapiential predecessors and gives his writings both originality and importance, however, are his views concerning the relationship between wisdom and the law. In a recent introduction to Jewish wisdom literature, James Crenshaw has saliently and usefully summarized the nature of ben Sira's distinctiveness in comparison with previous sapiential thought.

> "The theophany within the Book of Job bears eloquent testimony to an awareness that the experience of the living God belonged to the essence of any authentic search for knowledge. Sirach advanced beyond this cautious acknowledgment to a bold proclamation that true wisdom was hidden in the Mosaic law. The consequences of this conviction were far-reaching; in a word, they achieved a significant transition within wisdom."[5]

The strength of this analysis lies in the recognition that there is both continuity and discontinuity between the Book of Sirach and earlier Jewish wisdom. To agree with Crenshaw's assessment concerning the transitional significance of Sirach is not, then, to deny that there is obviously a considerable amount of traditional aphoristic wisdom in the work of ben Sira.[6] Neither does agreement entail a denial of the existence of valid and important precedents in earlier Judaism for the association that is made by ben Sira between wisdom and Torah,[7] or imply that this association exhausts what may be said to be innovative and distinctive in Sirach.[8] Assent does, however, enable us to pinpoint a principal theme within Sirach[9] which seems, from all indications, to have been comparatively new in its emphasis,[10] and of considerable significance both for ben Sira, and for those who succeeded him.[11]

As such, it is also a theme which is important to our investigation into the nature of wisdom, and the relationship between wisdom and spirit in the sapiential literature of Judaism in the Hellenistic-Roman period. In particular, it seems valuable to our inquiry to ask whether or not the new stress upon nomistic wisdom in Sirach caused any appreciable shift in thought with regard to the mediation and obtaining of wisdom. Older sapiential sources had often drawn conclusions about the universal accessibility of wisdom, and the common capability of humanity to achieve its possession through instruction and inquiry.[12] With the narrowing emphasis upon nomistic wisdom in Sirach however, is it possible to observe any related changes with regards to the process by which wisdom was thought to be gained? To put the question directly; did ben Sira's link between wisdom and law lead him in any way towards the establishment of a corresponding connection between wisdom and spirit?

We propose to address this question in the first instance by taking another look at some of the dimensions of the link forged by ben Sira between wisdom and Torah. On the basis of these findings, we will then turn our attention towards the question of the relationship between wisdom and spirit in Sirach concentrating our investigation upon an analysis of Sir 39.6 in its literary context. Finally, we will consider briefly some of the benefits associated with the possession of wisdom in the mind of ben Sira.

1.2 The 'Book of the Covenant' and the Locus of Wisdom: The Relationship between Wisdom and Law in the Book of Sirach.

"Wisdom will praise herself, and will glory in the midst of her people. 2) In the assembly of the Most High she will open her mouth, and in the presence of his host she will glory: 3) "I came forth from the mouth of the Most High, and covered the earth like a mist. 4) I dwelt in high places, and my throne was in a pillar of cloud. 5) Alone I have made the circuit of the vault of heaven and have walked in the depths of the abyss."... 23) All this is the book of the covenant of the Most High God, the law which Moses commanded us as an inheritance for the congregations of Jacob. 25) It fills men with wisdom like the Pishon, and like the Tigris at the time of first fruits. 26) It makes them full of understanding like the Euphrates, and like

10

the Jordan at harvest time.   27) It   makes
instruction   shine forth   like   light, like
the Gihon at the time of vintage."
                    -Sirach 24.1-5, 23-27

     In two   important and   influential   works,   Johann
Marböck has sought to show that there is more   than one
echo of the older sapiential stress upon the universal-
ity of wisdom in Sirach.[13]   The association   of wisdom
and creation motifs in   Sir 1.10   and 24.6, as   well as
the mention   of wisdom   in connection with   'all flesh'
and 'every people   and nation' in these same   verses is
evidence to   Marböck that the   particularistic emphases
of Sir 1.14, 16,   18-20 and 24,23-27 are balanced   by a
more traditional universalism.[14]

     However, together with E.P. Sanders, we must diss-
ent from the opinion that 'universalism'   and 'particularism' are of equal concern to ben Sira.[15]   For in Sir
1 and 24, the two principal passages adduced by Marbock
in an attempt to substantiate his thesis, it seems much
more probable to conclude that the   universalistic element has been introduced into the context   for apologetic and/or polemical purposes.[16]

     In Sir 1.10   for instance, it is easily   seen that
the wisdom that 'dwells with all flesh' is   only actualized and   brought   to life   for ben   Sira   through the
'fear of the   Lord'; that   is, as each   individual ach-
ieves an attitude consistent with, and fostered   by the
pious observance of the law.[17]   Similarly, in   chapter
24, the wisdom that has 'acquired a possession in every
people and nation'   is nonetheless still said to   be in
search of a 'resting-place' (24.7), and her   hospice is
found, according to 24.8-12 and 24.23, among God's covenant people   Israel, in   the 'book   of   the covenant';
that is, within the law itself.   So in Sir 1 and 24 we
do not, in fact, find a balance   between "universalism"
and   "particularism', but   rather an argument   that the
universal   wisdom inherent within   the divinely-created
order has been emodied in, and, at least in some sense,
superseded by   the wisdom of the law.[18]   Ben Sira himself summarizes this argument in Sir 1.26.

          "If you   desire wisdom,   keep   the command-
          ments,   and the   Lord will   supply   it   for
          you."

     Sirach 1 and 24, however, are by no means the only
passages in the book to express this conviction concer-

11

ning the relation between wisdom (σοφία) and law (νόμος). The strength of ben Sira's belief and its importance for his thought is equally apparent from the reappearance of this relation throughout the body of the book.[19] In Sir 6.37, for example, an admonition is found which both relies upon and bolsters the connection.

> "Reflect on the statues of the Lord, and meditate at all times on his commandments. It is he who will give insight to your mind and your desire for wisdom will be granted."

A comparable sentiment is expressed in Sir 15.1 following an exhortation to all to 'encamp under (Lady) wisdom's boughs' (14.26).

> "The man who fears the Lord will do this, and he who holds to the law will obtain her."

Finally, in Sir 29.9, ben Sira's understanding of the relationship between traditional wisdom and nomistic wisdom may be seen to be epitomized within the context of a single verse.

> "Help a poor man for the commandment's sake, and because of his need do not send him away empty."

Here the older gnomistic wisdom has been refounded upon a new nomistic basis. Ben Sira has intentionally redefined the established value of a well known sapiential axiom in terms of the Mosaic legislation, and in so doing has demonstrated the existence and the completeness of the merger between wisdom and law in his thinking.[20]

The extent to which law and wisdom are integrated and amalgamated within Sirach may also be illustrated in another way. The wisdom of ben Sira discloses a full acquaintance with, and in many instances, an interpretative reliance upon the law.[21] This is most obvious in Sir 44.1-49.16, a section written expressly in praise of the wisdom disclosed within Israel's history.[22] Allusions to Pentateuchal history are also frequent elsewhere, however, especially in relation to the lives of the patriarchs and the events associated

12

with them.[23] Furthermore historical narrative is not
the only part of the developing canonical tradition to
influence Sirach. Indeed, in the view of Robert
Pfeiffer, ben Sira;

> "discloses an expert knowledge (cf. 39.1)
> of the Mosaic legislation in all of its as-
> pects: ritual prescriptions (7.31; 45.6-
> 26; 50; etc.), moral and religious precepts
> (3.1-16; 3.30-4.10; 7.26f; 18.22f; 19.13-
> 17; 20.24f; 29.1,9). and civil legislation
> (7.6 cf. Lev 9.15; 41.19b, 20b, 21bc;
> etc.)."[24]

Finally, from statements in Sir 39.1 and 49.10, it
seems probable to deduce that the remaining two divisions of the Hebrew canon also informed the reflective
sapiential activity of ben Sira.[25] From all of this
one gathers that it was the law in its totality which
functioned for ben Sira as a guide to wisdom.

Consequently the identification of the law with
wisdom may be regarded as complete within Sirach. For
whether one examines the two concepts on the basis of
the explicit statements made in Sir 1 and 24 concerning
the embodiment of wisdom within the law, or gives attention to other allusions concerning the relationship
between law and wisdom, or chooses to address the issue
by investigating ben Sira's own practice, the conclusion is still the same. For ben Sira, the law is the
locus of wisdom, the place where wisdom may, at last,
be found; (cp. Job 28.12, 20 and Sir 1.6).

It is important, however, to observe that this
identification does not preclude the search for wisdom
in Sirach, nor relieve any individual of the obligation
to seek it out.[26] Indeed, in ben Sira's estimation, an
understanding of the link between law and wisdom leads
in precisely the opposite direction. For if the law is
the locus of wisdom, then the search for wisdom begins
in earnest with the study and interpretation of the
law. The evidence to indicate that ben Sira has drawn
this deduction may be set forward, initially at least,
by pointing to the way in which the traditional sapiential concept of instruction is modified and adapted in
the course of his writing.

That ben Sira makes use of the idea of instruction, or παιδεία within his work is not surprising giv-
en the powerful precedent set by prior wisdom litera-

ture which characteristically drew connections between
the notion of instruction and any talk of obtaining
wisdom.[27] However, within Sirach, on at least two occasions, one becomes aware that the meaning of παιδεία
is being subtly shifted so as to bring the definition
of this term into closer correspondence with the new
nomistic understanding of σοφία. This tendency is discernable, first of all, in Sir 24.27 where instruction
is not defined with respect to the broad advice of traditional wisdom, or the learned counsel of the sage,
but instead is associated with the law; for it is the
law that "makes instruction shine forth like light".

The same sort of thought is brought to expression
a second time in Sir 39.8, however, where it is said
that the one who devotes himself to the study of the
law and its wisdom, "will reveal instruction in his
teaching, and will glory in the law of the Lord's covenant."[28] Instruction then, in these two instances, is
no longer being used by ben Sira to denote the kind of
gnomic, or aphoristic teaching that may be drawn from
the store of a universal experiential knowledge. Instead, in much the same way as σοφία, the concept of
intruction, and the role of the wise man are being
brought under the influence of ben Sira's nomistic piety. Instruction is being associated with the law, and
the sage with the one who studiously devotes himself to
its meaning.[29]

This understanding of παιδεία, of the role of the
wise man, and of the link between the search for wisdom
and the interpretation of the law in Sirach receives
further support from the prologue where ben Sira's
thought has received an early and important interpretation.

> "Whereas many great teachings have been gi-
> ven to us through the law and the prophets
> and the others that followed them, on ac-
> count of which we should praise Israel for
> instruction and wisdom; and since it is
> necessary not only that the readers them-
> selves should acquire understanding but al-
> so that those who love learning should be
> able to help the outsiders by both speaking
> and writing, my grandfather Jesus, after
> devoting himself especially to the reading
> of the law and the prophets and the other
> books of our fathers, and after acquiring
> considerable proficiency in them was him-

self also led to write something pertaining
to instruction and wisdom, in order that,
by becoming conversant with this also,
those who love learning should make even
greater progress in living according to the
law."

Here, in an obvious attempt to extract the full
apologetic value from the wisdom-law association for
the sake of his readership, the grandson of Jesus ben
Sira has provided an eloquent testimony to the significant transition effected upon the idea of instruction
and the function of the sage by his grandfather's
work.[30] Both are now linked in an absolute and exclusive way with the law. Instruction, like wisdom is defined by means of a relationship to the law, and both
παιδεία and σοφία are treated as the results of ben
Sira's study of the law. The work of the sage and the
goal of instruction is thereby made clear.[31] An understanding of the law is that which is taught so that
each individual may learn to order his life according
to the divine will. Thus, although demonstrably later
than the rest of the Book of Sirach, the prologue still
witnesses to the continuing relevance of the links between wisdom and law, between instruction and interpretation, between sage and Torah student for a later gen-
eration, and to the source of these links in the teaching of Jesus ben Sira.

Passing back to the original composition, we wish
finally to notice two other passages within the Book of
Sirach that accord with the wisdom-law affiliation and
with the inference that the quest for wisdom is to be
pursued through the understanding and interpretation of
the law. The first of these is Sir 14.20-21.

"Blessed is the man who meditates on wisdom
and who reasons intelligently. He who reflects in his mind on her ways will also
ponder her secrets."

The following context (15.1) makes it clear that we are
meant to read ben Sira's words here, concerning personified wisdom, with reference to the law. Within that
context, however, the blessing pronounced upon the individual who reflects, or meditates upon wisdom may be
seen, in actuality, to be a blessing pronounced upon
the person who diligently pursues the study of the law.
Likewise, perhaps, the mention of wisdom's secrets
within this setting may be intended by ben Sira as an

15

allusion to things hidden in the law.[32]   A second passage appears to confirm these interpretations.   In Sir
39.7 we   find   the wise   man characterized   as   one who
"meditates on God's secrets".[33]   Once more the affirmation of continuity between wisdom and the law   is present   within the   immediate context   (39.8),   and   once
again, therefore,   it seems we are meant   to understand
ben Sira's words with reference to the study and interpretation   of the law.[34]   The sage   is the one who reflects upon the   meaning of   the law;   (cp.   Sir 39.3).
Taken together   with the   evidence of Sir   24.27, 39.8,
and the prologue therefore, Sir 14.20-21 and 39.7 reinforce the connection between the search for   wisdom and
the study of the law in Sirach.[35]

    We may summarize the results of this brief account
of the   relationship between   wisdom and law   in Sirach
with a quotation from Gerald Sheppard's book, Wisdom as
a Hermeneutical Construct.   Towards the   close of   his
analysis,   Sheppard observes   that   the   identification
made by ben Sira between wisdom and Torah in   Sir 24.23
is "both a promise and a hermeneutical   statement – the
Torah can be read as a guide to wisdom and resides as a
unique   possession of   Israel".[36]   Sheppard's two-fold
assertion both encapsulates and substantiates our findings.   For Sirach,   the law has become the   definitive
locus,   the consummate embodiment of   wisdom.   Consequently,   the   search for wisdom proceeds in   his advice
and work   through the   study and interpretation of the
law.

1.3 The 'Spirit of Understanding' and the   Mediation of
    Wisdom: The Relationship between Wisdom and Spirit
    in the Book of Sirach.

        "On the   other hand   he   who   devotes
    himself to the study of the law of the Most
    High will   seek out   the wisdom of   all the
    ancients, and will be concerned with proph-
    ecies; 2) he will preserve the discourse of
    notable men and penetrate the subtleties of
    parables; 3) he will seek out the hidden
    meanings of proverbs and be at home with
    the obscurities of parables. 4) He   will
    serve among great men and appear before
    rulers; he will travel through the lands of
    foreign nations, for he tests the good and
    the evil among men. 5) He   will set his
    heart to rise early to seek the   Lord who
    made him, and will make supplication before

16

the Most High; he will open his mouth in
prayer and make supplication for his sins.
6) If the great Lord is willing, he will be
filled with the spirit of understanding; he
will pour forth words of wisdom and give
thanks to the Lord in prayer. 7) He will
direct his counsel and knowledge aright,
and meditate on his secrets. 8) He will
reveal instruction in his teaching, and
will glory in the law of the Lord's covenant. 9) Many will praise his understanding and it will never be blotted out; his
memory will not disappear, and his name
will live through all generations. 10)
Nations will declare his wisdom, and the
congregation will proclaim his praise; 11)
if he lives long, he will leave a name
greater than a thousand, and if he goes to
rest, it is enough for him.

-Sirach 39.1-11

Sirach 39.1-11 is a key text in terms of ben
Sira's understanding of the role and work of the
sage.[37] As such, it tells us a good deal about how he
thought wisdom was actually obtained, and an important
part in the process is played, according to Sir 39.6,
by God himself. But before we come to consider this
thought more carefully, it will be well for us to place
this verse within its literary context by giving attention to the contents of Sir 39.1-5.[38]

The passage begins by way of contrast, differen-
tiating the scribe (Sir 38.24) from all of the other
workers and craftsmen (38.31) who demonstrate their
skill and ability in the course of their labor.[39] The
scribe is distinguished from such artisans by way of a
total vocational devotion to the study of the law
(39.1). At the head of this section then, ben Sira may
be seen to reiterate and reaffirm the close relationship between wisdom and the law. The law is the locus
of wisdom and the pursuit of wisdom is undertaken by
means of its study.

But in Sir 39.1b and c, two further sources, 'the
wisdom of all the ancients', and 'prophecies' are named
alongside the law in conjunction with the scribe's inquiry. These, however, are probably not to be construed as additional sources, independent of the law. Instead, in their present setting, the two expressions

17

are more likely indications that the scribe's study is
not to be confined or restricted, in ben Sira's opinion, to an examination of the Mosaic Torah alone.   The
wisdom seeker's research should include the developing
canonical corpus of prophecy and writings as well.[40]

The following two verses are somewhat more ambiguous. Do they indicate that the quest for wisdom inevitably carries the scribe back beyond the literary and
canonical boundaries established in Sir 39.1 to the
broader store of secular wisdom?[41] Or do they refer
instead to the inception of evolving Jewish traditions
concerned with the 'haggadic' and 'halakic' interpretation of the law?[42]   The choice is difficult, but may,
in the end, slightly favor the latter suggestion in
light of Sir 39.2a.   For the words διήγησιν ἀνδρῶν...
are, in all likelihood, a reference to oral interpretative tradition, 'the sayings of famous men', which were
handed down by ben Sira and other scribal sages of his
era until the time of their collation and codification
in tractates such as Pirke Aboth.[43]   The specific mention of 'proverbs' (παροιμιῶν; 39.3a), and 'parables'
(παραβολῶν; 39.2b, 3b) also accords with this judgment
since these are precisely the forms that are most common within the later rabbinical anthologies.   Thus Sir
39.2-3 broadens the sage's scope of inquiry, but not in
such a way as to diminish the central significance of
the law.[44]   Instead, the association between them is
strengthened by the encouragement to the scribe to make
full use of those interpretative traditions whose value
is recognized in his own attempt to obtain wisdom
through the study of the law.

The endeavor to obtain a more complete comprehension of nomistic wisdom is not solely a matter of study
however, for in Sir 39.4 the reader is told how the
scribe's grasp upon wisdom is to be strengthened and
enlightened through practice. His understanding of the
law and its wisdom is brought to maturity in his service among leaders and rulers, and in his travels among
the nations as he learns to decide upon the 'good' and
the 'evil' in line with its guidance.[45]

Up to this point in the passage, ben Sira has
placed an observable emphasis upon human effort in relation to the acquisition of wisdom.   Wisdom is to be
found in the law (39.1); through study (39.2-3) and
practice (39.4) its wisdom may be gained. But in Sir
39.5 this perspective begins to change as talk of
'prayer' (προσευχῇ) and 'supplication' (δεηθήσεται) in-

trudes into the discussion of the scribe's occupations. These terms conspicuously, if implicitly, presume that divine grace plays an important part in the obtaining of wisdom. but the idea they express seems, for the modern reader at least, to stand in some tension to the emphasis of the previous verses. Is wisdom in Sirach acquired by means of diligent study and reflection, or is it all, in the end, simply a matter of God's gift?

It is doubtful that the question would have occurred to ben Sira in this form, nor would he, in all probability, have understood the talk of tension in relation to human effort and divine grace. For him one suspects that the two ideas were not only compatible, but essentially complementary.[46] They could and should be set side by side in a discussion about the acquisition of wisdom.[47] As his previous comments have accented anthropocentric responsibility in relation to the obtaining of wisdom, so ben Sira's thought naturally turns in verse 5 to a balancing stress upon the indispensability of divine assistance.

The notion of wisdom as God's gift, a prominent motif elsewhere in the Book of Sirach,[48] is here allowed to remain just beneath the surface as ben Sira makes the transition from human activity (39.1-4) to the gracious action of God (39.6) via the reference to prayer.[49] And, for a second time, (as before in Sir 39.1), the scribe is placed in contrast to others; (cp. 39.5 and 38.24). He not only distinguishes himself by his studious pursuit of wisdom, but also by means of his expanded commitment to the prayerful search for the gift of wisdom; (cp. Sir 51.13). In this quest, moreover, special attention is to be paid to the need for supplication in regards to one's own sin; (39.4a). For the gift of wisdom, as other references make clear, comes only to the righteous (Sir 43.33), to those individuals who purify themselves in order that they might receive it; (51.20).

We are now in a position to assess the meaning and significance of Sirach 39.6. The importance of the verse lies not only in its contents but also in relation to its function in terms of the logic and flow of thought within the passage as a whole. Indeed verse six may be seen upon inspection to be something of a pivotal point. All of the activity, the training and study described in the five previous verses has been undertaken in the attempt of the scribe to acquire complete wisdom. He has made, as it were, every effort to obtain as much insight as possible from diligent study (39.1-3), and, desirous of still further understanding, he has sought to place himself firmly within the sphere of special divine favor; (39.5). In Sirach 39.6 we find ben Sira's account of the divine response to such efforts.

It is of equal significance, however to note that the succeeding verses of this section proceed logically and directly from the affirmation of verse 6 to speak of the scribe's service to his people, clearly presuming that the superlative wisdom sought so persistently has now become the scribe's possession. By placing verse 6 in between the descriptions of 39.1-5 and 39.7-11 then, ben Sira has given added importance to the point made within the verse, namely that the quest for wisdom is only brought to fulfillment and completion by the entrance of a 'spirit of understanding', that is, by an experience of divine, spiritual inspiration.

The close connection of verses 1-5 with the affirmation of verse 6 shows that ben Sira has in mind an experience which brings an understanding and wisdom beyond that which is possible for the created spirit of any man to obtain.[50] Even the gifted man of extraordinary natural capacity whose created intelligence has been honed by continuous theoretical and practical study (39.1-4) must still come to 'the Most High' and 'make supplication' (39.5). For the experience described in Sir 39.6 is clearly a matter of divine perogative alone; ('if the great Lord is willing'). Subsequent then to the gracious activity of God in the creation of the individual, the experience described by ben Sira takes place only after man's native intelligence has been brought to maturity, and only if a particular individual is made the object of special divine attention and favor.[51]

This perspective must also affect the way in which we understand the nature of the spirit which the sage is said to receive.[52] To be πληρῶθες πνεῦμα συνέσεως is to be filled with a spirit whose presence is not native to man, a spirit whose origin springs rather from God's presence and initiative. It follows then the πνεῦμα συνέσεως is to be identified not only with its recipient, but also with its source. Πνεῦμα συνέσεως is a spirit which comes from without to reside within. It is a spirit alien but amenable to the scribe prepared by his study of the law and purified by his repentance. It is a 'spirit of wisdom' which comes from God

20

and fills the scribe of his choosing.53

Further it is only consequent upon an experience of the inspiration of this spirit that a transition takes place, and the scribe who previously has sought out wisdom now becomes the sage whose possession of wisdom is readily apparent to all; (39.6b, 9-10). Just as the scribe is distinguished from other men therefore by his diligent pursuit of wisdom, so the truly wise man is set apart from the scribe by the experience of spiritual inspiration described in Sir 39.6.54

Hence we are presented in Sir 38.24-39.11 with the rough outlines of a discussion concerned with different levels, or different stages in relation to the acquisition and attainment of wisdom.55 On a first level are all of those individuals who are engaged in traditional vocations; (Sir 38.25-35). Each of them is skillful at their work, but, in ben Sira's estimation, their wisdom is negligible.56 At a second level is the scribe who devotes himself to the study and practice of the law, to prayer, and to the maintenance of covenantal righteousness; (39.1-5).57 The ultimate plateau of sapiential achievement is attained, however, only by the sage upon whom God freely and willingly pours out his 'spirit of understanding'; (39.6-11.)58 A stratification of individuals in relation to wisdom is thus apparent in Sir 38.24-39.11.

Against this background, the relationship between wisdom and spirit in Sir 39.6 takes on its proper prominence. It was not entirely new however, for earlier talk about wisdom had occasionally drawn connections between the acquisition of wisdom and the entrance of a spirit sent from God.59 In Exod 31.3 LXX, for example, we are told that God "filled" Bezaleel ben Urias ben Or with πνεῦμα θεῖον σοφίας καὶ συνέσεως καὶ ἐπιστήμης so that he might exercise skill and ability in his role as a craftsman; (cp. Exod 35.31). In Deut 34.9 LXX Joshua is similarly said to have been 'filled' with πνεύματος συνέσεως at the time of his succession to Israel's leadership. And a final liaison is uncovered in Isa 11.2 LXX; for upon the "shoot that will spring forth from the root of Jesse" there will rest, according to the prophet, πνεῦμα σοφίας καὶ συνέσεως.

Ben Sira, however, may be said to have advanced the relationship considerably and uniquely by relating both wisdom and spirit to the law. In order to under-

21

stand the association between wisdom and spirit in Sirach, one must begin with the sequence of thought that proceeds from the wisdom-law link. Wisdom is embodied in the law; yet wisdom is still to be sought. The law must be studied, interpreted, and understood if wisdom is to be gained. But to study the law in such a way as to come to a full comprehension of its meaning presupposes, for ben Sira, the aid and assistance of the spirit of understanding sent from God.[60] Thus ben Sira's conception of nomistic wisdom is closely related to the affirmation of Sir 39.6. By equating σοφία and νόμος, ben Sira united the content and locus of wisdom to the law. By relating παιδεία to nomistic wisdom and scriptural study, he linked the search for wisdom to the interpretation of the law. Finally, in Sir 39.6, by bringing both of these notions into connection with a notion of divine inspiration through the spirit of understanding sent from God, he linked ultimate success in the pursuit of the wisdom of the law to the help and collaboration of the spirit.

Sir 39.6b-11 goes on now to narrate the consequences of the sage's experience of inspiration in terms that confirm its nomistic and interpretative character. The illumined sage "pours forth words of wisdom",[61] and "meditates on God's secrets".[62] He "reveals instruction in his teaching", and "glories in the law of God's covenant".[63] The people laud "his understanding", and the "congregation proclaims his praise".[64] All of these different expressions indicate that the encounter with the spirit of understanding not only derives from (Sir 39.1-5), but also contributes to (Sir 39.6b-11), the sage's insight into the wisdom of the law.[65]

Sirach 39.6 and its reference to the spirit of understanding should not, therefore, be understood or interpreted in isolation from the nomistic piety of the rest of the book. The 'word of wisdom' both originates from, and is directed towards an understanding of the meaning of the law, and so may not be easily or simply equated with a more direct and independently authoritative 'prophetic word'.[66] Such an identification has sometimes been suggested on the strength of Sir 24.30-34, a passage in which ben Sira, caught up in the joy of his own learning, seems to assert a prophetic claim on behalf of his teaching.

"I went forth like a canal from a river and like a water channel into a garden. 31) I

22

said, 'I will water my orchard and drench
my garden plot'; and lo, my canal became a
river, and my river became a sea. 32) I
will again make instruction shine afar; 33)
I will again pour out teaching like prophecy, and leave it to all future generations. 34) Observe that I have not labored
for myself alone, but for all who seek instruction."

Here it would appear, at least, that ben Sira refers to
his own teaching as prophecy. But the force of the
comparative particle ὡς may not be so quickly dismis-
sed.[67] It seems much more reasonable, in the light of
its appearance, to conclude that ben Sira means the
reader to understand that his interpretative work has
been undertaken with the help of the divine spirit of
understanding (cf. Sir 39.6), and is, in that sense,
like prophecy.[68] Johannes Marböck concurrs with this
opinion.

"Die Vergleichspartikel ὡς zeigt auch, das
sich der Weise nicht einfach in der Reihe
der Geistbegabten Prophetischen Sprecher
stellen will, die in seiner Geschichtsschau
eine Grosse Rolle spielen, und die er als
Schriftgelehrter interpretiert, (39.1).
Aber er stellt sich in ihre Nahe, indem er
also erster Weisheitslehrer sein weisheit-
liches sprechen mit einer Gottlichen inspi-
ratio im Verbindung bringt."[69]

Accordingly, we may conclude that ben Sira does not
place himself among the prophets, but rather among the
wise.[70]

Our investigation of Sir 39.6 in its context has
discovered a complex of inter-relationships between
σοφία, νόμος, and πνεῦμα. The theme which unites all
three concepts in the thought of ben Sira, however, is
the search for wisdom. At the foundation of this quest
lies a facility for understanding that is common to humanity, and is displayed in human endeavor. The potential for attaining wisdom is actualized, however,
by the scribe who recognizes that wisdom has taken up
residence within the law of Israel, and takes advantage
of the insight, devoting himself to study, practice,
and prayer. The culmination of sapiential achievement,
however, as Sir 39.6 makes plain, occurs with the arrival of the divine spirit of understanding, for with

23

the reception of this spirit comes a greater understanding of the law, and the scribe becomes the sage.

1.4   The Blessings and Benefits of Wisdom

In the two previous sections of this chapter, we
have concentrated attention upon ben Sira's thought
with respect to the nature of wisdom, (wisdom is embodied in the law), and the pursuit of wisdom, (wisdom is
obtained by the sage through study and inspiration).
It would be wrong to conclude our work, however, without a brief survey of some of ben Sira's views concerning the possession of wisdom, and the gifts which accompany, or are associated with wisdom's receipt.[71]

A number of these, wisdom's cognitive associations, have been mentioned in the course of the previous
discussion. Wisdom is, as we have seen, linked with
knowledge, (γνῶσις),[72] and understanding, (συνέσεως);[73]
and more esoterically, there are several references to
wisdom's secrets; (τὰ κρυπτά).[74] Also allied to the
ownership of wisdom, however, are a variety of other
benefits. The possession of wisdom is a source of joy,
delight, and happiness.[75] Its acquisition brings security, for with wisdom comes help and life; divine
blessing and divine love. Such notions are summed up
in Sir 4.11-15.

> "Wisdom exalts her sons and gives help to
> those who seek her. 12) Whoever loves her
> loves life, and those who seek her early
> will be filled with joy. 13) Whoever holds
> her fast will obtain glory, and the Lord
> will bless the place she enters. 14) Those
> who serve her will minister to the Holy
> One; the Lord loves those who love her.
> 15) He who obeys her will judge nations,
> and whoever gives heed to her will dwell
> secure."

Also prominent in Sirach is the association of wisdom
with glory, honor, and an everlasting name.[76] Sirach
37.24, 26 is representative of this connection.

> "A wise man will have praise heaped upon
> him, and all who see him will call him hap-
> py. 26) He who is wise among his people
> will inherit confidence, and his name will
> live for ever."

24

More important perhaps, in light of their significance for later sapiential thought, are several other
passages where wisdom and its possession are connected
with righteousness and the gift of eloquence. We have
already noticed an implicit relationship between wisdom
and righteousness in Sir 39.5.[77] However, this liason
is also evidenced by ben Sira's denial that wisdom is
possessed by sinners, or transgressors of the law.[78]

"Foolish men will not obtain her, and sinful men will not see her. 8) She is far
from men of pride, and liars will never
think of her."

-Sir 15.7, 8

"All wisdom is the fear of the Lord, and in
all wisdom there is the fulfillment of the
law. 21) But the knowledge of wickedness
is not wisdom, nor is there prudence where
sinners take counsel. ... 24) Better is the
God-fearing man who lacks intelligence,
than the highly prudent man who transgres-
ses the law."

-Sir 19.20, 21, 24

Linked to such denials is also often the idea of wisdom's conviction, or discipline.[79] A belief is even
expressed on one occasion that the possession of wisdom
will prevent the entrance of sin.[80] All of this evidence alerts us to the very real bond in Sirach between
wisdom and righteousness.

A different sort of bond is found with respect to
wisdom and eloquence in Sirach. In Sir 39.6 for instance, as we have seen, the one who possesses wisdom
is characterized by his speech; "he will pour forth
words of wisdom," (ῥήματα σοφίας). The reason for this
characterization is explained in Sir 4.24.[81]

"For wisdom is known through speech, (ἐν
γὰρ λόγῳ γνωσθήσεται σοφία), and education through the words of the tongue."

For ben Sira then speech seems to function as something
of a criterion with respect to the discernment of wisdom.

25

Eloquence, righteousness, happiness, security, knowledge, and a whole variety of other benefits may be seen in Sirach to accrue to the sage as the possessor of wisdom. The quest for wisdom is therefore not simply a search for a cognitive understanding of the meaning of the law, but also for everything that comes with it. It is a quest, in the final analysis, for a more complete religious experience.

1.5 Conclusion

We began this first chapter by pointing to the transitional significance of the identification made in Sirach between wisdom and the law. Our subsequent investigations have uncovered again the fundamental nature of this relationship for ben Sira's thought. Since wisdom is embodied in the law, the study of the law becomes the path to sapiential achievement. Since wisdom is contained within the law, ultimately, in order to come to its full comprehension, one must rely on the assistance of the divine spirit of uderstanding. Since wisdom is located in the law, all of wisdom's gifts come to those who have achieved success in their pursuit of its meaning. In Sirach, therefore, it is the scribe and the scribe alone who has the potential to become the sage.

The significance of ben Sira's contribution to Jewish wisdom lies in these thoughts. Their impact upon subsequent sapiential authors must now be assessed.

CHAPTER TWO

WISDOM AND SPIRIT AT QUMRAN

2.1 Introduction

In an attempt to investigate Jewish ideas about wisdom and spirit in the historical period subsequent to the composition of the Book of Sirach, serious consideration must surely be given to the scrolls so recently discovered at Khirbet Qumran.[1] For if the principal documents do indeed originate in the years between 135 and 75 BCE in reaction to the rule of the Hasmoneans in Jerusalem, as is now coming to be accepted among scholars, then together they represent an extensive collection of source materials which have the potential to be highly relevant to our study.[2]

Moreover, this potential begins to be actualized when it is recognized that רוח and חכמה are both important words within the theological vocabulary of the Qumran Essenes.[3] The validity of this observation is easily and quickly substantiated with respect to רוח, for the frequency of the term, and its wide range of meaning within the scrolls clearly denotes that it is a word of significance within the community.[4] But a longer and more detailed demonstration is necessary if it is to be shown successfully that the concept of wisdom, despite the relative infrequency of the substantive חכמה and the adjective חכם , also plays a major part in the religious perspective of the sectarian community.[5] Verification on this point may be provided, however, in three ways: a) by examining the references to חכמה, חכם, and related words within the scrolls; b) by observing the esteem that is accorded to teachers of wisdom within the community; and c) by taking notice of the personification of wisdom in 11 Q Ps[a] 18.[6]

Statistics, of course, can very often be misleading if they are not placed in perspective, and this is certainly true with respect to the occurrences of חכמה and חכם in the Qumran scrolls. For although these terms are only occasionally employed in the literature that has come to light thus far, they are found in contexts that suggest that their significance for the sect should not be too quickly minimized. חכמה , for example, is used on four occasions in that section of 1 QS whose concern is with the role of the "two spirits" in relation to the manifestation of good and evil among men. In 1 QS 4.3, we are told that the "good spirit" is a spirit of, or imparting, "mighty wisdom", and 1 QS 4.22 speaks significantly about a "wisdom of the sons of heaven", which will be taught to the "perfect of the way" by the man who has received "the spirit of purifi-

cation".[7]   1 QS 4.18 makes a connection between "the
glorious wisdom of God", and the characteristic Essene
notion of the divine רו, (cp. 1 QS 11.5, CD 6.3, 1 Qp-
Hab 7.23), and 1 QS 4.24 describes the dualism of humanity under the influence of the 'two spirits' in
terms of "wisdom and folly".[8]

These verses certainly indicate that חכמה plays a
role in this particular passage quite out of proportion
to its statistical significance. More important still,
however, is the synonymity of חכמה, דעה, בנה, and שכל
in this section, for the phenomenon suggests that there
is justification in speaking about a broad concept of
wisdom, or knowledge, at Qumran which transcends the
consistent usage of any one word, and is expressed, in
fact, by a series of closely related terms.[9]   In light
of this, according to Martin Hengel, our conclusion
must be that the concept of wisdom, "probably possessed
the greatest importance for Essene theology".[10]

One is led to a confirmation of his judgment
through an investigation of the titular use of כהן in 1
QSa 1.28 and 2.16.   These texts are most often understood to denote a special group within the community
elsewhere designated as the משכילים.[11]   The function of
these individuals is specified in 1 QS 3.13-15, 4.22,
and 9.12-20.   The משכלים are to instruct their fellow
sectarians in the interpretations originally established by the Teacher of Righteousness, and in this way
guide them into wisdom and knowledge. The structure of
the Essene community may therefore be seen to accord
special honor and esteem to those who, having attained
to wisdom and knowledge themselves, are now able to
teach and instruct their fellow sectarians in relationship to these goals.

A final indication of the importance of the wisdom
concept at Qumran is found in the Psalms scroll from
cave 11, (11 QPsª).[12] Here, in a manner unique and
quite unparalleled elsewhere in the sectarian literature, personified wisdom appears, and her speech,
especially in 11 QPsª 18, is full of allusions which
bear witness to her position of eminence at Qumran.[13]

"For to make known the glory of the Lord is
wisdom given 6) and for recounting his many
deeds she is revealed to man; 7) to make
known to simple folk his might, and to
explain to senseless folk his greatness.
8) Those far from her gates, those who

32

stray from her portals ... 12) From the
gates of the righteous is heard her voice,
and from the assembly of the pious her
song. 13) When they eat with satiety she
is cited, and when they drink in community
together 14) their meditation is on the law
of the Most High, their words on making
known his might. 15) How far from the
wicked is her word, from all haughty men to
know her."

-11 Qps^a 18.5-8, 12-15

In the light of all of the evidence pointing to
the importance of the wisdom concept at Qumran, the in-
frequent use of חכמה and חכם remains puzzling. Why
should the sectarians choose to express a concept central to much of their thinking in a less than direct
way? Two factors appear to be able to account for
this. The first factor is a polemical one. According
to John Worrell, the 'non-use' of the specific words
חכמה and חכם is to be attributed to a conflict between
the leaders of the sectarian community and the Hasidim
outside Qumran.[14] In Worrell's estimation, the latter
group most likely lies behind the reference to חכמים in
1 QH 3.14 whose wisdom "shall be swallowed up in judgment". But if non-sectarian religious leaders had
adopted the title חכמים, as this passage seems to show,
then the avoidance of the words חכמה and חכם can be explained. These words have been excluded in the midst
of a developing controversy between the community and
outsiders in favor of synonyms like שכל , בנה , and
דעת.[15]

A second factor also may have played a part in
this situation. Otto Betz suggests that the choice of
בנה and שכל instead of חכמה could have been intended to
point to the special nature of wisdom at Qumran.[16]
Since the concept of wisdom, (as we shall see more fully in the next section of this chapter), is characterized for the sectarian community in terms of an understanding and insight into scripture, it is understandable, according to Betz, that they should prefer to
make use of terms like בנה and שכל in an attempt to reflect this conviction.

Either of these explanations, or perhaps some combination of both of them, would seem to account satisfactorily for the relatively rare appearance of חכמה
and חכם on the one hand, and the prevalence and importance of the wisdom idea on the other. Consequently, a

33

growing body of scholarship is coming to recognize that
wisdom is a key concept within the Qumran literature,
one whose meaning is integral to our understanding and
appreciation of the thought and the nature of the sectarian community.[17] Within the context of this development, we propose to carry out an investigation into
the relationship between wisdom and spirit at Qumran.
Two questions seem particularly critical to our research, and to the attempt to relate our findings here
to those of the previous chapter. First, can we become
any more clear about the meaning and definition that
was given to the concept of wisdom at Qumran? In what
ways, if any, is this concept related to the law, or to
a nomistic understanding of wisdom?[18] Second, what can
be said about the acquistion of wisdom among the
Essenes? In what way, if any, do the sectarian documents relate the possession of wisdom to the presence
of some spirit, or speak about the process of obtaining
wisdom in relation to a spirit sent from God?

2.2   The Nature and Content of Wisdom at Qumran

> "But God remembered the Covenant with the
> forefathers, and He raised from Aaron men
> of discernment and from Israel men of wis-
> dom, and he caused them to hear. 3) And
> they dug the Well: the well which the
> princes dug, which the nobles of the people
> delved with the stave (Num 21.18). 4) The
> well is the Law, and those who dug it were
> 5) the converts of Israel who went out of
> the land of Judah to sojourn in the land of
> Damascus. 6) God called them all princes
> because they sought him, 7) and their re-
> nown was disputed by no man. The Stave is
> the Interpreter of the Law 8) of whom
> Isaiah said, He makes a tool for His work
> (Isa 54.16); and the nobles of the people
> 9) are those who come to dig the Well with
> the staves with which the Stave ordained
> 10) that they should walk in all the age of
> wickedness and without them they shall find
> nothing 11) until he comes who shall teach
> righteousness at the end of days."
>   -CD 6.2-11

This passage from the Damascus Document provides
us with some important clues about the concept of wisdom at Qumran. The key to their analysis and use however, is only indirectly related to our ability to dis-

34

cern the identity of the 'Stave' and the 'men of wisdom'.[19]   The question important to this stage of our
inquiry concerns the rationale behind the designations.
Why should these individuals be singled out by the
writer and designated חכמים? A succession of three answers is seen to be given to this query within the passage.   The חכמים are wise because 'God has caused them
to hear' (6.2).   They are wise because they have 'dug
the well' (6.3,4).   They are wise, last of all, because
in their work they have labored with the 'staves' prepared for them by the 'Stave' (6.8,9).

The first two of these responses, and the second
in particular, indicates that there was a definite and
significant relationship between the title חכמים and
the law at Qumran.[20]   Since the 'men of wisdom' are
identified as those who 'hear' and 'dig' in הבאר התורה,
it follows that the law was regarded as the source, or
the locus of wisdom for the writer. But the third response concerning the identity and occupation of the
חכמים alerts the reader to an important qualification.
The relationship between wisdom and law was not one of
simple identity, or equation in Essene thought.   In
contrast to this, CD 6.8-11 demonstrates that the relationship was redefined and reformulated at Qumran in
accordance with the peculiarities of a sectarian consciousness.   Wisdom and the title חכמים are reserved
here for those who espouse the particular interpretations of the law that are provided by the 'Stave'; "and
without them they shall find nothing".[21] Wisdom at
Qumran, therefore, is not identical with the law per
se, rather it is co-essential with the sectarian understanding and interpretation of the law.[22]

The background to this kind of refinement in the
relationship between wisdom and law is most likely to
be found in Essene beliefs concerning the hidden nature, and the mysterious content of the law.[23] A telling example of the character of these beliefs surfaces
in an earlier passage from CD.

> "But with the remnant which held fast to
> the commandments of God, He made His Cove-
> nant with Israel for ever, 13) revealing to
> them the hidden things in which all Israel
> had gone astray.   14) He unfolded before
> them His holy Sabbaths and His glorious
> feasts, the testimonies of His righteous-
> ness and the ways of His truth, 15) and the
> desires of His will which a man must do in

order to live.   16) And they dug a well
rich in water; and he who despises it shall
not live."
                              -CD 3.12-16

Here the sectarian community is designated as "the rem-
nant which held fast to the commandments of God".   The
object of their concerted allegiance is promptly clarified, however, just as it was in CD 6.8-11, by the
succeeding context which speaks about the subject matter of the scriptural commandments in terms of נסתרות,
or 'hidden things'.   From the description of verses 14-
16, it quickly becomes evident that these things hidden
within the law touch upon a broad part of Israel's covenantal legislation.   Thus a distinctly sectarian perception comes to expression. Large portions of the law
and its wisdom have been hidden from all save the members of the sect.   Beyond the discernment of Israel,
these parts of the law are apparent and manifest to the
community alone, (cp. CD 4.8, 6.14).

     Similar convictions about the essential nature of
the law are also found in 1 QS.   In 1 QS 5.11-12, for
instance, the men of falsehood are denied access to the
covenant of God because;

          "they have neither inquired, nor sought
          after Him concerning His laws that they
          might know the hidden things in which they
          have sinfully erred".

In 1 QS 8.11-12, an exhortation is given to the community concerning the instruction and training of novitiates;

          "and the Interpreter shall not conceal from
          them, out of fear of the spirit of aposta-
          sy, any of those things hidden from Israel
          which have been discovered by him".

A final illustration occurs in 1 QS 11.5-6, in the Hymn
of the Community Rule, where the sectarian perspective
on the hiddenness of the law and its wisdom is actually
celebrated.

          "From the source of His righteousness is my
          justification, and from His marvellous mys-
          teries is the light in my heart.   My eyes
          have gazed on that which is eternal, on
          wisdom concealed from men, on knowledge and

                           36

wise design (hidden) from the sons of men;"

Essene opinion about the opaqueness of scripture and its wisdom is also apparent in the biblical commentaries of the sect. For here the characteristic interpretative comment, the פשר, which forms the bulk and substance of most of the commentaries, has its <u>raison d'etre</u> in the belief that prophetic scripture is <u>full</u> of mysterious wisdom, or hidden significance. The רז of the prophet is in need of interpretation before its message and meaning may be understood, and its contemporary relevance comprehended.[24]

> "... and God told Habakkuk to write down that which would happen to the final generation, 2) but he did not make known to him when time would come to an end. 3) And as for that which He said, <u>That he who reads may read it speedily</u>, 4) interpreted this concerns the Teacher of Righteousness, 5) to whom God made known all the mysteries of the words of His servants, the Prophets."

> -1 QpHab 7.1-5

The commentaries, therefore, not only affirm the sectarians' belief in the hiddenness of the law, they also widen the scope of that belief to embrace Israel's prophetic scripture as well.

In the light of these texts from CD, 1 QS, and 1 QpHab, two results emerge. On the one hand, we may conclude with some certainty that the Essene community at Qumran was fully and firmly convinced of the hidden nature, and the mysterious content of major portions of the Mosaic and Prophetic scriptures. On the other hand, however, these same sources indicate that the community believed itself to be in possession of a full and complete understanding of the Law and the Prophets.[25] We suggest, then, that the Essene concept of wisdom has been adapted specifically in order to take account of both of these beliefs.

Wisdom's relationship to the law is still strongly affirmed. This relationship functions as the presupposition of the sectarian view.[26] Full wisdom, knowledge, and understanding belong exclusively, however, to those within the Qumran community. Indeed, the community understands itself in very real terms to be constituted on the basis of a new and full interpretation of the law.[27] Outside the fellowship there is, apparently, a knowledge of sorts, (cf. 1 QS 1.8-10, 3.2; 5.20-22), but the deeper significance and the full wisdom of scripture continues to remain hidden from non-sectarian Israel.[28] Only within the Essene circle is the whole counsel of God, the wisdom of the law, unfolded as its hidden details are brought to light and its mysteries interpreted. The concept of wisdom at Qumran may, therefore, be seen to have been shaped by its relationship to Essene belief concerning the value and worth of scriptural interpretation within the fellowship, and by corresponding convictions about the hiddenness of scripture, and the incompleteness of wisdom and knowledge outside the bounds of the sectarian community. With these convictions about the nature and possession of wisdom, the community distinguished its membership from outsiders.

Inside the community itself, however, a further differentiation in connection with wisdom and understanding is evident. For each of the members of the sect is to be ranked in accordance with their cognitive and ethical perfection year by year.[29]

> "They shall inscribe them in the order, one after another, according to their understanding and their deeds, that every one may obey his companion, the man of lesser rank obeying his superior. 24) And they shall examine their spirit yearly, so that each man may be advanced in accordance with his understanding and perfection of way, or moved down in accordance with the offences committed by him."
> — 1 QS 5.23-24

> "Thou wilt give to the children of Thy truth (unending joy and) everlasting (gladness), and according to the measure of their knowledge, so shall they be honoured one more than another."
> —1 QH 10.27

Moreover, at the head of the Essene community appears a select company of persons, distinguished from the rest of the fellowship according to the same criteria.[30]

> "In the Council of the Community there shall be twelve men and three Priests,

38

perfectly versed in all that is revealed of
the Law, whose works shall be truth, righteousness,   justice,   lovingkindness,   and
humility."

                    -1 QS 8.1

     These texts seem to show, as the studies of Paul
du Plessis and Beda Rigaux have indicated, that a hierarchy was recognized in relationship to the perfecting
of wisdom and obedience within the community.[31]   Entrance into the community brings with it an initial
status above that of outsiders; (cf. 1 QS 1.11-13).
Novitiates entering the community were then subject to
two years of intensive training and study in the Essene
interpretation of the Law and the Prophets before they
could be enrolled among "the men of the lot of God who
walk perfectly in all His ways"; (1   QS 2.2, cf. 1 QS
3.3).   Within the fellowship, however, a still higher
status was accorded to those who had come into the possession of a superior degree of understanding and observance, that is to say, to the teachers, the "Council
of Holiness" within the broader "Council of the Community"; (cp. 1 QS 8.1, 17, 20, 9.17-20).

     On the basis of this analysis, it now seems possi-
ble to speak, much as we did in chapter one, about several broad levels, or grades of accomplishment, in relation to the acquisition and possession of wisdom.
Those outside the community form one group. Their wisdom and knowledge, however, is culpably incomplete
apart from the reading of the Law and the Prophets promulgated within the sect.   In order to acquire wisdom,
one must seek entrance into the community and undertake
a two year period of guided study in the interpretation
of the scriptures, and the discipline of the sect.
Successful completion of this probationary period enables one to pass into the full fellowship of the community,   and entails a recognition that wisdom, understanding, and perfection of way has come into the possession of the individual.   A further and final degree
of perfection in wisdom and lifestyle within the community is reserved, however, to a still smaller group
which stands at the head of the sectarian organization.

     Our study of the concept of wisdom at Qumran has
yielded two important results.   We have seen, first of
all, that the content of wisdom among the Essenes was
not primarily defined in terms of an identity between
wisdom and the law, but was understood instead to be
co-essential with the sectarian interpretation of the

                        39

law.   Secondly, we   have observed how this concept   of
wisdom is linked to a hierarchy of achievement in relation to the   acquisition and possession of wisdom.   It
now remains for us   in the next section to   examine the
concept of   spirit   at Qumran   as it   bears   upon these
findings.

2.3   Wisdom and Spirit at Qumran

        Having examined the major sectarian   writings with
respect to the   nature and   content of wisdom,   and the
relationship of wisdom to the law, it now   seems useful
to approach these same literary sources with   a different sort of question, namely, how has the   hidden meaning, the wisdom of the law, come into the possession of
the   sect,   and how   have the   mysteries   of prophetic
scripture come to be community knowledge at Qumran?   A
succint and significant response is made to   this query
fairly frequently in 1 QS and 1 QH.   The knowledge, or
wisdom, or understanding of the sect, its   insight into
the hiddenness of the law and the prophets, is a result
of   divine revelation   within the   community.   If   one
probes further,   however, into the means, or   agency of
this revelation,   the evidence   becomes   somewhat   more
varied.

        In a number   of instances, the wisdom of   the sect
is portrayed   as a product of   direct   God-given revelation.

> "Blessed art Thou, my God, who   openest the
> heart of Thy servant to knowledge!   18) It
> is   Thou who   has taught all   knowledge and
> all things come to pass by Thy will."
> 　　　　　　　　　-1 QS 11.15, 18

> "These   things I   know by the   wisdom which
> comes from Thee, for Thou hast unstopped my
> ears to marvellous mysteries."
> 　　　　　　　　　-1 QH 1.21

> "I (thank Thee, O Lord), for Thou   hast en-
> lightened me through Thy truth.   27) In Thy
> marvellous   mysteries, and   in   Thy loving-
> kindness to   a man (of vanity, and)   in the
> greatness of Thy mercy to a perverse heart,
> Thou hast granted me knowledge."
> 　　　　　　　　　-1 QH 7.26-27

Another group of passages, however, relates the revelation of wisdom and understanding within the community to the influence and activity of God's Spirit.

> "I, the Master, know Thee, O my God, by the Spirit which Thou hast given to me, and by Thy Holy Spirit I have faithfully hearkened to Thy marvellous counsel. 12) In the mystery of Thy wisdom Thou hast opened knowledge to me, and in Thy mercies (Thou hast unlocked for me) the fountain of Thy might."
>
> -1 QH 12.11-12

> "And I know Thee through the understanding which comes from Thee, that in Thy goodwill towards (ashes Thou hast shed) Thy Holy Spirit (upon me) 13) and thus drawn me near to understanding of Thee."
>
> -1 QH 14.12-13

> "Bowing down and (confessing all) my transgressions, I will seek (Thy) Spirit (of knowledge); cleaving to Thy Spirit of (holiness), 7) I will hold fast to the truth of Thy covenant, ..."
>
> -1 QH 16.6-7

A third set of texts seem to speak even more differently about an awakening, or enlightenment of the spirit which God has placed within the person.[32]

> "(But what is) the spirit of flesh that it should understand all this, and that it should comprehend the great (design of Thy wisdom)?"
>
> -1 QH 13.13

> "The way of a man is not established except by the spirit which God created for him to make perfect a way for the children of men, ..."
>
> -1 QH 4.31

> "Thou hast favoured me, Thy servant, with a spirit of knowledge, (that I may choose) truth (and goodness) and loathe all the ways of iniquity."
>
> -1 QH 14.25

The relationship and/or integration of these texts is a difficult and problematical issue, but one factor seems to point us towards a solution.[33] The first type of text, which speaks of the means of divine revelation in terms of the direct activity of God is noticeably more common within the scrolls than either of the other two idioms, and this would probably indicate that these passages represent a basic understanding about the revelation of wisdom within the sect.[34]

God himself is the ultimate and primary source of the interpretation of the law in Essene thinking, and their wisdom is his gift.[35] Thus is it God's gracious activity in granting wisdom that is being further defined and described with reference to the divine and the human spirit in the second and third type of text. God has acted through the power of his Spirit to bring insight and wisdom into the created spirit of chosen individuals so that the sectarian community might comprehend the hidden significance of the scriptural wisdom.[36] In this sense, then, it seems quite proper to speak about an inspired wisdom at Qumran, and to relate talk about the acquisition and possession of wisdom in Essene thought to the mediating assistance of God's Spirit.[37] Wisdom, the gift of God, is a product of the inspiration of the divine Spirit, and the illumination of the human spirit.[38]

In light of the work of Otto Betz, Heinz Kuhn, and Frederick Nötscher, however, the nature of revelation at Qumran may be further clarified by giving attention to the Essene anthropology, and the relationship between Torah-study and purification.[39] In accordance with their findings, it is worthwhile to take notice of the fact that stress is placed upon the holiness of the human spirit within the scrolls.[40] It is equally important, though, to recognize that this conception of human nature is balanced within the sectarian literature by a corresponding emphasis upon the defiled state of the human spirit outside the sectarian community (cf. CD 5.11, 1 QS 2.21-3.6), and by a profound and acute awareness within the community itself of the corrupted nature of this spirit; (cf. 1 QH 1.22, 33, 3.20-22, 5.5-16, etc).[41] The hope of the individual in regards to salvation and revelation lay, consequently, in the cleansing, or purification of his spirit within the community where such purification and perfection was achieved by individuals in varying measure through their study and observance of the law.[42] To those who attained to the highest degree of perfection of spirit,

the community awarded the office of teacher and the title הנבים.[43] From such persons, the community expected
to receive its inspired interpretation of the law and
its wise teaching.[44]

It follows then that Essene belief was convinced
of a need for spiritual perfection in the quest for
wisdom, and that the Qumran community conceived of such
perfection as occurring in several stages, linking progress in wisdom to parallel progress in spirituality.
Outside the community there is 'defilement of spirit'
and only a limited 'knowledge'; (CD 5.11, 1 QS 3.2).
Within the community in general there is a 'spirit of
holiness' among the members of the fellowship and an
opportunity for advancement in 'understanding'; (1 QS
3.5-8, 9.3, 15). At the head of the sectarian organization stand the teachers and leaders. Perfect in
'holiness' and perfect in 'wisdom' (1 QS 8.1, 17, 20),
they receive and instruct their fellows in an inspired
interpretation of the law (1 QS 9.17-20, 1 QH 2.13,
4.27-28), following the lead of the Teacher of Righteousness to whom "God made known all of the mysteries
of his servants, the prophets"; (1 QpHab 7.5).[45]

2.4 Conclusion

Our study of the Qumran literature has led us to
results which correlate in significant ways with our
findings in chapter one.

1. At Qumran, as in Sirach, the content of wisdom is
closely related to the law. As we have seen, this relationship is more nuanced in the Essene literature,
and is influenced especially by the exclusivity of the
sectarian perspective. But the law is still the primary locus of wisdom at Qumran. In the law, the wisdom
of God has been hidden to be revealed by the sectarian
interpretation.

2. At Qumran, as in Sirach, there are recognizable levels of attainment and achievement in relationship to
the understanding of the law, and the acquisition of
wisdom. Those outside the community, community members, and the leaders, or teachers of the community
constitute three separate groups in the Essene documents, distinct from one another in terms of their understanding of the law, and in terms of their purification, or perfection of spirit. A higher spirituality
is closely related to a higher degree of wisdom and understanding.

3.   At Qumran, as in Sirach, there is a connection between the acquisition of wisdom, and the aid, or activity of God's Spirit.   The חכם is qualified to teach and
instruct the community based upon an inspired understanding of the Law and the Prophets.   God, working
through the inspiration of his Spirit, illuminates the
perfect spirits of the חכמים so that they might lead
the community in the true interpretation of the law.

These conclusions indicate that the concept of
wisdom at Qumran is similar to the understanding of
wisdom in Sirach.   The implications of this must be
left aside for the moment, however, until we have had a
chance to add and assess the evidence from chapter
three.

CHAPTER THREE

WISDOM AND SPIRIT IN PHILO

3.1 Introduction

The extant sapiential literature from the latter half of the first century BCE and the first decades of the Common Era is largely dominated by two contributions which emanate from the Alexandrian diaspora. The first of these is the Book of Wisdom, (or the Wisdom of Solomon), an anonymous exhortatory and apologetic treatise concerned with the wisdom displayed in Israel's past and present.[1] The second is not, in fact, one book, but instead a whole series of books about the pursuit of wisdom authored over a space of some fifty years by a single individual, Philo Judaeus.[2]

The geographical and chronological proximity of the two works suggests from the outset that the Book of Wisdom and the Philonic literature might be examined and evaluated most profitably for our purposes together rather than separately. The rationale underlying such an approach is not, however, entirely dependent upon external considerations. At least as important is an internal coherence and similarity which becomes evident in the light of numerous and varied linguistic and conceptual parallels.[3] Among the agreements, moreover, there appears a singular confluence of purpose and concept. Both Wisdom and Philo seem to be intent upon describing a paradigmatic pattern in which wisdom is both the means and the immediate object of a religious quest whose ultimate goal is an immortal life of fellowship with God.[4]

Each author, of course, can express the theme in his own way. For Wisdom, the sapiential quest described in chapters 6-9, and enjoined upon the reader in 6.9-25, is narrated under the pseudonymous guise of a Solomonic confession.[5] Solomon reveals how he has passed from a common existence among men in his youth (Wisd 7.1-6, cp 8.19-20, 9.15), to friendship with God (7.14, 27-28, 9.4) and immortality (8.12,17) via the reception and possession of wisdom. In the Philonic literature the quest appears as a journey. In greater detail, and in relation primarily to the lives of the Patriarchs, Philo relates an account of the "migration of the soul" (Heres 98); from body, sense, and passion, to spirit, mind and virtue; from earthly existence via wisdom's way (Immut 143, 160) to communion with God; (1QG 4.140, QE 4.47)[6] However, a general similarity of interest, intent, and approach is not obscured by these differences of description, and both authors may be seen to depict an archetypal pattern of religious

49

achievement involving the acquisition and retention of
wisdom.[7]

Thus, external proximity in provenance and date,
copious agreements of language and concept, and a central thematic harmony all combine to indicate that the
Book of Wisdom and the Philonic treatises share in
large measure a common context of meaning and outlook.
It is within this shared context of meaning, therefore,
that we propose to examine more closely the understanding of wisdom in both sources especially in relation to
νόμος and πνεῦμα. Since, however, the Philonic literature is much more extensive and more detailed in these
regards, we propose to adopt Philo's presentation as
the basis for our study in this section.[8]   How then
does Philo relate νόμος and πνεῦμα to wisdom and the
sapiential journey?   The following two sections will
attempt to respond to this question.

3.2   Wisdom and νόμος: The Way of Wisdom

> "The wise man is ever longing to discern
> the Ruler of the universe.   As he journeys
> along the path that takes him through know-
> ledge and wisdom, he comes into contact
> first with the divine words and though he
> had meant to go the remainder of the way,
> he comes to a stop for the eyes of his un-
> derstanding have been opened."
>
>   - Post 18

> "Having related in the preceding treatises
> the lives of those whom Moses judged to be
> men of wisdom, who are set before us in the
> sacred books as founders of the nation,
> within themselves unwritten laws, I shall
> now proceed in due course to give full de-
> scription of the written laws. And if some
> allegorical interpretation should appear to
> underlie them, I shall not fail to state
> it.   For knowledge loves to learn and ad-
> vance to full understanding, and its way is
> to seek the hidden meaning rather than the
> obvious."
>
>   - Decal 1

> "So behold me daring not only to read the
> sacred messages of Moses, but also, in my

50

love of knowledge, to peer into each of
them and unfold and reveal what is not
known to the multitude."

- Spec 3.6

"I hear once more the voice of the Invisi-
ble Spirit, the familiar secret tenant saying, 'Friend, it would seem that there is a
matter great and precious of which thou
knowest nothing and this I will ungrudging-
ly show you for many other well-timed les-
sons have I given you."

- Som 2.252

It is obvious perhaps, but still essential and
useful to observe that the majority of the Philonic
literature openly endeavours to provide its reader with
an exposition or interpretation of some portion of the
Torah.[9] By common consensus almost three-quarters of
the Philonic treatises concern themselves primarily, or
in some cases exclusively, with this exegetical task.
Most often Philo's exposition centers upon some portion
of the Mosaic law, but a quick check is enough to show
that neither the Prophets nor the Writings are completely neglected in his work. The implication is obvious, as Chrysostom Larcher points out; "le souci
d'interpréter la Pentáteuque restè au cèntre de toute
l'activité intellèctuelle de Philon".[10]

But one must inquire further than this. Why
should Philo, in fact, choose to concentrate his efforts in this direction, and what connection, if any,
does this focus upon scriptural interpretation have
with wisdom? The answer to this question is undoubtedly complex, but the main lines of a response appear to
us to be suggested, at least, by the material which has
been cited at the head of this section. Torah is important to Philo, because, allegorically interpreted,
it provides the wisdom-seeker, and indeed Philo himself, with a path to the knowledge of God.[11]

"The wise man", says Philo in Post 18, "is ever
longing to discern the ruler of the universe". The
knowledge of God in both an objective and a subjective
sense is his goal. But an immediate obstacle stands in
his path, namely, the incomprehensibility of God.
Philo stresses the incomprehensibility of God repeatedly in his works, characteristically describing God, in

51

his essence, as τὸ ὄν, 'The One', or perhaps, "The One unlike any other'; ineffable, (ἄρρητος) unnamable, (ἀκατονόμαστος) and incomprehensible, (ἀκατάληπτος).[12] The hope of the aspirant lies exclusively, therefore, in God's gracious self-disclosure. If he is to reach his goal, according to Philo, then he must "journey along the path that takes him through knowledge and wisdom". He must seek to follow the wisdom of God back to its source.

That way, however, is neither short nor easy, despite the condensed account of it which Philo employs here in Post 18. For divine wisdom is found in differing degrees among several sources, and it is through these, according to Philo, that the aspirant must journey if he is, in the end, to reach his goal. The main stages of the sapiential journey may be summarized, then, as follows.

There is, first of all, a wisdom present within and revealed by creation. Hence, in Philo's estimation, the aspirant should begin the journey here. For the 'school subjects' of the ancient world, such disciplines as science, mathematics, and logic, reflect in their contents the wisdom which God has placed within creation.[13] A more complete wisdom, however, is revealed to the sojourner through the study of philosophy rightly pursued. For reflection upon the 'school subjects' should press the enquirer, in Philo's opinion, towards a knowledge of the cause behind such phenomena, towards a knowledge of God's existence, and an accurate appraisal of the individual's place in the divinely created cosmos.[14] Yet, from philosophical reflection too the aspirant is urged to pass on, this time to the 'genuine philosophy' of the Torah, in order to be purified of passion, desire, and wickedness, and be guided into a life of virtue and righteousness.[15] Finally, the God-seeker is ready, however, for the wisdom which, according to Spec 3.6, "is not known to the multitudes"; for the deeper meaning that may be discerned within scripture by means of allegory.[16] Through a meditation upon this sense of the law, Philo asserts, the sojourner is at last led out of the cognitive confines imposed by earthly existence, and called upon into to fellowship and communion with τὸ ὄν.[17]

From this short resume of the journey of the God-seeker in the philonic literature, we may draw two conclusions in regards to the relationship between wisdom and νόμος. First, we may observe that while Philo is

52

reluctant to limit wisdom in a comprehensive sense to the revelation contained in the law, he does appear to maintain a consistent distinction of degree and completeness between Torah on the one hand, and other sources of wisdom on the other. Wisdom, though it may be found in part outside of the Jewish law, is nonetheless for Philo predominantly and pre-eminently associated with it.[18] Insofar, then, as the λόγος, the full expression of divine wisdom, has been embodied or embedded in any one source, it has been most fully and most clearly manifested for Philo in the law.[19] It is surely for this reason as well that Moses appears in Philo's works, as elsewhere in Hellenistic Judaism, not simply as a 'law-giver', but also as τὸ πανσόφος ἄνθρωπος.[20] The search for wisdom and the knowledge of God is inextricably linked in Philo's mind to an exegesis and interpretation of the Mosaic law. It is here that the God-seeker must "come to a stop"; (Post 18).

Secondly, we should also notice how Philo maintains that the wisdom of the law exists, or functions, on two separable levels. "Philo assumes that scriptural texts have a two-fold meaning; a literal, (ρήτή), or obvious, (φάνερα) meaning, and an underlying meaning, (ὕπονοια) also called by him allegory, (ἄλληγόρια)."[21] On the first level, Torah functions, according to Philo, as a source of instruction, purification, and guidance for all of its students. But on a higher level, reached by means of an allegorical exegesis, (cf. Decal 1 and Spec 3.6), scripture provides the pathway for a journey that each of us can make to fellowship and communion with God.[22] Thus, while Philo never completely abandons the literal sense of any passage, (and indeed, he is strongly critical of those who do neglect this basic level of meaning),[23] he is chiefly concerned, as the majority of his writing shows, with the interpretation of the law on the allegorical level, a level at which Torah ceases to be simply νόμος, and instead becomes a paradigmatic description of Jewish religious experience as recorded by Moses. Ultimately then, by way of aspiration and emulation, the law becomes a pattern or a guide to the experience of everyone who searches out divine wisdom and communion with God.[24] The individual who reaches this goal no longer reads the covenant in its written form, but looks beyond this to the genuine covenant in its highest sense, to the deeper meaning of the law which mediates a personal experience of the divine presence; (QE 2.42).[25]

53

In accordance with this, in Decal 1 and Spec 3.6, Philo speaks of his own exegesis along the same lines. His is an attempt to look into the hidden significance of the law, which is the way to wisdom, by means of allegory. But this sort of interpretation, by his own account, does not rest simply upon an innate or natural skill. Instead, as he indicates in Som 2.252, it depends upon spiritual assistance.[26] In order to set Philo's allegorical expositions in their proper perspective, therefore, we must examine the concept of spirit in the Philonic literature and attempt to analyze those texts which speak about the Spirit or spiritual inspiration in relationship to the task of exegesis.

3.3 Wisdom and πνεῦμα: A Light in the Soul

To begin, it may be useful for us to survey briefly the range of meaning associated with the term πνεῦμα in the Philonic literature.[27] The citations may be broken down, to some extent at least, into three broad categories; the cosmological use of πνεῦμα, the anthropological use of πνεῦμα, and the theological use of πνεῦμα.[28] Philo uses the word in the first sense to represent the element of air or wind. Thus, in Cher 111, we find πνεῦμα placed in parallel with ἀήρ , (cp. Sac 97, Gig 22, Abr 160), and, as air in motion, πνεῦμα is both a "well-tempered breeze", (as in Opif 41), and a "violent head-wind"; (cf. Agr 174). The anthropological use of πνεῦμα encompasses both a physical and psychological manifestation. Thus, πνεῦμα is life-breath, the vital physical principle of all living beings, (cf. Gig 10), but it is, at the same time, a part of our psychological constitution, the substance, or οὐσία of the soul, or rather, as Philo regularly says, of its higher and most dominant part, the mind; (cf. LA 1.42, Spec 4.123, Heres 55-56, Det 83, QG 2.59).[29] In a theological sense, Philo uses πνεῦμα to represent the divine Spirit, (τὸ πνεῦμα θεῖον), the Spirit of God; (cf. Opif 144, Gig 19, 22, 29, 53, 55, Plant 24, etc.: cp. Ex 31.3; 35.31, Job 27.3; 33.4 LXX).

There is, however, a conspicuous and considerable overlap in the Philonic corpus between the anthropological and the theological use of πνεῦμα, and this possesses a good deal of significance for our understanding of Philo's concept of spirit. Hence, we may continue our study of πνεῦμα in Philo by noting the nature of this overlap as it is illustrated in LA 1.36-38 and Plant 23-24.

54

"Breathed into, (ἐνεφύσησεν, Gen 2.7), we
note, is equivalent to inspired, or besoul-
ing the soulless; for God forbid that we
should be infected with such monstrous folly as to think that God employs for in-
breathing organs such as mouth or nostrils;
for God is not only not in the form of man,
but belongs to no class or kind. Yet the
expression clearly brings out something
that accords with nature. For it implies
of necessity three things; that which inbreathes, that which receives, and that
which is inbreathed. That which inbreathes
is God. That which receives is the mind.
That which is inbreathed is the spirit or
breath. What then do we infer from these
premises? A union of the three comes about
as God projects the power that proceeds
from himself through the mediant breath,
(τοῦ μέσου πνεύματός), till it reaches the
subject; and for what purpose save that we
may obtain a conception of him? For how
could the soul have conceived of God had he
not breathed into it and mightily laid hold
of it? For the mind of man would never
have ventured to soar so high as to grasp
the nature of God had not God himself drawn
it up to himself, so far as it was possible
that the mind of man should be drawn up,
and stamped it with the impress of the powers that are within the scope of its understanding."

                    -LA 1.36-38

"This is why those who crave for wisdom and
knowledge with insatiable persistence are
said in the sacred oracles to have been
called upwards; for it accords with God's
ways that those who have received his down-
breathing should be called up to him. For
when trees are whirled up, roots and all,
into the air by hurricanes and tornadoes,
and heavily laden ships of large tonnage
as though objects of very little weight,
and lakes and rivers are borne aloft, and
earth's hollows are left empty by the matter as it is drawn up by a tangle of vio-
lently eddying winds, it is strange if a
light substance like the mind is not ren-

dered buoyant and raised to the utmost
height by the native force of the divine
Spirit, overcoming as it does in its bound-
less might all powers that are here below."

- Plant 23-24

The interpretation of ἐνεφύσησεν from Gen 2.7 LXX
comes as the second part of a four part analysis of the
verse as a whole, and provides us with an informative
statement of Philo's views about the nature and capacity of the spirit that God has breathed into the soul
of created humanity. Its nature, according to Philo's
account, is manifestly divine, for it proceeds, and is
derived from God himself; (LA 1.37).[30] The effect of
God's action, moreover, is made equally clear. It ren-
ders the individual capable of receiving a knowledge of
God; (1.38). The process of theological cognition is
then elucidated in Plant 23-24 where Philo illustrates
how the mind receives wisdom and knowledge as it is
drawn up into God's presence by the force of the divine
Spirit.[31] Thus Philo may be seen to assert that the
spirit breathed into each person at creation provides
the individual with a cognitive, spiritual capacity, a
capacity that is actualized in the experience and encounter with the Spirit of God.[32]

To unite these two texts so immediately, however,
is, in some sense, to do violence to Philo's thought,
for in his estimation all persons have not achieved the
prerequisite necessary to actualize their spiritual potential, or prepare themselves for the reception of divine inspiration. The pre-condition in his mind is a
state of purity which consists in an absence of passion
and fleshly desire. For him it is the flesh that is
the "chief cause" of theological ignorance, since it is
"impossible" for the divine Spirit to remain in the
mind that has been contaminated with the appetites and
cravings of the flesh; (cf. Gig 19, 20, 29-31, 53-55).
Accordingly, the divine Spirit seeks out a dwelling-
place among all, but does not long endure among the majority, "because men are flesh and the nature of the
flesh is alien to wisdom so long as it is familiar with
desire"; (QG 1.90). Philo seems to acknowledge, then,
that all receive occasional flashes of the Spirit's
illumination, but these must inevitably be but brief
interludes because so few achieve a consciousness de-
void of passion and desire for more than a temporary
interval. Even among those that do:

"Nothing is harder than that the divine
Spirit should abide forever in the soul
with its manifold forms and divisions, the
soul which has fastened onto it the greiv-
ous burden of this fleshly coil".

- Immut 2

Thus virtue, purity, and the renunciation of physical
desire are not only preliminary, but also continuing
conditions necessary to the one who seeks to free the
spirit within to receive inspiration in the encounter
with God's Spirit.[33]

In what way, however, are virtue and the absence
of passion to be achieved? Philo's answer is that
these qualities are attained gradually or progressively
by the one who undertakes the pursuit of wisdom and attempts to follow wisdom's way.

"Accordingly it is impossible to grow fruit
trees before migrating into the country given by God; for the words are when ye shall
have entered into the land, ye shall plant
every tree yielding food, (Lev 19.23), so
that while staying outside we shall be unable to cultivate such trees. And this is
what we might expect; for so long as the
mind has not come near and entered the way
of wisdom, but turns in another direction
and wanders away far off, its attention is
given to trees of wild growth which are either barren and yield nothing, or though
they are productive, bear no edible fruit.
But when the mind has stepped onto the way
of insight, and in the company of its
teachings comes into and runs along that
way, it will begin instead of those wild
trees to cultivate trees of the orchard
bearing orchard fruits, instead of passions, freedom from them, knowledge in
place of ignorance, good things in the
place of evil."

- Plant 96-98

Progress in wisdom and progress in virtue, or the elim-
ination of fleshly desire may consequently be seen to
function as complementary and concommitant notions in
philonic thought.[34] Advancement in wisdom inevitably

brings with it a corresponding advancement in virtue
and moral freedom from the passions of the flesh. It
is through the wisdom of the law, that one is freed,
according to Philo, from fleshly passion and desire,
and prepared, as a result, to receive the inspiration
of the divine Spirit.[35]

With this, however, we may return directly once
more to the relationship betwwen spirit and wisdom in
Philonic literature, and to Philo's claim that the
Spirit has enabled him to penetrate into the allegorical meaning of the law and obtain the wisdom which
leads to fellowship with God.[36]

Franz Klein, who has made a careful and thorough
study of the relationship between those texts in the
philonic corpus which speak about inspiration, and
those that speak of the illumination of the soul or the
mind, has shown that Philo reasons in this matter by
way of analogy.[37] If our normal human perception is
dependent for ordinary understanding upon the medium of
natural light, then, Philo argues, in a comparable manner, the higher wisdom, and the knowledge of God must
come as the mind's eyes are irradiated by a further illumination; a divine light shed into the soul by the
Spirit of God.[38] This kind of an experience of spiritual illumination in its purest and most potent form
lies, according to Philo, behind the phenomenon of prophetic ecstasy where the rational perception of the
mind is literally overwhelmed and set aside by the power of the divine light that shines when the Spirit is
fully present.[39] Indeed, Philo himself, in his highest
moments, claims to have enjoyed an analagous kind of
ecstatic, or mystical experience of being in God's presence.[40] But the unadulterated illumination enjoyed in
such ecstasy is also, to a lesser extent, experienced,
according to Philo, by all of those who have received
insight into the deeper meaning and significance of the
scriptural word with the aid of the Spirit who brings
"seeing" and "understanding".[41]

For Philo, therefore, Torah is not only a word to
be read or understood in its literal sense, but rather,
as Klein concludes; "die Worte Gottes indes haben also
die Möglichkeit in der Seele gesehen zu werden".[42] The
divine Spirit illumines the mind to enable it to grasp
the full wisdom of the scriptural narrative. By the
Spirit, the 'eyes' of the God-seeker's 'understanding'
are 'opened' to the hidden or allegorical meaning within the law, and, in reflection upon this, the soul is

intermittently borne up by the force of the Spirit into the very presence of God; (cf. Plant 23-27). Such wisdom, however, is not achieved by the student who simply studies Torah in order to be guided by its commandments in their literal sense. It is reserved instead for the individual who searches within the law for a deeper meaning, and aided by the light that comes with the inspiration of the Spirit seeks, by way of his insight, to imitate the Patriarchs and the Prophets, rising like them, to a regular experience of mystical or ecstatic communion with God.[43]

To the person who has ascended to this level of sapiential achievement, Philo attributes a whole array of titles and capabilities. To consider all or even a large proportion of these in depth, however, would certainly take us well beyond the limited scope of this inquiry.[44] Several of them, nonetheless, are of direct relevance to the later stages of our investigation, and consequently deserve to be noted, if only very briefly, at this point.[45] The first of these is the title σοφός which is employed consistently and exclusively in Philo to designate the person of higher religious attainment, and to distinguish this person from the μορός, the μανθάνον, and the σοφιστής.[46] The second is the designation τέλειος which Philo uses in a very similar way, and in parallel with σοφός, to distinguish the sage as a person of perfection from the προκοπτόντος, or the individual only making progress towards wisdom.[47] The third is not a title, but instead a capability attributed to individuals of higher sapiential status, namely, the faculty of εὐλογία, or παρρησία; the gift of eloquent or powerful speech.[48] In each of these three ways, Philo marks out the person possessing the higher wisdom of the Spirit from others who have not yet attained to such wisdom.

We have attempted in this section to delineate something of the shape of the relationship between wisdom and πνεῦμα in the Philonic literature. We began by examining Philo's use of πνεῦμα in general, then concentrated our attention upon the inter-relationship between the anthropological and the theological use of πνεῦμα. In this way, we were able to demonstrate Philo's belief in a divinely-created human capacity to receive the knowledge of God. Such a capacity, however, must first be freed from the downward pull of fleshly desire. Hence, through the way of wisdom, purity must be successively attained until, through an obedience to wisdom and virtue, the soul is at last

made ready   to receive the illumination of   the Spirit,
the higher   wisdom of   allegory, and the   experience of
being drawn up into communion with God.

3.4 Conclusion

     Martin Hengel, in his massive and important study,
Judaism and Hellenism, has proven that a rigid   or consistent   distinction between   Palestinian Judaism   and
Hellenistic   Judaism in   the Greco-Roman era   cannot be
successfully maintained.   In view of the extensive and
detailed   demonstration   of   this   thesis   provided   by
Hengel, it   should occasion   little or no   surprise for
the reader to discover that our more limited investigation   of sapiential   phenomena within   the   same period
leads us to advance a similar sort of conclusion.   For
we have   found, in fact, several significant   points of
contact between   the notion of wisdom which   figured so
prominently in the Hellenistic Judaism of   the Philonic
literature,   recurring, at   points within   the   Book of
Wisdom, and   the wisdom   concept as   it   was manifested
within the literature of Palestinian Judaism.

     The   first of these congruencies, evident   in each
of the sources that   we have examined, is the   link between   wisdom and   Torah.   It appears   first and   most
forcefully in the   Book of Sirach, but from   that point
onwards, the understanding of the Torah as   the definitive locus of wisdom, in one way or another, appears as
a dominant   influence upon the whole of   the subsequent
sapiential enterprise within Judaism.   At Qumran, it is
reshaped by sectarian convictions about   the hiddenness
of the law's meaning outside the community.   In Philo,
it is modified in relation to the larger concept of the
λόγος,   and redefined   by the methodology   and presumptions of allegorical exegesis.   But in   both cases, as
in Sirach, the search for wisdom proceeds by way of the
interpretation of the law.   In   a very real   sense,
therefore, the relationship between wisdom and   the law
must be considered   to be a basic and   fundamental premise underlying all of the later Jewish literature that
concerns itself with the pursuit of הנכמ or σοφία.

     A   second point of analogy and   comparison between
the materials analyzed in our study may be discerned in
regard to the understanding of the law and the acquisition of wisdom.   For each of the sources differentiates
or distinguishes in some manner between   different levels   of   sapiential   attainment   or   achievement.   In
Sirach, the   distinction is   related in   the   first in-

stance to vocation, and in the second to diligence and divine grace. At Qumran, the community as a whole differentiates itself in terms of its wisdom and its obedience from outsiders, but also simultaneously distinguishes among its own members, recognizing a hierarchy of perfection in spirit and understanding. For Philo, discrimination in connection with the possession of wisdom is integrated and amalgamated into a discussion about the migration of the soul, and the stages along the way of that journey which mark distinct levels of progress in relationship to the sapiential and spiritual goal. Each of our literary witnesses, however, though they approach the subject from differing perspectives and form their treatment of the subject in accordance with these perspectives, comes to a similar and comparable conclusion. Wisdom is attained to a greater degree by some, and to a lesser degree by others. A variable pattern of sapiential attainment or achievement may thus be said, like the wisdom-law link, to characterize pre-Christian Jewish wisdom.

A third correlation between the different documents occurs in regard to the relationship between wisdom and spirit with respect to this pattern. For the highest degree of sapiential attainment in the literature that we have surveyed may be seen to be consistently attributed to the person who has had an experience of inspiration and gained wisdom with the help of the Spirit. In Sirach, it is attributed to the scribe who has been filled with the divine Spirit of understanding and is enabled, as a result of his experience to perceive and pour forth words of wisdom as a sage. At Qumran, it is attributed to the teachers and leaders of the sect who receive a knowledge of the hidden meaning of the Law and the Prophets through such divine revelation. For Philo, it is attributed to the wise man who has purified his soul enabling it to receive the higher wisdom of allegory and to experience a mystical transport into the divine presence by way of the illumination of the Spirit. Again, the terms in which the theme is stated, and the description of the process may be seen to vary. In each instance, however, the person of higher sapiential status is said to have obtained the wisdom that differentiates him from others through the assistance of God's Spirit.

Finally, we may note a last confluence in terms of the titles and qualities that are used in our literature in conjunction with descriptions of persons attaining to the highest level of sapiential status. The agreement here also is not complete, but it is still substantial. Sirach and Philo, for example, concur in attributing a surpassing eloquence of speech to this person; Qumran and Philo in denoting him as τέλειος or חכם. All three of our sources, moreover, are in accordance in reserving the designation σοφός or חכם to this individual, and in associating his wisdom with righteousness and virtue. The evidence suggests, then, that a group of titles and capabilities were somewhat, though not fully, standardized, and that these were customarily associated to a greater or lesser extent with the claim to a higher sapiential status.

In four instances, then, we are able to indicate broad areas of agreement, or analogy which cut across the geographical and cultural diversities of Jewish sapiential literature in the Hellenistic-Roman era. To recognize such points of contact and similarity is not, however, to attempt to speak of the later Jewish wisdom movement as a completely homogeneous entity. Rather, as our studies should indicate, a concern for wisdom, and the pursuit of wisdom, comes to expression in a significant way within three different portions of post-biblical Judaism. The fact that common themes are nonetheless recognizable does, however, allow us to give definition to the phenomenon of wisdom as it existed and developed across a broad spectrum of post-biblical Judaism, and it is against this background that we now propose to investigate and analyze the manifestation of wisdom at Corinth, and Paul's response to it.

CHAPTER FOUR

WISDOM AND SPIRIT AT CORINTH: THE PAULINE CRITIQUE

4.1 Introduction

It will be useful for us to begin our analysis of 1 Co 1-3 by giving attention to the overall form of this portion of the epistle. However, it is interesting to notice in this regard that up until a comparatively recent date as far as Pauline scholarship is concerned little effort has been spent on this task. As a result of this, and somewhat, then, by way of default, 1 Co 1-3 has been considered for the most part to be primarily an ad hoc composition whose parameters have been determined entirely spontaneously by Paul in response to the particular situational demands of the Corinthian conflict. Increasingly, however, over the past few decades of research, scholars have pointed out that there are solid indications within this passage which enable one to argue a contrasting conclusion with considerable plausibility.

Chief among these has been Wilhelm Wuellner who has strongly supported a proposal which assigns Paul's evaluation of wisdom in these opening chapters of 1 Corinthians, on a form-critical basis, to the "haggadic homily genre" of post-biblical Judaism.[1] Wuellner bases his contention upon an analysis of the data utilizing criteria for the detection and recognition of the homily genre first developed and presented by Peder Borgen. According to Borgen and Wuellner, then, there are three main features which are characteristic of the homiletic pattern.[2]

1. There is a correspondence between the opening and closing statements of the homily. The closing statement picks up words and/or phrases from the opening statement in a reprise of the central theme.

2. In addition to the main scriptural quotation which occurs in the opening statement, there is always at least one, and sometimes several subordinate scriptural quotations interspersed throughout the homily.

3. Key words and phrases from the opening scriptural quotation, and sometimes from the subordinate scriptural quotation(s) recur throughout the homily either as quoted or paraphrased.

67

Turning again then to 1 Co 1-3 with these three criteria in mind, Wuellner finds that 1 Co 1.18-3.20 meets all of the qualifications necessary for inclusion within the homily genre.

1. There is a definite correspondence between 1 Co 1.18-20 and 1 Co 3.18-20. The latter section picks up words, (i.e. σοφός and μώρια), and phrases, (i.e. σοφία τοῦ κόσμου), from the former passage.

2. There is a scriptural quotation in the opening section, (in 1 Co 1.19; cf. Isa 29.14), and in the closing section, (in 1 Co 3.19-20; cf. Job 5.12, 13, and Ps 93.-11). Subordinate quotations are discernable at 1 Co 1.31, (cf. Jer 9.24), 1 Co 2.9, (cf. Isa 64.4?), and 1 Co 2.16, (cf. Isa 40.13). Possible scriptural allusions occur in 1 Co 1.20, (cf. Isa 19.-12; 33.18, and 44.25), 1 Co 1.26, (cf. Jer 9.22, 23), 1 Co 2.10, (cf. Job 11.7), and 1 Co 3.13; (cf. Prov 20.27).

3. Both words, such as σοφία, (cf. 1 Co 1.-20, 21, 22, 24, 30, 2.1, 4, 5, 6, 7, 13, 3.19), σοφός, (cf. 1.20, 25, 26, 27), and μώρια, (cf. 1 Co 1.21, 23, 3.19); and phrases, like σοφία τοῦ κόσμου, or σοφία τοῦ αἰῶνος τούτου, (cf. 1 Co 1.20, 2.6), recur in the passage. Further, the ideas they express are also conveyed paraphrastically; (cf. 1 Co 1.28, 2.8, 10, 11, 12, 14).

On the strength of these observations, Wuellner has argued that one is able to make out a strong case for the recognition of a coherent and cohesive homily pattern behind the successive subsections of Paul's argumentation in 1 Co 1.18-3.20.

But what of the rest of 1 Co 1-4? How does the remainder of the evidence in these chapters integrate with this thesis? Wuellner has responded to this point making use of research by Carl Bjerklund,[3] and Nils Dahl[4] in order to show that the παρακαλῶ exhortations in 1 Co 1.10 and 4.16 provide an applicational framework for the more closely structured wisdom homily.[5] Paul's discourse, then, is intentionally bounded

68

by introductory comments, (1 Co 1.1-17), and concluding remarks, (Co 3.21-4.21), whose exhortations are meant to show that the Corinthian situation provides an appropriate context for the applications that may be drawn out of the discourse.

Recently, James MacDonald, in the couuse of a separate study of the forms of early Christian communication, has also come to quite similar conclusions concerning the genre of 1 Co 1.18-3.20. Based upon a comparative analysis, and drawing upon a much wider range of parallels than Wuellner, MacDonald has affirmed that Paul's evaluation of wisdom is cast in the form of a 'paraclesis', as a Pauline homily intended to convey apostolic teaching.[6] However, his findings also carry the thesis beyond those of Wuellner in three important respects.

First of all, MacDonald has discovered that a further feature common to the homily genre is a "proneness to the use of antithesis".[7] Antithesis appears consistently within any given subsection of the argument, and also serves to structure the overall form of the discourse. Following MacDonald, then, a fourth criterion may be added to those of Borgen and Wuellner. The homily genre displays a thematic structure based on antithesis; (compare 1 Co 1.18-2.5 and 2.6-3.20).[8]

Secondly, he has confirmed an important observation with regard to the motivational rationale underlying the employment of the 'paraclesis' form. According to MacDonald, who follows the earlier research of Nils Dahl, the customary aims of 'paraclesis' are fourfold: instruction, consolation, exhortation, and admonishment.[9] Thus, if Paul does employ a homily form in 1 Co 1.18-3.20, then it is probable that his intention is guided by these aims.[10]

Thirdly, MacDonald has pointed to other comparable homilies elsewhere in the Pauline corpus.[11] The clearest and most helpful parallel is provided in Rom 1.18-4.25 where Paul's exposition is built upon the thematic statement of Rom 1.16-17. It is concluded with Rom 4.16-25 and the discussion of the righteousness reckoned to Abraham; (cp. Rom 1.16-17 and 4.22-25). Subordinate scriptural quotations and allusions are also apparent throughout, (i.e. quotations in Rom 2.24, 3.4, 10, 11-18, 4.3, 7-9), as are key words and concepts, or ideas from the opening statement. Further, the structural development is by way of antithesis upon the stated theme with a movement from the negative aspects of the theme, (cf. Rom 1.18-3.20), to the positive development of the topic; (cf. Rom 3.21-4.25). MacDonald concludes, therefore, that Rom 1.16-4.25 is "a thematic homily, antithetical in structure, and expounding systematically the initial statement of the theme".[12] As such, Rom 1.16-4.25 provides an important parallel to 1 Co 1.18-3.20, particularly informative in terms of its antithetical negative to positive development.

In evaluating the significant contributions that Wuellner and Macdonald have made to the interpretation and understanding of 1 Co 1.18-3.20, it is clear that full weight should be given to their conclusions as far as they go.[13] Accordingly, Paul's words here do not simply represent a spontaneous, immediate attempt to resolve the problems that have arisen at Corinth. In the light of the evidence, they must also be seen as a unified, organized, and considered attempt to respond to the situation that confronted Paul especially with respect to the phenomenon of wisdom.[14] This is not, however, to argue that the ad hoc and the formal approach are necessarily antithetical. Instead, it seems best to conclude that in 1 Co 1.18-3.20 they are complementary. The homily pattern has provided Paul with a useful and natural structure for the formation of his response.[15] The Pauline corrective has been intentionally brought to the problem in the general and comprehensive terms of an overall definition and evaluation of the experience of wisdom within the Christian context; an evaluation whose positive and negative facets are specifically highlighted by the use of a thematic antithetical structure.

In this section of the thesis, therefore, which concentrates on Paul's attitude to wisdom and on his response to the Corinthian claim to wisdom, we will want to proceed on the structural basis supplied to us by these observations.[16] We propose, in addition, however, to analyze more closely the negative (1 Co 1.18 -2.5), and positive (1 Co 2.6-3.17), portions of the Pauline discourse from the perspective afforded to us as a result of our research in part one in order to test the hypothesis that the manifestation of wisdom at Corinth and Paul's response to it are convincingly explained against the background of later sapiential Judaism.

4.2   Wisdom: Content,   Definition   and Locus;   (1 Co
       1.18-25)

        Paul opens his   discourse in   1 Co 1.18-20   with a
combination of quotation   and allusion drawn   from the
text of Isaiah.[17] The appropriateness of his choice is
apparent from the original context where both quotation
and   allusion occur   in connection   with   the prophetic
critique of   Israel's wisdom   which had failed   to perceive the pattern   of God's   activity in the   course of
contemporary events.[18]   That Paul also intends to critique the   Corinthians with   regard to   the   failure of
their wisdom to perceive the meaning of   God's activity
in the cross of Christ is made clear from   the concluding interpretative comment of 1 Co 1.20b.   As we shall
see, however, a closer examination of   Paul's quotation
in 1 Co 1.19   will serve to show more   specifically how
Paul makes this point with reference to the   content of
the Corinthian wisdom.

        It is virtually certain that Paul has obtained his
version of the citation   in 1 Co 1.19 from   the Septuagint rather than the Hebrew text as it agrees   word for
word with   the   former and   not the   latter.   However,
there is a single significant exception to   this observation.   The final word of the quotation seems to have
been altered by   Paul from κρύψω to ἀθετήσω.[19]   But if
this   is indeed the apostle's own   deliberate adaption,
then his alteration might provide us with a clue to the
meaning and the usage of the citation within   its Pauline context.

        It is interesting,   as a   point of entry   into the
discussion of 1 Co 1.19, to notice the virtual uniform-
ity and   unanimity of   the translations that   have been
given to ἀθετήσω in 1 Co 1.19b.   Thus the   <u>Authorized</u>
<u>Version</u> renders the clause, "and (I) will bring to not-
hing the understanding of the prudent"; a translation
which the   <u>New English Bible</u> and   the   <u>Jerusalem Bible</u>
have been content to follow exactly as far as the meaning of ἀθετήσω is concerned.   Moreover, the   rendering
receives further support from the <u>Revised Standard Ver-</u>
<u>sion</u> and   the   <u>New International Version</u> which   have
adopted the   synonymous alternatives, "I   will thwart",
and "I will frustrate", respectively.

        However, despite this unusual solidarity among the
English versions, the meaning that has been chosen as a
rallying point is somewhat surprising.   For it is only
in a derivative sense that ἀθετήσω may be   construed in

this way.   The primary meaning of ἀθετήσω, which comes
from the root verb τίθημι is,   "to set aside".[20]   So,
for example, in Mk 7.9, Jesus' accusation is that the
scribes and the pharisees ἀθετεῖτε τὴν ἐντολὴν τοῦ θεοῦ
ἵνα τὴν παράδοσιν ὑμῶν στησῆτε.   The center of the
charge, therefore, is surely that the scribes and pharisees have 'set aside' one thing for another; (in this
case, the law for their traditions).   So, while it is
certainly true enough to go on to say that in so doing
they have brought the law to no effect, (cf. Mk 7.13),
this does not alter the primary meaning of ἀθετέω in Mk
7.9 which is meant to show how this effect has come
about.[21]   Pauline usage also conforms to this meaning
as is shown by 1 Th 4.8 where Paul warns the Thessalon-
ians that his words cannot be 'set aside' in favor of
another ethic.[22]

   Presumably, the translators have been influenced
by the parallelism within the Pauline citation, and
feel that the nuance of ἀθετήσω in 1 Co 1.19b must be
inferred from the verb ἀπολῶ in 1 Co 1.19a.   But is it
possible, especially given the probability that ἀθετήσω
represents a Pauline alteration to the Septuagint
text, that the influence should be taken as proceeding
in the opposite direction as far as Paul's usage of the
citation is concerned? Is it possible, in other words,
that the deliberate, or apparently deliberate change of
verb in 1 Co 1.19b implies that a different nuance must
be given to ἀπολῶ in 1 Co 1.19a, and consequently also
to the verse as a whole?

   We wish to suggest that this is precisely the
case, and that, accordingly, ἀπολῶ should be translat-
ed, 'to do away with', so that the entire verse conveys
a single idea; that God has done away with the wisdom
of the wise and the understanding of the prudent in the
sense that he has set such wisdom and understanding
aside.[23]   It has been superseded by 'the cross of
Christ', (1 Co 1.17), and 'the word of the cross'; (1
Co 1.18, cp. 1.21).[24]

   In the same way, as Hans Conzelmann brings out in
his commentary on this passage, verse 20 follows a similar pattern of thought, and comes, as a result, to a
similar conclusion.   Succeeding Paul's three pointed
questions about where God's activity has left the
σοφός, the γραμματεύς, and the συζητητὴς τοῦ αἰῶνος
τούτου; "the judgement on ἡ σοφία τοῦ κόσμου is passed
in the form of a question; not by reasoning, but by asserting an act of God".[25]   Furthermore, if, following

C.K. Barrett, and, more especially, A.J.M. Wedderburn, one takes ἐν τῇ σοφίᾳ τοῦ θεοῦ as a prepositional phrase of accompanying, or attendant circumstances, rather than in a casual, temporal, or spatial sense, then verse 21 also complements Paul's scriptural argument in 1 Co 1.19. For it asserts that it has always been a part of God's intention, in light of the ultimate incompleteness of ἡ σοφία τοῦ κόσμου to arrange the circumstances under which such wisdom would be transcended and set aside by 'the folly of what we preach', (1 Co 1.21); namely, 'Christ crucified', (1 Co 1.23), 'the power of God and the wisdom of God'; (1 Co 1.24).[26]

Finally, however, if we turn our attention back now to 1 Co 1.18 in the light of these findings, then even the puzzling contrast between μωρία and δύναμις begins to resolve itself. The 'wisdom of the world', which regards the cross and the kerygma as 'folly' in comparison to its own understanding, is perishing, as are those who hold to it. It has been set aside and superseded, transcended by God's act in Christ.[27] But as for those who have recognized God's activity in the cross, they are being saved and brought into fellowship with God by the proclamation of the divine deed.[28]

Now all of these assertions take on an added relevance if, in reality, the phenomenon of wisdom at Corinth was nothing other than a manifestation of Torah-centric σοφία. Moreover, as Nils Dahl has pointed out, there are indications within the passage itself to support the conclusion that the Corinthians, "exercised their wisdom as interpreters of scripture".[29] This result, Dahl suggests, is indicated principally by the designations that Paul assigns to those whom he critiques in 1 Co 1.20. The idea has been taken further, by Kenneth Grayston and R.G. Hamerton-Kelly, who have deomonstrated that Jewish and not Greek culture provides the most probable background for the conjunction of the titles σοφός, γραμματεύς, and συζητητής.[30] Thus, within 1 Co 1.20, there exists evidence to bolster the possibility that Paul's response is shaped by an attempt to depreciate the value of a claim to Torah-centric wisdom at Corinth.[31]

However, if 1 Co 1.20 is indeed an indication of the background to the Corinthian controversy, then we can see more clearly how, over against the Corinthian concept of wisdom centered upon the prior revelation of God in the Torah, Paul strives to set the new act of God in Christ. He does so by way of a scriptural argument, contending along the lines presented to him by his prophetic citation, that God has made the former wisdom into foolishness by revealing himself anew and more completely in Christ.[32] The kind of wisdom upon which the Corinthians were now relying had proved itself, in the final analysis, to be incomplete and inadequate in the light of the cross; (cf. Deut 21.22-23).[33] Therefore, says Paul, God has done away with it in the sense that it has been superseded by a more complete revelation which has given a new content and definition to wisdom.

> "In direct antithesis to their understanding of wisdom, Paul asserts that Christ is God's wisdom -Christ crucified. Divine wisdom is manifested in the cross and its proclamation."[34]

In this way, then, a new locus has been given to the wisdom of God. Christ, cross, and kerygma have replaced Torah as the definitive loci of divine wisdom.[35]

In summary, it may be useful to draw together our comments concerning Paul's critique by noticing that the Corinthian wisdom which is the subject of his polemic is characteristically styled by the apostle as σοφία τοῦ αἰῶνος τούτου, or σοφία τοῦ κόσμου.[36] For if indeed these phrases are of Jewish origin denoting the time before the 'messianic age', or the 'age to come', (cf. Lk 18.30 and 20.35), then either phrase serves to encapsulate the Pauline critique.[37] The Corinthian wisdom is a wisdom which has not yet reckoned with the full implications of the Christ-event, and especially with the significance of the cross. For there God has brought in a new age and transcended the wisdom and revelation that was present before the coming of "Christ, the power of God and the wisdom of God'; (cf. 1 Co 1.24). This is the message which Paul has been sent to preach, (cf. 1 Co 1.17), and, far from 'folly', it is 'the power of God', (cf. 1 Co 1.18), and God's wisdom; (cf. 1 Co 1.21).

4.3   Wisdom: Purpose, Function, and Status; (1 Co 1.26-31)

In this section, in contrast to 1 Co 1.18-25, the scriptural citation comes at the conclusion rather than the commencement of the discussion. Nonetheless, it is still quite plausible to treat the citation as an important factor as far as the structure and content of the argument is concerned. Here also, for instance, as in 1 Co 1.18-25, it is apparent that the citation derives from another prophetic text which takes up the critique of wisdom and the wise man in much the same way as Isaiah 29.14. More specifically, 1 Co 1.31 appears to represent an abbreviated form of Jer 9.24; (cp. Jer 8.4-9 and 9.12-16).[38] Out of this context, Paul has deliberately chosen to focus attention on what he considers to be the most crucial and relevant element of Jeremiah's polemic, namely the boastful confidence which has been produced as a result of a reliance upon wisdom. This aspect of the citation Paul will now apply to the Corinthian situation; in this case to Corinthian ideas about the purpose and function of wisdom within the community.

Further, (as also in 1 Co 1.18-25), it appears likely that Paul's line of reasoning within this section rests upon the meaning and nuance of the verb that is employed within the scriptural text.[39] Interestingly, whether the citation derives from the Septuagint or the Hebrew text may make little difference in this case. For καυχάομαι, which represents a translation of הלל, preserves virtually the same connotations as the Hebrew verb; the chief feature of both being the fact that they may be used in either a positive or negative sense.[40] So it should not surprise us to see Paul use καυχάομαι in both ways in 1 Co 1.29 and 31, especially as such antithesis is characteristic of the homiletic genre which Paul's discourse reflects.

But what is the boast ἐνώπιον τοῦ θεοῦ which Paul rejects, and what is the boast ἐν κυρίῳ which he commends? Judging from the context which is supplied to us by the intervening verse, (1 Co 1.30), Paul seems to be making a distinction between a boast in God, as the 'source of our life in Christ Jesus', (so 1 Co 1.30), and a boast before God, a boast that apparently has laid claim to a more complete experience of salvation. It may be, then, that the underlying issue in 1 Co 1.26-31, an issue highlighted by the positive and negative uses of καυχάομαι in verse 29 and verse 31, is one of attainment, or status within the Christian community. If so, then the distinction drawn by some within the Corinthian fellowship may have been similar to the distinction drawn within later sapiential Judaism, and especially clearly in Philo, between persons at different levels with respect to the acquisition and attainment of wisdom.

Thus, for example, we have observed the characteristic contrast that is drawn by Philo between the
τέλειος, (representing the one who has arrived at complete perfection in wisdom and full communion with
God), and the νήπιος , (depicting the one who has only
begun to progress towards the full possession of wisdom
and fellowship with God).[41] Furthermore, it can be
shown that a whole host of cognate terms, words such as
σοφός, δυνατός, εὐγενής, πλούσιος, and βασιλέυς are all
associated with the person of higher status in Philo,
and that these terms form an important link connecting
the Corinthian controversy with a background in Jewish
wisdom.[42] We wish to suggest, therefore, that the intention within this section of Paul's argument is to
critique the devotees of the Corinthian sophia in terms
of their predilection for descriptive titles which per-
petuate a belief in distinctions of status with regards
to wisdom and the experience of communion with God.
The starting point for an analysis of the Pauline critique is the scriptural citation from Jer 9.24a and its
immediate context in Jer 9.23 and 9.24b.

The triadic form of 1 Co 1.26 has always been
something of a puzzle for interpreters.[43] For although
the three-fold motif of wisdom, power, and well-being
is widely attested in comparative literature, at least
in terms of its individual components, still there
exists no parallel to the precise arrangement found in
1 Co 1.26.[44] The difficulty may be resolved, however,
if we assume that the apostle is working in 1 Co 1.26
with a dual reference in mind; to the self-designations
of the Corinthians on the one hand, and to the scriptural citation from Jeremiah and its context on the
other. Thus, the particular terms employed in 1 Co 1.-
26 would appear to be derived not from Paul, but from
the Corinthians; (cp. 1 Co 4.10). Σοφοί , δυνατοί, and
εὐγενής are all applicable to those who, because of
their possession of wisdom, think of themselves as
wise, powerful, and well-born.[45] But it also seems
that the particular arrangement of these three terms,
and the modification of the second element of the
triadic formula in 1 Co 1.27, (δυνατοί is changed to τὰ
ἰσχυρά), are indications that Paul has taken up these
terms not only with reference to the Corinthian usage,
but also in the light of the context of his scriptural
citation; (cf. Jer 9.23). Hence, we may conclude that
Paul intends to criticize the use of this kind of terminology among some of the Corinthians, who spoke of
themselves by virtue of a claim to wisdom as those who
had achieved a higher religious status and a more inti-

76

mate experience of communion with God than their fellow
believers. But his approach is by way of an attempt to
show a connection between the attitude of the Corinthians who use these titles, and the kind of boasting
that is explicitly criticized in scripture. For inasmuch as these Corinthians have been content to distinguish themselves from others in terms of these designations, they are boasting before the Lord ἐν τῇ σοφίᾳ,
ἐν τῇ ἰσχυΐ, and ἐν τῷ πλουτῳ.46

Now in the context in Jeremiah, it is stated that
such boasts are to be rejected in favor of a boast 'in
the Lord', (so Jer 9.24a), and this, as we have already
noted, is the element which Paul wishes to lay particular stress upon in his use of the scriptural citation
in 1 Co 1.31 and, indeed, in the section as a whole.
In the first part of 1 Co 1.26-31, Paul gives emphasis
to his point by centering his remarks around the theme
of God's call.47 In 1 Co 1.26-29, then, it is the
apostle's intention to remind the Corinthians of the
circumstances in which they first entered into an experience of fellowship with God. Then, Paul says, as
they themselves will recall if only they will consider
it, (cf. βλέπετε; 1 Co 1.26), it was God's call, God's
own powerful act that had brought them salvation and
fellowship with him. Their initial experience of God's
grace had come to them, therefore, apart from any capabilities in terms of wisdom, and apart from any distinctions of status, through the kerygma.

Now Paul's appeal makes particularly good sense
if, as has been alleged, some of the Corinthians
thought that they had found a pathway to a more complete experience of salvation and fellowship with God
through another means, namely, through the contempla-
tive study of the Torah subsequent to the time of
Paul's departure. In that case, Paul's argument is
that the Corinthians are being inconsistent. If their
initial experience of salvation and fellowship with God
has come to them through God's call in the kerygma, it
can hardly be completed by turning back to the study of
the Torah, or to a Torah-centric wisdom. Indeed, in
the light of the scriptural citation that Paul adduces,
the Corinthians should recognize that they are in danger of making a 'boast before the Lord', rather than a
'boast in the Lord' by turning back to such wisdom and
to the distinctions of status which accompany it. For
if such distinctions represent a claim by some to have
achieved a more complete experience of salvation, then
they do so by asserting that this experience has been

obtained not through the kerygma, but through a Torah-
centric wisdom which claims to confer upon its adherents a superior status.

Nevertheless, while Paul clearly rejects the
Corinthians' wisdom as a means to a more complete experience of salvation, there may also be a sense in
which he is willing to accommodate himself to sapiential language and imagery. For he seems ready in 1 Co
1.30 to commend a wisdom ἐν Χριστῷ Ἰησοῦ, a wisdom that
is, in fact, δικαιοσύνη τὲ καὶ ἁγιασμὸς καὶ ἀπολύτρωσις.
This element of his argument may also, however, derive
from Jer 9.24. For, in that verse, there is commendation for the person who 'boasts in the Lord' and in the
'knowledge and understanding of God'; (a phrase which
is taken in context to include a knowledge of God's actions 'in the earth'; cp. Jer 8.12ff.). Hence Paul's
point in making reference to wisdom in 1 Co 1.30 would
be similar to the one which he made in 1 Co 1.18-25.
The search for wisdom within the law has been set aside
by a knowledge of God's act and the wisdom that has
come into being in Christ; (cf. ἐγενήθη). Therefore
those who 'boast in the Lord' boast in their understanding of God's act in Christ in which a new wisdom
has come into being, providing life, righteousness,
holiness, and redemption.

4.4   Wisdom: Source, Authentication, and Inspiration;
       (1 Co 2.1-5)

In the previous two sections of the discourse,
Paul has successfully critiqued the manifestation of
wisdom at Corinth on the basis of its content and its
effects, and this in light of God's action in Christ.
Now, in 1 Co 2.1-5, he turns to a third and concluding
aspect of his critique, to the question of the source
and authentication of wisdom.[48]

Although, in contrast to the previous two sections
of the discourse, we possess no scriptural citation
within 1 Co 2.1-5 which might alert us to the central
issue in this portion of Paul's presentation, we do
have in 1 Co 2.5 a short, epigrammatical statement that
appears to operate in much the same way. In this
verse, which draws a concise and climatic antithesis
between σοφία ἀνθρώπων and ἡ δύναμις θεοῦ, Paul appears
to revert back to the implied contrast of the theme
statement of the homily in 1 Co 1.18. Here, however,
the exposition of the contrast is not developed in
terms of the respective contents of the Corinthian wis-

dom and the Pauline kerygma, but instead it is drawn on the basis of the source and form of these two messages, (cp. ὁ λόγος μοῦ, and πειθοῖς σοφίας λόγοις in 1 Co 2.-4).[49] The former aspect of source comes to expression quite clearly in the two genitival constructions of 1 Co 2.5, (i.e. σοφία ἀνθρώπων and δυνάμει θεοῦ), and the latter aspect of form in the twice repeated disclaimer of eloquence; (cf. 1 Co 2.1 and 4; cp. 1 Co 1.17, 2.13, 4.19-20).[50] Thus, the question which presses upon the one who would endeavour to grasp the thrust of Paul's argument at this point in its development is why these two particular aspects of source and form have been brought together in the context of 1 Co 2.1-5 as the focal point of this section.

Here, as before in the course of our investigations into 1 Co 1.18-25 and 1 Co 1.26-31, later sapiential Judaism would appear to be of assistance in finding a perspective that will enable us to understand Paul's intention within this passage. For, as we have noticed, eloquent speech plays a significant part in the Jewish wisdom traditions that appear to be related to the manifestation of wisdom at Corinth. One observes, for instance, that within these traditions, wisdom is frequently and characteristically associated with eloquence; so much so, in fact, that in some of the sources a tendency can be noticed to regard eloquent or persuasive speech as a special sign or indication of the one who is truly in possession of divine wisdom.[51] Now, if we also recall at this point that God is consistently regarded by these same sources as the giver of wisdom, and that God is often said to mediate his wisdom through the Spirit, then it is not too difficult to conceive of a group at Corinth who could have looked upon eloquence as a key criterion in regard to the evaluation of the worth of any message and the authentication of its divine, spiritual source.[52] Indeed, it seems quite possible to conclude that it was the Corinthians who had in this way made a connection between the form of a message and its source, regarding eloquence as an important standard to be used in assessing the inspiration of a speaker and evaluating the wisdom and worth of his message.[53]

But Paul, while apparently prepared to concede to others at Corinth a certain superiority of word, (ὑπεροχὴν λόγους; 1 Co 2.1), and a certain persuasiveness, (πειθοῖς σοφίας λόγοις; 1 Co 2.4), is nonetheless unwilling to accept the conclusion that the Corinthians have reached concerning the value of such eloquence.

For him, there is a very real danger in a 'wisdom of words', a danger that the Corinthians' faith might come to be falsely founded upon superficial impression and appearance rather than the 'power of God'. Consequently, Paul disputes the Corinthian claim that inspiration is authenticated by eloquent and persuasive speech. His criticism comes to expression in 1 Co 2.4 and 5.

In the former verse, by way of two parallel dative constructions, Paul sets up a strong contrast between one sort of authentication, (ἐν πειθοῖς σοφίας λόγοις), and another, (ἐν ἀποδείξει πνεύματος καὶ δυνάμεως).54 Especially worthy of notice, however, is the element of the contrast that is highlighted by the use of ἀπόδειξις, for, as is regularly noted, ἀπόδειξις is a technical rhetorical term which serves in both Jewish and Greek sources to denote a conclusive and compelling proof.55 What is less often observed, though, is that these same sources preserve a consistent distinction between this superior sort of proof and an inferior validation specifically in terms of an antithesis between πειθώ and ἀπόδειξις .56 Almost certainly then ἀπόδειξις is meant to be contrasted with πειθός in 1 Co 2.4 in this same way, and Paul's point is two-fold.

First, drawing upon a technical distinction particularly appropriate to his purpose and audience, given the Corinthians' admiration for rhetoric and eloquence, Paul argues that his preaching possesses a convincing and compelling demonstration of its spiritual origins vastly superior to the proof of persuasion offered by the Corinthian wisdom with its eloquent speech. The Corinthians, with a view to the external form of their language have attempted to authenticate an inspired wisdom surpassing the kerygma. But, as Paul makes plain in 1 Co 2.4, the conclusive and definitive demonstration of inspiration is not found in external manifestations such as eloquence. It can be observed rather in an internal conviction, in the power produced by the Spirit in conjunction with the preaching of the kerygma; (cp. 1 Co 2.5 and 1 Th 1.5).57 Hence, secondly, Paul's message not only possesses the more convincing demonstration of its origins, but also the only demonstration adequate to prove that it emanates from a divine source. The true power of spiritual conviction must be clearly differentiated, Paul argues, from the sort of persuasion and eloquence that belongs to the wisdom at Corinth. The one finds its source ἐν δυνάμει θεοῦ ; the other is merely a product of ἡ σοφία ἀνθρώπων.58

4.5   Conclusion

Our investigation of the first half of the Pauline discourse in 1 Co 1.18-2.5 has disclosed that it is quite possible to interpret the manifestation of wisdom at Corinth and Paul's critical response to its phenomena against the background of later sapiential Judaism. Indeed, the three-fold polemic of the passage pertaining to the content of wisdom in 1 Co 1.18-25, to distinctions of status in 1 Co 1.26-31, and to the relationship between eloquence, wisdom, and inspiration in 1 Co 2.1-5 may be coherently and consistently explained with reference to those precise elements that have been found to be most characteristic of later Jewish wisdom. It seems reasonable to conclude, therefore, that the wisdom of the Corinthians, which provides the focus for Paul's criticisms within this text, was closely related to some form of later sapiential Judaism. This result may be confirmed, however, by an analysis of 1 Co 2.6-3.20.

CHAPTER FIVE

WISDOM AND SPIRIT IN THE PAULINE TEACHING

5.1 Introduction

In 1 Co 2.6ff., as most of those who have attempted to interpret Paul's words about wisdom in 1 Co 1.18-
3.20 would be prepared to admit, the apostle's argument
undergoes a significant shift, equally apparent in
terms of content and in terms of expression, or tone.[1]
Up to this point, for instance, Paul's comments concerning wisdom have been predominantly, if not quite
exclusively negative,[2] (so 1 Co 1.19-21, 26, 27, etc.),
and such sentiments have been brought to a climax in 1
Co 2.1-5 where Paul strongly disclaims wisdom for himself, (his message was not ἐν πειθοῖς σοφίας λόγοις),
and draws a sharp contrast between faith ἐν σοφίᾳ
ἀνθρώπων and faith ἐν δυνάμει θεοῦ. Yet, in 1 Co 2.6
the apostle seems to change direction completely. He
now not only admits the validity and the legitimacy of
some sort of wisdom, but also actually asserts that he
himself speaks such wisdom, (σοφίαν δὲ λαλοῦμεν), among
the mature, (ἐν τελείοις), in direct antithesis, apparently, to the denials of 1 Co 2.1 and 2.4.[3]

One also perceives a surprising shift in relation
to Paul's evaluation of the Corinthians' religious vocabulary in this section, or so it seems. For within 1
Co 2.6-3.4 both the τέλειος-νήπιος and the πνευματικός-
ψυχικός contrast are not criticized, as we have seen
Paul do with reference to some of the other terminology
of the Corinthians, (in 1 Co 1.26ff., for example), but
instead, their terms here are taken up in a much more
positive way, in order, apparently, to allow Paul to
claim that he himself is among the τέλειοι and the
πνευματικοί.[4] Thus, the question of the relation of
this section to the previous context confronts us directly and immediately.

Ulrich Wilckens, Martin Winter, and Walter
Schmithals, in view of these basic contrasts between 1
Co 1 18ff. and 1 Co 2.6ff. have come to the conclusion
that the latter passage, at least for the most part,
reflects the opinions of Paul's opponents rather than
those of Paul himself.[5] Paul, they argue, would hardly
have contradicted his earlier statements about a personal renunciation of wisdom in 1 Co 2.1-5 so soon and
so dramatically in 1 Co 2.6. Therefore, his use of the
concepts and terminology of Corinthian wisdom within
this section of the letter must be interpreted as an
imprecise, ambiguous, and largely unsuccessful attempt
to enter into a pastoral dialogue with the wayward theology of the Corinthians.

But, as Robert Funk has reponded, the declaration of 1 Co 2.6 need not necessarily be understood to represent a contradiction in Paul's argumentation. Rather, given the presence of the connective δέ the indication is that 1 Co 2.6a and the following material, while undeniably in contrast to Paul's previous remarks, is nevertheless intended as a qualification to what Paul has said about wisdom.[6] This grammatical argument is reinforced, moreover, by 1 Co 2.6b and c which contain two further limiting clauses that seem, in the same way, to be intended to set off the wisdom about which Paul is now speaking positively from the wisdom that previously formed the basis for Paul's antitheses in 1 Co 1.17ff. and 1 Co 2.4 and 5.[7] Finally, as Wilckens, Winter, and Schmithals admit, Paul's introduction of θεοῦ σοφία in 1 Co 1.24 appears to militate against the conclusion that in 1 Co 2.6 Paul is exclusively reflecting the postion of his opponents, and makes λαλοῦμεν in 1 Co 2.6 look very much like a resumption of κηρύσσομεν from 1 Co 1.23.[8]

The contrast between 1 Co 2.6 and Paul's former criticisms of wisdom, therefore, is not absolute but relative, and Paul's acceptance of wisdom in 1 Co 2.6 must be understood in such a way as to modify the earlier disclaimers. What Paul actually disclaims both there and here is only a certain kind of wisdom; σοφία λόγου, (1 Co 1.17), σοφία τοῦ κόσμου, (1 Co 1.20, 2.6), and σοφία ἀνθρώπων ; (1 Co 2.5).[9] It is going beyond the evidence, then, to conclude that Paul rejects all wisdom as something which is out of accord with the gospel. Instead, in antithetical style, he moves from a critique of false wisdom in 1 Co 1.18-2.5, to an exposition of authentic wisdom in 1 Co 2.6-3.17; from the negative to the positive portions of his presentation.[10]

The second objection raised by Wilckens, Winter, and Schmithals as to the language of the passage is also adequately answered along similar lines. Paul's purpose in taking over a portion of the terminology of the Corinthians in 1 Co 2.6ff. is admittedly apologetic, for it is certainly true to say that the terms used in 1 Co 2.6ff. show that he is responding to his opponents in such a way as to try and produce a meaningful dialogue between his position and theirs. But in utilizing their terminology, it is not clear that Paul is capitulating to their definitions as is implied by Wilckens, Winter, and Schmithals. Nor is Paul's use of terms so imprecise or ambiguous as to render the attempt at dialogue a failure in that the whole passage may yet be read in a 'gnostic' sense.[11] Instead, in a directly polemical way, Paul has redefined the basic terms of the Corinthians, altering their meaning so that they are now inapplicable to the present situation; (cp. 1 Co 2.6 and 3.1).[12] Moreover, as James Reese has indicated, Paul's purpose in redefinition need not be seen solely as a polemical device.[13] It is equally possible to infer that he is seeking, at least to some extent, not only to rebuke the Corinthians, but also to instruct them. In the latter case, he would be attempting in a didactic way to correct an inadequate understanding of the terms commonly employed at Corinth by conveying to his readers the true sense in which such terms may legitimately be utilized.

Hence, the presence of terms that seem to come from the Corinthians in 1 Co 2.6ff. need not be decisive, as Wilckens, Winter, and Schmithals have argued, against the thesis already proposed, namely, that 1 Co 2.6-3.17 represents a shift in the predominant orientation of Paul's argument; a shift from the critique of the Corinthian position to an exposition of Paul's own understanding of wisdom.

But if 1 Co 2.6-3.17 is indeed meant as something of a balance to the previous sections of the Pauline discourse, then it becomes at least likely, prima facie, that this section is intended to be in correspondence, in organizational terms, with the main lines of Paul's presentation of the wisdom theme in 1 Co 1.18-2.5.[14] Thus the two-part structural division of 1 Co 2.6-16 that has been noticed by Hans Conzelmann and Anthony Hanson brings 1 Co 2.6-9 into line with 1 Co 1.28-25, and 1 Co 2.10-16, (or indeed, as we think, 1 Co 2.10-3.4), into relationship with 1 Co 2.1-5.[15] In 1 Co 2.6-9, Paul returns to the question of the content of wisdom, and in 2.10-3.4 to the question of the source or origin of wisdom.[16] Both questions, though, are taken up from a new perspective and treated positively in contrast to Paul's previous discussion. Finally, then, by way of three successive illustrations, the discourse reverts back to the question of the function of wisdom within the community, (cp. 1 Co 1.26-31), before it closes with a reprise of the opening statement in 1 Co 3.18-20.

Having dealt with the question of the relation of 1 Co 2.6ff. to its context, the question of Paul's use of Corinthian terminology within this section of his argument, and the question of the organization of 1 Co 2.6-3.20 as a whole, we may now turn our attention to an analysis of Paul's wisdom as he presents it in 1 Co 2.6-3.17. As was the case in our exposition of the Pauline critique in 1 Co 1.18-2.5, the scope of our investigation must be restricted. We will not be able to discuss all of the material within this portion of 1 Corinthians, but instead will concentrate our focus upon the concept of wisdom which is here presented, and upon the relationship between that wisdom and the Spirit. Three questions arising out of a realization of the link between 1 Co 2.6-3.17 and 1 Co 1.18-2.5 may serve to guide our study. First, what is the nature of the wisdom that Paul offers to the mature and how is its content to be distinguished from the sort of wisdom already rejected in 1 Co 1.18-25? Second, how does Paul wish to define the relationship between wisdom and spirit? Third, what is his estimation of the purpose or function of wisdom? How is it intended to affect the community and operate within it? Trying to provide answers to these questions will supply us with more than enough material for investigation.

5.2 Wisdom: Content, Definition, and Locus; (1 Co 2.6-9)

5.21 Introduction

Following the declaration of 1 Co 2.6a, which represents, as has just been seen, a sharp, though not inexplicable shift in the direction of the Pauline argument, it is fairly safe to assume that we may interpret the succeeding context through verse 9 as an attempt to define, or at least to describe, the content of θεοῦ σοφία. This explanation is also indicated by the two qualifying negative clauses which immediately follow in 1 Co 2.6b and c, and the series of parenthetical expressions and relative clauses which occur in 1 Co 2.7-ff. Subsequent to this, we find a quotation which appears to be intended as an authoritative conclusion to the thought of 1 Co 2.6-8 and as a basis for the introduction of new ideas in 1 Co 2.10ff. It would seem, then, that Paul wishes in this section as a whole to define carefully the wisdom which he speaks with reference to three topics; negatively, first of all, with reference to σοφία τοῦ αἰῶνος τούτου and τῶν ἀρχόντων τοῦ αἰῶνος τούτου in 1 Co 2.6b and c, then positively, with respect to the 'mysterious' and 'hidden' θεοῦ σοφία in 2.7, and finally, both negatively and positively with reference to the text which we find before us in 1 Co 2.9. Thus we propose to examine each of these areas of Paul's discussion in turn.

5.22 The Wisdom and Ignorance of the Ἄρχοντες

What was, in Paul's view, ἡ σοφία τοῦ αἰῶνος τούτου, and who were οἱ ἄρχοντες τοῦ αἰῶνος τούτου? It is beneficial, as Robin Scroggs points out, not to pass by the first of these two questions too quickly, or to allow one's attention to be attracted solely by the second.[17] For if οὐδέ carries its normal correlative force, then the relationship between the two phrases is meant to be mutually clarifying.[18] It is helpful for our understanding of both clauses to recall that Paul has already introduced ἡ σοφία τοῦ αἰῶνος τούτου in 1 Co 1.20 where the phrase is used in parallel with the expression ἡ σοφία τοῦ κόσμου. In reality, the two expressions are so close in meaning here and elsewhere within the Pauline corpus as to be virtually synonymous and this allows us to be more certain of the meaning of Paul's initial qualification in 1 Co 2.6b.[19] Paul is carefully distinguishing between the wisdom which he claims to speak in 1 Co 2.6a, and the kind of wisdom which has been the focus of his earlier critique in 1 Co 1.20 and 1.18-25 as a whole.

Furthermore, if our prior analysis of 1 Co 1.18-25 is reliable, then this would enable us to conclude that Paul's intent in 1 Co 2.6b is to mark off his wisdom quite clearly from an exclusively Torah-centered σοφία. The Torah as a locus of wisdom had, in Paul's mind, been superseded by a fuller wisdom that had been revealed in Christ, and particularly in his death and resurrection. Torah as the former embodiment of σοφία had been succeeded by a more complete embodiment of God's wisdom in Christ. Christ's death and resurrection have not only inaugurated the age to come, but are also to be regarded as the consummate and definitive expression of wisdom within that age.

Torah, accordingly, can be identified with ἡ σοφία τοῦ αἰῶνος τούτου because it represents an expression of wisdom designed for a prior world order, an eschatologically conditioned expression of wisdom in contrast to the wisdom of Christ, "the all-embracing, final, eschatological revelation of God."[20] Just this sort of differentiation would have been necessary within the Corinthian context as it has been envisioned in the previous portions of this study, but especially so if, as has been suggested, we are to see in 1 Co 1.24 and 30 the first occasion upon which an equation had been drawn by Paul between ὁ χριστός and ἡ σοφία.[21]

A knowledge of the relationship which appears to exist between ἡ σοφία τοῦ αἰῶνος τούτου and the Torah-centric wisdom of 1 Co 1.18-25 may also, perhaps, assist us in formulating a response to the very difficult question of the identity of the ἄρχοντες in 1 Co 2.6c. Three principal solutions have been offered in which the ἄρχοντες have been variously aligned with the human religious and political powers contemporary with the cruccifixion,[22] or with the supernatural demonic powers thought to dominate the present world order,[23] or with a combination of both of these two groups in which the influence of demonic beings is seen to lie behind the actions of the human authorities.[24] It is undoubtedly difficult to come to a final decision here, but Wesley Carr has recently advanced an argument which is extremely persuasive on behalf of the first of these three options.

Carr brings forward three separate kinds of evidence in support of his position. First of all, he points to general lexical evidence for the meaning of the term in secular and biblical Greek prior to the New Testament. Such evidence indicates with unanimity that οἱ ἄρχοντες is normally employed with reference to human religious and political rulers.[25] Particularly telling, however, is the additional fact that all of the other occurrences of the plural, οἱ ἄρχοντες within the New Testament literature refer clearly and unambiguously to human officials including the only other certain Pauline reference in Rom 13.3.[26] As Carr points out, the weight of this evidence is undiminished, by the use of the singular ὁ ἄρχων to designate Satan as ὁ ἄρχων τῶν δαιμονίων, (cf. Mt 9.34, 12.24, Mk 3.22, Lk 11.15), or ὁ ἄρχων τοῦ κόσμου; (cf. Jn 12.31, 14.30, 16.11). For in both cases it is apparent that Satan is being named as the sole ruler within his kingdom, and there is no sense, therefore, in which the domonic powers might be called οἱ ἄρχοντες beside him.[27]

Next, Carr domonstrates how the lexical evidence is strengthened by a consideration of the contextual relation between 1 Co 2.6-8 and 1 Co 1.18-25.[28] He maintains that a reference to domonic rulers can only be sustained if one is prepared to separate the object of Paul's disclaimer in 1 Co 2.6c from that of 1 Co 2.6b, for the qualification expressed in the latter

90

clause is firmly connected with Paul's previous critique of ἡ σοφία τοῦ κόσμου and those who espouse it, including the σοφός, the γραμματεύς, and the συζητητής τοῦ αἰῶνος τούτου, (1 Co 1.20), all, undoubtedly human figures. The parallelism of thought is not confined, however, to this example, for in both sections ἡ σοφία τοῦ κόσμου or ἡ σοφία τοῦ αἰῶνος τούτου is contrasted with ἡ σοφία τοῦ θεοῦ, (cf. 1 Co 1.21, 2.6, 8); in both, the climax of the contrast occurs in relation to a perception of the meaning and significance of the cross, (cf. 1 Co 1.23, 24, 2.8); and in both, a group is designated, who, because they are adherents of an inferior wisdom are ignorant of the divine wisdom that God has revealed in Christ.

Finally, Carr presents an argument based on certain form-critical similarities between Paul's remarks in 1 Co 2.6b and c and early Christian kerygmatic tradition as recorded in Acts.[29] He calls attention particularly to the mention of the ἄρχοντες in Acts 3.17, 4.26, and 13,27, (cp. also Lk 23.34-35), and notices that the three points which are made in these texts, (i.e. "the ignorance of those who crucified Jesus; the fact that is was the rulers in particular who so acted; and the centrality of the cross"), are closely related to Paul's emphases in 1 Co 2.6-8.[30] It is most probable, therefore, that Paul is echoing the primitive Christian kerygma here in 1 Co 2.6-8 as he does, admittedly, elsewhere within the epistle, most noticeably, for example, in 1 Co 15.3ff.

Thus, bringing together lexical evidence, contextual considerations and a form-critical argument, Carr makes out what, on any reckoning, must be considered to be a very substantial case for treating the ἄρχοντες in 1 Co 2.6 and 8 as the Roman and Jewish authorities responsible for Jesus' crucifixion.[31] There is, accordingly, every reason to conclude that when Paul used the phrase σοφία τοῦ αἰῶνος τούτου he intended to critique, at least in the case of the Jewish authorities, the allegiance of these individuals to a transient Torah-centric wisdom that led to the rejection and condemnation of Jesus.[32] Despite their possession and understanding of the law, they were still ignorant as to the nature and outcome of their actions in relation to the wisdom of the divine plan; (θεοῦ σοφία, 1 Co 2.8).[33] In this way, Paul thoroughly distinguishes the wisdom of which he speaks, (1 Co 2.6a), from a purely Torah-centered σοφία τοῦ αἰῶνος τούτου, (1 Co 2.6b), and separates himself co-ordinately from the chief representa-

91

tives of that wisdom, the ἄρχοντες of the Jewish people; (1 Co 2.6c).

If it is clear, however, that the object of their
ignorance was θεοῦ σοφία, it is not yet clear how Paul
intends to define that expression. We must therefore
turn our attention at this point to 1 Co 2.7 in an attempt to come to an understanding of Paul's description
of θεοῦ σοφία as the mysterious and hidden 'wisdom of
God'.

5.23 The Wisdom of God

In a carefully marked contrast, (ἀλλά), to the
wisdom of which he has been speaking in the previous
two clauses, Paul moves now in verse 7 to an expansion
of his preliminary assertion in 1 Co 2.6a. This expansion is achieved by means of a remarkable series of
four modifying expressions which, in a manner similar
to 1 Co 2.6b and c, are set in close co-ordination with
one another.

The first of these, the genitive θεοῦ, is obviously an important addition as far as the structure of
Paul's discourse is concerned, for it serves to bring
the wisdom of which he speaks here in 1 Co 2.7 into relationship with previous comments about ἡ σοφία θεοῦ in
1 Co 1.21, 24, and 30. There, as we have seen, ἡ σοφία
θεοῦ is placed in antithesis to ἡ σοφία τοῦ κόσμου,
(cf. 1 Co 1.20), and it denotes both the plan of God as
a whole, (1 Co 1.21), and especially the Christological
center of the plan; (1 Co 1.24, 30). Thus it seems
possible that both aspects of the earlier discussion
might also be in view here in 1 Co 2.7 as well.[34]

The correctness of this judgement is verified by
means of an investigation of the second expression
which Paul uses to modify and define σοφία in 1 Co 2.7,
the prepositional phrase, ἐν μυστηρίῳ.[35] For μυστήριον
within those letters which are either authored by Paul,
or authored under the influence of his thought, refers
either to the plan of God as a unity, (cf. Eph 1.9,
3.9), to the focus of that plan in Christ and kerygma,
(cf. Rom 16.25, Col 2.2, 4.3), to various other important individual constituent parts of that plan, (cf.
Rom 11.25, 1 Co 15,51, 2 Th 2.7), or, finally, to the
sum of the parts as representative of the whole, (cf. 1
Co 4.1, 13.2).[36] Thus the use of the term overall is
quite similar to the range of meaning associated with
σοφία.[37] Yet, in the same way that Paul lays special

stress in 1 Co 1.24 and 30 on the centrality of Christ and kerygma with regard to σοφία, he also puts emphasis on exactly these same elements in his references to the divine μυστήριον, so we may say that, for Paul, the Christ-event is the place where all of God's mysteries, past, present, and future, converge; the place from which all of them must now be interpreted.[38] Christ is the locus of the mystery, then, in the same way that he is the locus of God's wisdom, and he displaces the claims of the Torah in this regard in the same way as was the case with regards to wisdom.[39]

To these two closely associated expressions is now added a third, the adjectival participle, τὴν ἀποκεκρυμμένην, and once more the inter-relationship is obvious. For in its occurrences within the canonical Pauline corpus, ἀποκρύπτω is used only in connection with either σοφία, or μυστήριον, or both.[40] Furthermore, as has also been true of the latter two terms, the object of ἀποκρύπτω, what is hidden, may be either the plan of God, (as in Eph 3.9), or the significance of the Christ-event in relation to that plan, (as in Col 1.26).

A further point arises in relation to Paul's use of the hiddenness motif, however, and it will be worthwhile to notice it briefly here. For, as Nils Dahl has demonstrated, the hiddenness motif, employed in 1 Co 2.7, is integral to one of the basic patterns of early Christian preaching, the "revelation-schema".[41] Characteristic of this pattern is the theme that what was present in the plan of God from eternity, but hidden, has now been revealed in Christ. Thus σοφία, μυστήριον, and ἀποκρύπτω may be united utilizing the results of Dahl's research. What was planned by God has now been brought to actuality and fulfillment in Christ. Hence the reason why Christ stands at the center of God's wisdom and represents the central mystery of the divine will is because in Christ what was hidden formerly has now been revealed; in Christ the plan of God has come to its crucial, determinative expression.[42]

This, however, brings us to a second conclusion with respect to the hiddenness motif in 1 Co 2.7. For it seems likely that Paul's christological focus in relation to this motif should, like the previous two elements of 1 Co 2.7, be set over against the prior claims of the Torah to be the definitive locus of God's hidden wisdom. Here, as James Dunn has observed, it is salient to recall that in pre-Christian Judaism,

> "the problem for the pious was precisely the hiddenness of God and the difficulty of knowing his will; the wisdom tradition within Judaism solved the problem by reference to the Torah, but the Christians solved it by reference to Christ".[43]

Paul's claim to christological wisdom stands in opposition, then, to the widespread claim made among the Jewish people of Palestine and the diaspora that it was within the Torah that God had hidden wisdom.[44] Paul asserts, however, that it is pre-eminently in Christ and not in Torah, that all of the treasures of wisdom and knowledge are hid; (Col 2.3, cp. 1 Co 1.24, 30). The Christ-event has displaced the Torah as the most complete source for a knowledge of the divine design and intention.

Finally, then, we come to the fourth co-ordinate element in 1 Co 2.7, the relative clause ἣν προώρισεν ὁ θεὸς πρὸ τῶν αἰῶνος εἰς δόξαν ἡμῶν. Here too, in light of the use of προόριζω, the thought of God's plan, and of Christ's place within it comes to the forefront.[45] The decisive point, εἰς δόξαν ἡμῶν, Paul asserts, has now been reached in Christ enabling a new comprehension and revelation of the divine intent. Such is Paul's assertion both here and throughout 1 Co 2.7.

In 1 Co 2.8, however, the discussion returns to the Jewish rulers and the object of their ignorance, and although we have given preliminary consideration to this question in the previous section, we are now in a position to come back to it and in so doing summarize the results of our investigation to this point. Having added considerable precision to the concept of θεοῦ σοφία in 1 Co 2.7, we may initially confirm our conclusion that the object of the rulers ignorance was nothing other than the plan of God, and its christological crux in particular.[46] Utilizing Paul's earlier references to θεοῦ σοφία, however, it seems possible to become more specific. What they failed to understand was the meaning of the crucifixion and the real significance of their actions in relation to the plan of God as a whole. If they had appreciated either, Paul asserts, then they would not have crucified the "Lord of Glory". The underlying polemic which has been discerned behind each of the expressions of 1 Co 2.7 seems, then, to be present here in 1 Co 2.8 as well. For despite their possession of the Torah, the Jewish rulers were still in ignorance of θεοῦ σοφία. Thus throughout 1 Co 2.7 and 8 Paul shows how the incompleteness of the wisdom of the Torah has been demonstrated by the event of the crucifixion.

5.24 The Meaning and Significance of 1 Co 2.9

Having described the wisdom which he speaks both positively and negatively, Paul now seeks to conclude his argument by means of an appeal to scripture.[47] In order to do so he must have been certain of the origin and authority of his citation. We, unfortunately, cannot be so sure, as least as far as the source of the citation is concerned.[48]

A more pressing question, however, is whether or not Paul means, as we have just suggested that he does, to apply this citation directly to the previous discussion of 1 Co 2.6-8. For it has been claimed by some that the language of Paul's citation here points more clearly towards a parenthetical and eschatological interpretation.[49] Proponents of this position argue that Paul is speaking proleptically about the blessings of the age to come.[50]

But there are three obstacles, in our opinion, to an acceptance of this result, and two of these, moreover, point us back towards the conclusion that has been reached above. First, and most generally, there is a problem of date, for the rabbinic sources that are normally cited in support of an eschatological meaning for this sort of citation cannot be placed prior to Paul with certainity.[51] Second, as Andre Feuillet observes, the argument from context does not support the proposal that Paul's citation may be treated parenthetically.

> "Il faut dire à tout le moins que l'interprétation strictement eschatologique et futuriste du passage n'est guère en conformité avec le context, soit antécédent, soit subséquent, qui parle seulement de la transcendence de la sagesse Chrétienne, inacessible à la science des 'archontes' et à toute science humaine, et que l'on ne connàit que par révélation divine."[52]

A third factor, however, seems especially decisive against the eschatological interpretation and in support of Feuillet's suggestions about an alternative interpretation. For it is not certain that the relative pronoun should be left without an antecedent so that the content of 1 Co 2.9 remains unspecified. And if a referent can be supplied, or implied, then this eliminates, presumably, the possibility that the theme of the citation is the unspecified blessings of the coming age.[53]

The difficulty here is not the relative itself which seems to continue the sequence of relative pronouns begun in 1 Co 2.7, but the plural number. For until now Paul has been speaking in the singular of θεοῦ σοφία, but, as this point, he picks up a citation whose object appears instead in the plural. The problem, however, may be obviated to a great extent by the recognition that the expression θεοῦ σοφία may be used with a collective sense whereby,

> "the whole is taken to signify its parts; wisdom which primarily signifies the totality of the revelation of God's plan, also stands for the individual contents of that plan ... the 'things which God has prepared for those who love him'".[54]

So the referent or antecedent of the relative in 1 Co 2.9 need be nothing other than the collective elements of θεοῦ σοφία, the details of the divine plan. Indeed, in 1 Co 2.10, Paul continues to speak in the plural in this same way about τὰ βάθη τοῦ θεοῦ, a metaphor employed elsewhere in connection with God's wisdom and the hidden details of his plan and activity.[55]

Thus good reasons exist to support the rejection of the common eschatological interpretation of 1 Co 2.9 and to affirm instead an understanding of the citation which sees in it a concluding attempt on Paul's part to describe the wisdom that he speaks both polemically and didactically. Polemically, the 'things' unseen, unheard, and unconceived denote the hidden elements of God's wise plan that remain unknown to the ἄρχοντες.[56] Didactically, however, Paul's claim is that it has become possible for the individual in Christ to comprehend the whole plan of God, (θεοῦ σοφία),[57] in and through the light of the Christ-event which is its central and most significant aspect.[58]

5.3 Wisdom: Source, Authentication,   and Inspiration;
(1 Co 2.11-3.4)

5.31 Introduction

Certainly one of the most noticeable features of
this section is how much it depends upon and is linked
with Paul's previous comments in 1 Co 2.6-9.   One observes, for instance, that the statement about the role
of the Spirit in 2.10a is formed in apparent antithesis
to 2.8-9.[59]   In contrast to the   ignorance of
the full scope of divine wisdom stands the assertion
that 'these things God has revealed to us through the
Spirit'.[60]   In 1 Co 2.10a, then, we can see contrast
and affirmation, a polemical and a didactic thrust.[61]

Furthermore, as Raymond Humphries has indicated,
full attention must be paid to the fact that 1 Co 2.10-
16 is united with 1 Co 2.6-9 by means of a repetition
of key terms and a consecutive series of relative pronouns.[62]   This may be convienently illustrated by com-
posing an outline of the major declarations in both
sections and underlining recurring words and phrases.

1 Co 2.6 σοφίαν δὲ λαλοῦμεν

2.6 σοφίαν δὲ οὐ τοῦ αἰῶνος τούτου

2.7 θεοῦ σοφίαν

2.7 ἣν προώρισεν ὁ θεὸς πρὸ τῶν αἰώνων

2.8 ἣν οὐδεὶς τῶν ἀρχόντων τοῦ αἰῶνος
τούτου ἔγνωκεν

2.9 ἃ ὀφθαλμὸς οὐκ εἶδεν

2.9 ἃ ἡτοίμασεν ὁ θεὸς

2.10 τὸ γὰρ πνεῦμα πάντα ἐραυνᾷ

2.10 καὶ τὰ βάθη τοῦ θεοῦ

2.11 τὰ τοῦ θεοῦ οὐδεὶς ἔγνωκεν

2.12 τὰ ὑπο τοῦ θεοῦ χαρισθέντα ἡμῖν

2.13 ἃ καὶ λαλοῦμεν

2.14 τὰ τοῦ πνεύματος τοῦ θεοῦ

97

2.15 ὁ δὲ πνευματικὸς ἀνακρίνει τὰ πάντα

Diagrammed in this way, it is possible to see that a string of repeated or related terms along with a continuous use of antithesis; (in 1 Co 2.6, 8, 12, 13, 15), is a pervasive and characteristic feature of both 1 Co 2.6-9 and 1 Co 2.10-16. But this fact is more than simply a matter of shared form and style. It reflects, as Humphries has argued, a common purpose behind both sections. Paul is involved in both places in a "continuous process of redefinition", giving a new and more adequate meaning to the terms that the Corinthians found so significant to their own religious thinking.[63]

While it is important to recognize the connection between these two sections in terms of form and purpose, it is also necessary to acknowledge that the two sections are distinguishable from one another on the basis of content and subject matter. For while 1 Co 2.6-9 concentrates on a definition for wisdom, 1 Co 2.10-3.4 focuses instead upon the role of τὸ πνεῦμα, or τὸ πνεῦμα τοῦ θεοῦ in relation to the mediation of wisdom. In 1 Co 2.6 and 7, Paul's assertions focus on the wisdom of God, while in 1 Co 2.10, 12, and 13, their counterparts describe the work of the Spirit of God. It appears, then, that as wisdom was redefined christologically in 1 Co 2.6-9, so here, the concept of πνεῦμα is being likewise reformulated with reference to the results of that previous discussion.

Additionally, it seems probable to infer that Paul's remarks in 1 Co 2.10-3.4 are influenced to some extent by his earlier critique of Corinthian notions about the source and authentication of wisdom; (cf. 1 Co 2.1-5).[64] There, the apostle was concerned, as we have already seen, to reject the Corinthian contention that the eloquent 'word of wisdom' functioned as the primary indicator of spiritual inspiration. It is natural, then, to expect to find an answer in 1 Co 2.10-3.4 to questions about how the Spirit actually does function in relation to the giving and receiving of divine wisdom. What does distinguish or mark out the one who possesses true spiritual wisdom?

The basic structure of the passsage as a whole seems to follow along from these observations as to its theme and purpose, and from a recognition that this section appears to be constructed as an expansion, in chiastic form, upon the terms of Paul's initial statement in 1 Co 2.10a.[65]   Thus 1 Co 2.10b and 2.11, which speak of τὸ πνεῦμα and τὰ βάθη τοῦ θεοῦ, may be related back to the prepositional phrase διὰ τοῦ πνεύματος, while 1 Co 2.12 and 13, which discuss the source of the knowledge, (εἰδῶμεν), and proclamation, (λαλοῦμεν), of τὰ ὑπο τοῦ θεοῦ χαρισθέντα ἡμῖν, ('things', we take it, of God's wisdom), may be referred back to the verb ἀπεκάλυψεν.   So also, the verses from 1 Co 2.14-3.4, which talk about the identity of the πνευματικός, may be read as an allusion back to the indirect object of 1 Co 2.10a, ἡμῖν, completing the pattern.

This tripartite structural analysis by no means resolves all of the grammatical and syntactical ambiguities that fill this section of 1 Corinthians, but it does enable us to perceive a degree of differentiation in Paul's discussion between three closely related topics. The communication of wisdom to the πνευματικός by the Spirit involves three aspects: a) a source for such communication, b) the act or process of communication itself, and c) a recipient for the communication. Paul identifies the source with God's Spirit, (1 Co 2.-10, 11), describes the process in terms of receiving, understanding, and speaking, (1 Co 2.12, 13), and restricts the reception of the Spirit's communication to the πνευματικός, (though he radically redefines the term in relation to the Corinthian usage in 1 Co 2.14-3.4).

Moreover, the structural analysis has another advantage in enabling us to clarify the subject(s) which stand behind the use of the first person plural in 1 Co 2.10-16.   The issue has been a persistent problem. Is the 'we' of these verses to be taken so as to include all of the Christians in the congregation at Corinth, in opposition to the exclusivistic 'we' of the pneumatics?[66]   Or, is it simply a rhetorical device used in the same manner here as in 1 Co 1.23 and 2.6, as a circumlocution for Paul?[67] Advocates of both alternatives acknowledge some difficulty in maintaining a consistency of meaning for these expressions in 1 Co 2.10-16, and this has led, in turn, to a recent proposal that would combine the previous positions by referring the plural in "verbs of communication" to Paul, and the plural in "verbs of reception" to all Christians, including Paul.[68]

If, however, we are correct in linking the ἡμῖν of 1 Co 2.10a with Paul's discussion in 1 Co 2.14-3.4, then a solution to this problem becomes, perhaps, a bit

clearer.   The use of the first person plural   in each
instance would   then refer   to the πνευματικοί of whom
Paul is one.[69]   This conclusion does not   immediately
clarify all of the exegesis either, (for one thing, as
we have said,   the definition   that Paul gives   to this
group at each   stage of the argument remains   to be
seen), but the   proposal does   seem to offer   a natural
guide to the   sense of the first person plural expressions, one that   is keeping with the context,   and one
which does not import a meaning into each usage solely
on the basis of presupposition.[70]

     Finally, an   analysis of the   three-part structure
of 1 Co 2.10-3.4 furnishes us with a   practical format
for our own presentation.   Thus, we propose in what
follows to take up three successive questions that reflect the threefold form of Paul's argument: the
question of source, the question of means, and the
question of scope.

5.32 Divine Wisdom: A Question of Source; (1 Co 2.10b-11)

     If we are right to discern a kind of programmatic
significance to Paul's statement in 1 Co   2.10a, then
the immediate repetition of πνεῦμα in 2.10b should probably be understood epexegetically in relation to the
last phrase of 2.10a.   Paul's affirmation there is, as
we have seen, that God has indeed revealed the 'things'
of his wisdom, (cf. 1 Co 2.9).   We have also argued
that this assertion is meant to be contrasted with previous remarks about the ignorance of the 'rulers';
'things' that were formerly hidden to 'them' have now
been revealed to 'us'.[71]

     To put Paul's assertion in this form, however, is
to neglect a crucial element in his argumentation.   For
if God's wisdom remained hidden to the ἄρχοντες despite
their access to ἡ σοφία τοῦ αἰῶνος τούτου, then how is
a knowledge of the new wisdom, (θεοῦ σοφίαν   ἐν
μυστηρίῳ), to be gained?   Paul's answer, of course, is
that a knowledge of divine eschatological wisdom has
been made available to the Christian διὰ τοῦ πνεύματος.
1 Co 2.10b and 11 together, then, contain the justification and rationale, (cf. γάρ in both 2.10b and 2.11),
for Paul's contention that the Spirit functions as the
source of christological wisdom.

     Once more, though, (as was the case with much of
the material in 1 Co 2.6-9), Paul's remarks may be tak-

en in either a polemical or a didactic way; (i.e. 'only the Spirit is able to reveal God's new wisdom', or, 'the Spirit is able to reveal even the hidden details of God's plan'). To try and interpret the passage exclusively by means of one or the other of these approaches is, probably, a mistaken attempt.[72] Yet as was the case in the previous section, we seem to be warranted in emphasizing the didactic intent as the primary intention, and the polemical thrust as subsidiary to this.

A related concern is the question of whether or not 1 Co 2.10b and 11 reflect the viewpoint of Paul's Corinthian opponents, and if so, to what extent.[73] The evidence brought forward in support of a positive response consists of the 'uncharacteristic' vocabulary of 1 Co 2.10b,[74] and the 'unusual' use of the 'like-by-like' analogy in 1 Co 2.11,[75] so that the greater amount of the passage is quite often attributed to the Corinthians on these grounds. But if one admits that Paul's basic aim in this part of the discourse is one of redefinition understood didactically as well as polemically, then this evidence loses much of its power to convince us that the usage here must reflect Corinthian and not Pauline theology. This is not, however, to deny the possibility of a Corinthian origin for this material, but rather to assert that Paul is here taking over language and concepts that are familiar to his Corinthian audience expressly in order to give them new meaning, or to set them in a different context. This kind of redefinition has already been accomplished with respect to the content of wisdom in 1 Co 2.6-9 where Paul has shown that θεοῦ σοφία must be defined more broadly than ἡ σοφία τοῦ αἰῶνος τούτου so as to include the 'things' of 1 Co 2.9. Paul now pursues a similar aim with reference to the work of the Spirit in relation to the mediation of divine wisdom; the Spirit is able to discover and reveal even the hidden details, the 'things' of God's eschatological wisdom.

The thought of 1 Co 2.10b is opened up for us in two ways; first, by the force of the καί which connects its two clauses, and second, by the vocabulary of the clause. We shall deal with the latter consideration first, and then return to the other.

The vocabulary of 1 Co 2.10b is, as is often noted, very 'un-Pauline' language, especially ἐραυνᾷ and τὰ βάθη.[76] In view of this, it is regularly concluded that these terms derive from the Corinthians and not, originally, from Paul.[77] As a result, however, several important questions arise. What is the background for the use of these words at Corinth? What is Paul's response to this background and usage? How does Paul himself wish to define and utilize these terms? Finally, how does this vocabulary, understood in Pauline terms, serve to support Paul's assertion that the revelation of God's wisdom has come διὰ τοῦ πνεύματος?

Of course, only tentative answers can be proposed with respect to the Corinthian context. However, if our assessment of the Corinthian pattern of religion, (based on Paul's arguments in 1 Co 1.18-2.9), is accurate, then we should probably relate both of these examples of the Corinthian vocabulary back to the Torah-centered wisdom of pre-Christian Judaism. Gerhard Delling seems to confirm this conclusion when, following some notations on the secular sense of ἐρευνάω, he points to the relatively large number of cases where ἐρευνάω is used, "for the study of the scripture", and in some cases, "as a technical term for the work of the scribe".[78] He directs our attention to examples of this in Philo and the LXX. Thus, in Det 141, for instance, we find that Philo's question, τὰ δ᾽ἑξῆς ἐρευνήσωμεν, is answered immediately with a quotation from the Torah, (Gen 4.13). Again, in Cher 14, ἐρευνάω and Torah-study are closely connected by Philo when he says, "what scripture would indicate by these last words, let us investigate; (ἐρευνήσωμεν)". Moreover, in almost one-third of the occurrences of ἐρευνάω in Philo, the word bears this sense.[79] It is in fact, therefore, one of the words that Philo uses repeatedly in order to denote his own allegorical investigation into the meaning of the Torah. In the LXX, the clearest examples of the same meaning for ἐρευνάω are to be found in Psalm 118, a Psalm that is generally recognized as having been composed under the influence of the wisdom tradition.[80] The Psalm commences with a blessing utilizing a close cognate of ἐρευνάω; μακάριοι οἱ ἐξερευνῶντες τὰ μαρτύρια αὐτοῦ; (cp. verse 129). It continues, however, even more explicitly by making the object of ἐξερευνάω first τὸν νόμον σοῦ, (vs. 34), and then, τὰς ἐντολάς σοῦ; (vs. 69). It is not surprising, then, to find that the New Testament literature employs the verb ἐραυνάω quite often within this same context of meaning. Thus, for example, in Jn 5.39, it is used, (once more according to Delling), "in the sense of seeking the divine revelation in Holy Scripture, (the

Old Testament), which is the actual locus of the living divine revelation"; (cf. also Jn 7.52).[81]

All of this evidence combines to reinforce the conclusion that the Corinthians probably used the term ἐραυνάω to denote a search for wisdom that concentrated and focused itself upon an investigation of the meaning of the Torah. Paul, however, as we have seen, has rejected the Torah as the pre-eminent locus of God's new wisdom and pointed to its grave inadequacy in 1 Co 2.6-9. Why then should he choose to take up a term tinged with associations of Torah-study? Moreover, how does he intend, having taken up the term, to use it in the context of his own argument which emphasizes the christological nature of divine wisdom in relation to all of the detail of God's wise plan?

In our estimation, the key to Paul's use of ἐραυνάω in 1 Co 2.10 lies in an understanding of its object, (what it is that is searched), and its subject, (who it is that does the searching). The first matter can be clarified by defining more precisely the reference for πάντα in the opening clause of 1 Co 2.10b. For while it is true that πάντα used in an absolute sense, without the article, most often means 'all things' without any further definition as to extent, it is also important to note that the absolute sense of πάντα is often capable of restriction with reference to the context.[82] In view of this, we are certainly warranted in asking whether or not the scope of πάντα in 1 Co 2.10b can also be narrowed by giving attention to the context. Given the relationship between 1 Co 2.10a and 2.9 on the one hand, and the linking conjunction between 2.10a and b on the other, it seems possible to interpret πάντα more narrowly with reference to the double relative in 2.9a and c. Paul's assertion in 2.10a was that these 'things', (the 'things' of 2.9), have now been revealed to us in contrast, (δέ), to the ignorance of the ἄρχοντες. Now, in 2.10b, he supports that assertion, (γάρ), by revealing its premise. The Spirit is able to reveal the full detail of divine wisdom because the Spirit has investigated that wisdom completely; 'for the Spirit searches into all these things'.

That brings us back to the subject of ἐραυνάω. In the parallel passages that have been cited from Jewish wisdom literature, the subject is always man himself.[83] The reason for this also seems clear. Since the locus of divine wisdom had been made available to all in the Torah, it remained for those who would know God's wisdom to diligently search out Torah's truths.

Paul's perspective, however, is markedly different. First, he stresses that God's wisdom has found a new locus in Christ; (1 Co 1.24, 30, 2.7). But he is faced, at the same time, by the fact that the new locus of divine wisdom has been hidden, as it were, in history; (1 Co 2.8, 9). How then is a person to know the real significance of the life and death of Jesus in relation to God's wise plan? Paul's answer is that if one is to come to a knowledge of the hidden aspects of divine wisdom, aspects that transcend the previously revealed wisdom of the Torah, then this knowledge must be brought to each by the Spirit; first the knowledge of the meaning of the Christ-event, then, the knowledge of its implications. For by the light of God's act in Christ, every facet of his plan has been illumined. Thus the wisdom that was placed within the Torah has been superseded by the christological wisdom brought by the Spirit.[84]

Our understanding of the meaning of 1 Co 2.10b is enhanced, in a similar way, by the realization that τὸ βάθος was also employed within pre-Christian wisdom circles.[85] Thus, one finds instructive instances of the use of the term or a cognate in Job 11.8, Prov 18.-4, and Ecc 7.24, (where what is called βαθὺ βάθος is probably σοφία; cf. vs. 23). Philo also links βάθος with σοφία and ἐπιστήμη in Ebr 112 and Som 2.271.[86] The most helpful parallel in terms of discerning Paul's intention in 1 Co 2.10b, however, is probably to be found in Rom 11.33. The passage is certainly later and not earlier than 1 Co 2.10, but it is, significantly, the only other occasion where Paul uses βάθος in connection with θεός, and it is perhaps safe to assume some measure of continuity in Paul's meaning given his very limited use of the word. The passage from Romans reads as follows.

"O, the depth, (βάθος), of the riches and wisdom and knowledge of God! How unsearchable are his judgements and how inscrutable his ways!"[87]

Here, it is evident that βάθος πλούτου ... is paralleled by the more explicit expressions in Rom 11.33b, enabling us to conclude that, for Paul, at least in Romans, the depth of God's wisdom lay in his unsearchable judgements and his inscrutable ways.[88] Perhaps,

then, in 1 Co 2.10a, τὰ βάθη τοῦ θεοῦ is to be similarly defined with reference to the plans and actions
which are hidden in θεοῦ σοφία. This would present us
with a reason for the use of the plural, (for the reference could once again go back to the plural relatives
in 1 Co 2.9), and Paul's thought would then be that the
Spirit searches into the furthest and deepest details
of God's decisions and activities. This interpretation
also fits in well with the epexegetical καί, and the
thought of 1 Co 2.10a; and this, after all, may be what
is truly determinative.

Having clarified the meaning of 1 Co 2.10b, we can
now go on to analyze the purpose and function of the
analogy that Paul employs in 1 Co 2.11 with more confidence. It is meant to provide confirmation for the
Pauline assertions regarding the Spirit and the
Spirit's capabilities in 1 Co 2.10, as the repetition
of the γάρ also shows.[89] This syntactical conclusion,
however, is not unimportant since it indicates that the
analogy of 1 Co 2.11 is not, (as has often been too
easily assumed), utilized by Paul primarily in prepara-
tion for the subsequent denial and affirmation of 1 Co
2.12.

The use of the 'like-by-like' idea, belongs, in
large part, to the same wisdom milieu as the vocabulary
of 1 Co 2.10b,[90] and, in the opinion of Birger Pearson
and several other scholars, this makes it likely to
suppose that the analogy found a place in the Corinthians' thinking, since much of the rest of their thought
seems to emanate from this background.[91] According to
Pearson, then, the usage that was made of the 'like-
by-like' principle at Corinth would have been intended,
(as the background materials indicate), to emphasize
the existence of a 'consubstantiality' between man's
spirit and the Spirit of God; (cf. Gen 2.7 LXX). This
similarity of essence seems to have been taken as providing an epistemological basis for a cognition of God's
wisdom, and so one may go on, accordingly, to interpret
the analogy in 1 Co 2.11, according to Pearson, as a
Pauline attempt to employ the same 'like-by-like' principle as his opponents in order to disprove any continuity between ὁ πνεῦμα τοῦ ἀνθρώπου τὸ ἐν αὐτῷ, and, τὸ
πνεῦμα τοῦ θεοῦ in anticipation of 1 Co 2.12.[92]

But, while it may be possible, or even probable to
conclude that Paul has derived the 'like-by-like' idea
from his Corinthian opponents, it does not necessarily
follow that he must have used it in the same way as

105

they did: to prove or disprove any continuity between the two πνεύματα in connection with a discussion of the capability of created man to receive divine revelation. Paul does indeed have a response to make to the Corinthian position in this regard, (as is apparent from 1 Co 2.12 and 14), and the δέ of 1 Co 2.12 could suggest that he is aware of a use of the 'like-by-like' analogy among his opponents in line with the suggestions of Pearson.[93] But Paul's own use of the 'like-by-like' idea is meant, we submit, to address a different sort of question. The analogy of 1 Co 2.11 does not concern itself with questions of man's capability to receive revelation, but instead it focuses upon the Spirit's capability to bring revelation. It is meant, therefore, to prove that the Spirit of God can reveal even the deepest and most secret aspects of God's inner thoughts and intentions, the 'things' which are hidden beyond the sight and hearing of humanity, θεοῦ σοφία in all of its fullness and detail.[94]

The analogy of 1 Co 2.11 has, accordingly, the force of a Qal Vahomer argument.[95] Even a human being has within him secrets of his own that no other person can penetrate, but which are known solely to his own spirit. How much more then is this true of God as the divine being.[96] Understood in this way, the analogy as Paul employs it is a direct confirmation of the central thought of 1 Co 2.10a in both its polemical and its didactic aspect. Polemically, it stresses the hiddenness of the wisdom of God in contrast to the wisdom of the world. Didactically, however, the analogy emphasizes the capability of the divine Spirit in light of the hidden nature of God's wisdom. The Spirit of God is the one source fully privy to God's innermost thoughts and plans, so the Spirit is competent to reveal to us the whole wisdom of God, even τὰ βάθη τοῦ θεοῦ.

In summary, then, the results of this section of our analysis can be put down quite briefly. For Paul, the Spirit alone is a complete and reliable guide to all of divine wisdom. Torah, even Torah fully and completely interpreted is not. Its incompleteness and inadequacy has been decisively shown up by the event of the crucifixion, (cf. 1 Co 2.8-9), but, through the Spirit, God has now revealed to us not only the significance of that event, but also, in its light, all of the rest of God's wisdom has been laid open to us.

5.33 Divine Wisdom: A Question of Means; (1 Co 2.12-13)

Whether or not one chooses to lay particular stress on the 'emphatic' position of the personal pronoun in 1 Co 2.12, ἡμεις plainly marks a noteworthy and important change in the direction and thrust of the Pauline discussion.[97] For while in the previous verses the focus has been on the Spirit's relation to God and his wisdom, in 1 Co 2.12 and 13 the focus is shifted and concentrated upon the Spirit's relation to 'us'. The transition, however, is perfectly reasonable. For if Paul has succeeded in putting his point across in 1 Co 2.10-12 as to the reliability and exclusivity of the Spirit as the source of christological wisdom, then it follows that the next question which will need to be addressed in his presentation is the question of means. How does the Spirit's wisdom come to be ours? How have we come to know that which is known only by the Spirit, namely, the christological nature of θεοῦ σοφία in all its richness and detail?

The isolation of these questions is important because it allows us to navigate our way more certainly through a sea of exegetical difficulties and semantical ambiguities within this section. What, for instance, does Paul have in mind in the antithesis of 1 Co 2.12 when he speaks of τὸ πνεῦμα τοῦ κόσμου, and similarly, what is the meaning of the phrase, τὰ ὑπὸ τοῦ θεοῦ χαρισθέντα ἡμῖν? Or again, what does the genitive expression ἀνθρωπίνης σοφίας in 1 Co 2.13a actually modify? Or, perhaps most notorious of all, what is the gender of πνευματικοῖς and the meaning of συγκρίνοντες in 1 Co 2.13b? All of these questions have long attracted the time and the talents of exegetes, but what has been virtually ignored is the meaning and importance of the three principal verbs in 1 Co 2.12 and 13; ἐλάβομεν, εἰδῶμεν, and λαλοῦμεν.

What is so striking about these three verbs is not only their individual connotations, but even more their collective significance. For their inter-relationship reveals as much, if not more, about the progression of Paul's thought in 1 Co 2.12 and 13 than any of the exegetical and semantic questions that are normally taken to be the keys to a proper interpretation of the passage. Indeed, taken together, they provide us with an answer to the central question of this section, the question of means. How has the wisdom of the Spirit come to be ours? The basic outline of the Pauline answer is both direct and succint. We have received God's Spirit, (ἐλάβουμεν τὸ πνεῦμα τὸ ἐκ τοῦ θεοῦ), that we might know, (ἵνα εἰδῶμεν), and speak, (καὶ λαλοῦμεν), the wisdom of God; (τὰ ὑπο τοῦ θεοῦ χαρισθέντα ἡμῖν).

The full significance of this verbal sequence remains to be seen, but a preliminary conclusion as to its meaning may help to guide our investigation. Thus, even at this stage, one thing seems clear. For Paul, in regard to wisdom, it is the experience of receiving the Spirit that is primary. Both the knowledge and the communication of wisdom are in some way made dependent upon it. The reception of the Spirit forms the basis, or the starting point, therefore, in understanding and imparting Christian wisdom. Indeed, it is here that the Pauline idea distinctively begins. With this in mind, we may turn back now to a more thorough analysis of the verbal sequence to see how this point is worked out in the detail of the Pauline presentation.

The first two considerations that help us to fill out the meaning of the verbal sequence are grammatical ones. One must come to a decision about the force of ἵνα in 1 Co 2.12b and καί in 1 Co 2.13a, for these two conjunctions give us an initial indication as to how Paul meant to relate the three verbal actions of receiving, knowing, and speaking. The interpretation of ἵνα is probably the more significant of the two, but it is also much more potentially complicated. For ἵνα within the period of the New Testament literature, as is commonly known, is broadening in its usage so as to have, in some cases, a consecutive force, (expressing the actual result achieved), and in others a sub-final force, (expressing the contemplated or expected result), as well as the normal final force, (expressing the intended result or purpose.[98] Which of these three meanings is to be given to the ἵνα of 1 Co 2.13? The answer appears to depend upon the interpretation of the phrase τὰ ὑπο τοῦ θεοῦ χαρισθέντα ἡμῖν, for if the 'things that God has freely given us' are actually all now possessed by us, then ἵνα must be understood in a consecutive way. But if, on the other hand, these 'things' as a whole are not yet fully ours, then ἵνα εἰδῶμεν will denote either the expected or the intended result of our receipt of the Spirit.

Given the plural, (τὰ χαρισθέντα), it seems most likely that the phrase should be related back to 1 Co 2.9.[99] The 'things' that God has freely given us are

108

all of the 'things' that God has prepared for us; the 'things' that constitute θεοῦ σοφία. As we have seen, however, the central core of this many-faceted wisdom is the knowledge contained in the kerygma. But, as has also been suggested, θεοῦ σοφία, in the sense of God's wise plan, goes beyond the Christ-event in its scope to encompass other dimensions of the divine intention and activity which can now be interpreted in the light of God's act in Christ.[100] We would propose, then, that this wider concept of wisdom is in view here in 1 Co 2.12b. A knowledge of all of the implications of God's act in Christ has been made freely available to us in the light of the cross.

This interpretation of 1 Co 2.12b, however, suggests in turn that we should probably construe ἵνα with either a final, or a sub-final force. We do not yet know all of God's wisdom, (cp. 1 Co 13.12), but all of it is potentially knowable to us, for the christological key to its meaning has already been revealed to us by the Spirit. The reception of the Spirit and the kerygma has opened up the possibility for us to come to know God's wisdom completely. This is the intended, or perhaps even the expected present result, (εἰδῶμεν), of our prior receipt of the Spirit, (ἐλάβομεν). But, as Paul points out, (cf. 1 Co 3.1ff.), all are not yet fully mature or spiritual in this sense.

The opening phrase of 1 Co 2.13 continues this idea and forms an important sequel to the thought of 1 Co 2.12.[101] For if the Spirit's wisdom does not come to all of us at once, or to all uniformly, then the 'things' of divine wisdom must be spoken and shared. But the consecutive καί also implies that the sharing of spiritual wisdom is dependent upon both the initial reception of the Spirit and the growth in wisdom that is implied by ἐλάβομεν and ἵνα εἰδῶμεν in 1 Co 2.12b. It is a product of our initial receipt of the Spirit and of a maturing understanding of the whole divine purpose and its center in Christ.[102]

Thus, we may summarize Paul's argument in the verbal sequence of 1 Co 2.12 and 13 as follows. Our receipt of God's Spirit forms the basis for a growing understanding of divine wisdom. In the kerygma, the christological core of divine wisdom has been made known to us by the Spirit. A full comprehension of all of the implications of the Christ-event does not, however, take place at the time of our first experience of receiving spiritual wisdom. The intended, or expected result of our possession of the Spirit is that we might come to know the whole wisdom of God, but such knowledge is only progressively realized by the one who is maturing in the Spirit as he takes part in the speaking and sharing of spiritual insights.

Keeping the positive aspects of Paul's teaching in mind, it may now be possible to come to an understanding of the negative and polemical aspects of the passage which are contained primarily in the antitheses of 1 Co 2.12 and 2.13a. It is important, though, to observe at the outset that the results which may be achieved in this way must remain much more tenative than those that have been outlined above. For the difficulties involved in the interpretation of the antitheses are a good deal more formidable than those which we faced previously in regards to the verbal sequence of 1 Co 2.12 and 13.

What, for example, does Paul mean when he denies in 1 Co 2.12 that we have received τὸ πνεῦμα τοῦ κόσμου? The problem to be faced here is not only the lack of any terminological parallel in the background materials, but also the brevity of the expression itself.[103] If, then, the first of these two factors seems to favor the possibility that the phrase is of Pauline origin, then the second effectively prevents us from being able to give it any great amount of definition. It is probable, however, that the phrase has a polemical ring to it, especially when it is taken together with the rest of 1 Co 2.12.[104] Either, then, Paul is defending himself against a claim that has been made by the Corinthians about him,[105] or he is seeking to address himself to some aspect of the Corinthians' own thinking with respect to the spirit by means of a shorthand catchphrase.[106] A third alternative, however, is that Paul has simply coined the phrase for the purpose of denoting a hypothetical source for ἡ σοφία τοῦ κόσμου.[107]

It is the last of these three views that has commended itself to exegetes most frequently, but the strength of this view lies precisely in the lack of a more convincing reason as to why Paul might choose to coin the phrase. Perhaps, however, the sort of rationale that is required may be obtained by giving more attention to the second alternative outlined above.

What leads us to believe that Paul may be attempting in his own words to dismiss an aspect of the Corinthian position is the presence of the opening conjunction, δέ, which seems to point to some sort of contrast between 1 Co 2.12 and the preceding context. Now in 1 Co 2.11, as we have already seen, Paul makes use of a 'like-by-like' principle which he seems to have derived from the Corinthians.[108] In the previous section, of our investigation, (5.32), it was necessary for us to argue against the view of Birger Pearson that Paul's usage of the 'like-by-like' idea was formally identical to the Corinthian usage. However, if the results of Pearson are correct with respect to the usage of the 'like-by-like' analogy at Corinth, then Paul's redefinition of that principle in 1 Co 2.11 could conceivably have led him on to a passing renunciation of the Corinthians' thinking such as the one we find here in 1 Co 2.12a.

The Corinthians, according to Pearson, appear to have used the 'like-by-like' analogy to argue for a similarity in nature between the Spirit of God, and the spirit in man as a created being. This similarity meant that each individual possessed a divinely created capacity to receive the Spirit's revelation, a capacity which might be cultivated and actualized through the knowledge and practice of wisdom, enabling one to rise to experiences of spiritual illumination, or to a spiritual level of existence.[109] Now if we accept, for the moment, that this sort of analysis does indeed describe the Corinthian thinking accurately, then Paul's denial in 1 Co 2.12a may be seen to strike with precision, if fleetingly, at the root of the Corinthian pattern of religion.

According to Paul in 1 Co 2.11, τὸ πνεῦμα τοῦ ἀνθρώπου τὸ ἐν αὐτῷ is only illustrative of the activity of the Spirit of God. As he uses the illustration, therefore, there is no thought of an essential connection between the two spirits at all. However, because Paul is aware that the Corinthians have made a different use of the same analogy to prove just such a connection, he denies in passing that our capability to know wisdom is based upon a divinely created capacity to receive spiritual insight. What enables us to recieve the 'things that God has freely given us' is not the spirit within us, but the 'Spirit which we have received from God'. The former spirit belongs to us as a part of the created κόσμος; the latter is God's new gift, and it is this gift which forms the basis, according to Paul, for our knowledge of divine wisdom.[110]

111

A second and equally difficult antithesis is found in 1 Co 2.13a. The uncertainty in this case, however, arises out of a grammatical difficulty, namely, the use of διδακτοῖς and the genitive expression ἀνθρωπίνης σοφίας. The normal interpretation reads διδακτοῖς as a simple verbal adjective, and takes ἀνθρωπίνης σοφίας as a subjective genitive. However, it is important to notice that there is a close parallel between 1 Co 2.13a and 1 Co 2.4 which might suggest a different rendering.[111] There, we find exactly the same grammatical elements as here; a verbal adjective, (πειθοῖς), followed by a genitive, (σοφίας), preceding the dative object, (λόγοις), of the preposition, (ἐν). But there are further similarities as well, for in both cases Paul employs this peculiar construction in setting up an antithesis, and in both cases, the antithesis appears to be between two different ways of speaking.[112]

All of this seems to us at least to hint at the fact that a better translation of the phrase ἐν διδακτοῖς ἀνθρωπίνης σοφίας λόγοις in 1 Co 2.13 might be formed on analogy with 1 Co 2.4, and, in that case, Paul's antithesis might well be less symmetrical and more directly polemical than it is normally understood to be; an antithesis, in fact, between speech 'in learned words of human wisdom', and speech 'in words taught by the Spirit'.

The Corinthians seem to have valued learned words taking them to be a sign of the Spirit's inspiration.[113] But Paul corrects this perception asserting that eloquence belongs solely to 'human wisdom'. What learned words signify is merely the human facility for expression.[114] True wisdom does not reside in profound speech, but in speech inspired with the power of the Spirit. Consequently, Paul's speech, though not 'in learned words of human wisdom', is nevertheless, (ἀλλα), in words that are the product of authentic spiritual inspiration, and, as such reflect fully the powerful new wisdom of God.

This interpretation of the antithesis of 1 Co 2.-13a also assists us in coming to a decision about the meaning of 1 Co 2.13b. As is well known, the alternatives here are practically equivalent in terms of relative probability. Either Paul, in anticipation of 1 Co 2.14ff. 'interprets spiritual truths to spiritual men', or, with reference back to the preceding antithesis, he concludes his thought by saying that he 'interprets spiritual truths by means of spiritual words'.[115] With

112

the evidence so finely balanced, the most one can do is
to express a preference here, and ours is for the latter meaning. For the phrase forms a fitting conclusion
to the antithesis of 1 Co 2.13a. Spiritual truths are
communicated in words inspired by the Spirit, and that,
not eloquence, is what is really determinative in regards to an evaluation.[116]

Thus, the two antitheses in 1 Co 2.12 and 13 serve
to refute the thinking of Paul's Corinthian opponents
with regard to the process by which spritual wisdom is
gained, and with regards to the criterion by which it
is authenticated. The capability to receive spiritual
wisdom does not lie in created human nature, nor is
such wisdom authenticated by learned, or eloquent
words. These two antitheses complement Paul';s positive presentation by highlighting the points of difference between the apostle and his opponents.[117] What is
even more interesting, however, is that both antitheses
appear to point back to a unified pattern of thinking
on the part of the Corinthians, a pattern which seems
to have viewed an experience of the Spirit as the culmination of individual religious experience. By contrast, as can be seen initially from 1 Co 2.12, and
more fully, as will be seen from 1 Co 2.14ff., Paul put
such an encounter at the very start of the Christian
experience and predicated further growth in the knowledge of divine wisdom upon the continued possession of
God's Spirit.

5.34 Divine Wisdom: A Question of Scope, (1 Co 2.14-
     3.4)

Two of the most noteworthy features of 1 Co 2.14-
3.4 are, undoubtedly, the πνευματικός – ψυχικός antithesis in 1 Co 2.14-16, and the corresponding contrast
between the πνευματικός and the νήπιος ἐν χριστῷ in 1
Co 3.1-4. In the case of the antithesis, our judgement
has been supported by a large amount of scholarly research that has sought to investigate the background
and interpretation of the πνευματικός - ψυχικός language
as it might have been used in Corinth, and as it was
actually employed by Paul. That 1 Co 3.1-4 is an
equally important and integral part of Paul's discussion has been less widely recognized. Yet, in spite of
this comparative neglect, the contrast set up in 1 Co
3.1 between the πνευματικός and the νήπιος ἐν χριστῷ
does seem, prima facie, to provide a close connection
to 1 Co 2.14-16, and one which appears from its proxim-

ity at least to be intended to supply a further modification to the earlier discussion. As such, the πνευματικός-νηπιός contrast surely deserves to be treated at the same time, and with the same care, as the πνευματικός-ψυχικός antithesis.

The fact that both distinctions have a similar sort of point to make adds further weight to this methodological assumption. Thus, if one reviews the contextual background of 1 Co 2.14-3.4, it may be seen that a) having established the Spirit as the source of Christian wisdom in 1 Co 2.10-11, and b) having described the process by which such wisdom comes to us in 1 Co 2.12-13, Paul now turns in 1 Co 2.14-16 to a consideration of those who receive the 'things' of the Spirit, and those who do not. Then, in a metaphorical but no less forceful way, in 1 Co 3.1-4, he turns back to the situation at Corinth, distinguishing between those who are ready for a 'feeding' of 'solid food', and those who remain on a diet of 'milk'. The two distinctions, then, are alike in that both of them propose to deal with persons who do receive something, as opposed to others who do not, and another correspondence, allied to this general similarity, is to be noted in the use of πνευματικός in both of the distinctions. It seems reasonable, therefore, to conclude that the two distinctions should be treated as complementary.

But can one become any more specific about the nature of their relationship? Can it be determined why Paul has brought these two contrasts into conjunction with one another? It is our contention that an answer can be supplied to both questions by supposing a unified purpose as the underlying basis of continuity behind the use of both distinctions. Paul is attempting, first in 1 Co 2.14-16, and then in 1 Co 3.1-4, to redefine the Corinthian concept of the πνευματικός, and, at the same time, to use the new concept as the foundation for his own discussion about the recipients of spiritual wisdom. We propose, then, to examine this hypothesis in relation to both of the distinctions; first, with respect to the πνευματικός-ψυχικός antithesis in 1 Co 2.14-16, and then in relation to the contrast drawn in 1 Co 3.1-4 between the πνευματικός and the νήπιοι ἐν χριστῷ.

The place to begin in any consideration of the πνευματικός-ψυχικός antithesis is surely with the observation that the language of the contrast almost certainly belongs to the Corinthian context. This is in-

114

ed to supply a further modification to the earlier discussion. As such, the πνευματικός - νήπιος contrast
surely deserves to be treated at the same time, and
with the same care, as the πνευματικός - ψυχικός antithesis.

The fact that both distinctions have a similar
sort of point to make adds further weight to this methodological assumption. Thus, if one reviews the contextual background of 1 Co 2.14-3.4, it may be seen
that a) having established the Spirit as the source of
Christian wisdom in 1 Co 2.10-11, and b) having described the process by which such wisdom comes to us in
1 Co 2.12-13, Paul now turns in 1 Co 2.14-16 to a consideration of those who receive the 'things' of the
Spirit, and those who do not. Then, in a metaphorical
but no less forceful way, in 1 Co 3.1-4, he turns back
to the situation at Corinth, distinguishing between
those who are ready for a 'feeding' of 'solid food',
and those who remain on a diet of 'milk'. The two distinctions, then, are alike in that both of them propose
to deal with persons who do receive something, as opposed to others who do not, and another correspondence,
allied to this general similarity, is to be noted in
the use of πνευματικός in both of the distinctions. It
seems reasonable, therefore, to conclude that the two
distinctions should be treated as complementary.

But can one become any more specific about the nature of their relationship? Can it be determined why
Paul has brought these two contrasts into conjunction
with one another? It is our contention that an answer
can be supplied to both questions by supposing a unified purpose as the underlying basis of continuity behind the use of both distinctions. Paul is attempting,
first in 1 Co 2.14-16, and then in 1 Co 3.1-4, to redefine the Corinthian concept of the πνευματικός, and, at
the same time, to use the new concept as the foundation
for his own discussion about the recipients of spiritual wisdom. We propose, then, to examine this hypothesis in relation to both of the distinctions; first,
with respect to the πνευματικός-ψυχικός antithesis in 1
Co 2.14-16, and then in relation to the contrast drawn
in 1 Co 3.1-4 between the πνευματικοί and the νήπιοι ἐν
χριστῷ.

The place to begin in any consideration of the
πνευματικός-ψυχικός antithesis is surely with the observation that the language of the contrast almost certainly belongs to the Corinthian context. This is in-

dicated both by the fact that ψυχικός is found only in
1 Corinthians, and by the fact that πνευματικός, though
it occurs elsewhere in Paul's epistles, is found no
less than fifteen times in 1 Corinthians. In view of
this evidence, it is mostly presumed that the
πνευματικός-ψυχικός contrast has been taken over by
Paul from the Corinthians.[118]

This, however, leads one to ask about the meaning
which the Corinthians themselves gave to the antithesis. Unfortunately, Paul leaves us with very much
less information than we would like to have at this
point, yet his use of the πνευματικός -ψυχικός language
does provide us, both directly and indirectly, with
some evidence as to the meaning and use of these terms
among the Corinthians. To begin with, there is a correspondence between the πνευματικός -ψυχικός antithesis
and the other terminological antitheses discernable
within 1 Corinthians 1-3, and this analogy suggests
that the Corinthians used the πνευματικός -ψυχικός contrast, as they seem to have used the other antitheses,
to separate themselves off from the rest of the
church.[119] They called themselves πνευματικοί and distinguished themselves in this way from the remaining
believers in Corinth, whom they designated ψυχικοί.

One can go further, however, by noticing that the
same group appears to have placed a particular value on
wisdom, claiming to be 'wise' as well as 'spiritual'
men; (cf. 1 Co 3.18). Now, of course, it might be possible to regard these two claims as completely unrelat-
ed. But, it certainly seems more likely that the Corinthians connected their claim to be 'wise' and their
claim to be 'spiritual', asserting that their wisdom
was a result, or a product of their spirituality.[120]
It would appear possible, then, to move to a preliminary definition of the meaning of the πνευματικός-
ψυχικός distinction in its Corinthian setting purely on
the basis of the evidence that Paul has left to us.
The πνευματικός is one who possesses spiritual wisdom.
The ψυχικός is one who does not.

This initial definition, however, is still a fairly basic one. For although it does tell us what the
Corinthians valued, and shows us, as a result, the basis upon which the πνευματικός -ψυχικός distinction
rests, it does not tell us how the Corinthians claimed
to have come into the possession of such spiritual wisdom, nor why they should have reserved this wisdom ex-

116

clusively to themselves and denied it to the other Corinthian Christians. In order to answer questions like
these, more evidence is needed beyond that which is
available to us from within the context of 1 Corinthians. As a consequence, no less than three major attempts have been made in recent years to uncover a
background to the πνευματικός-ψυχικός language in comparative literature.

The first of these seeks to understand the Corinthian antithesis against the variegated background of
Gnosticism.[121] In this case, the terminological and
conceptual distinction between the πνευματικός and the
ψυχικός is said to rest upon and reflect gnostic notions of a cosmological and anthropological dualism.
Among different groups of gnostics, this dualism is
conceived of as either a dualism between men, (some are
constituted with a 'pneumatic' nature, and so have the
possibility, by means of 'gnosis', to rise back again
to the divine, while others are created solely with a
'psychic' nature and have no such prospect), or, as a
dualism within man, (in the world and in mankind
'pneumatic' and 'psychic' elements have been mixed so
that each man has the possibility, through knowledge,
to return to God).[122]

On its behalf, proponents of this explanation of
the terminological contrast between the πνευματικός and
the ψυχικός in 1 Corinthians can point to a usage of
the specific terms of the antithesis within existing
gnostic literature.[123] But the very closeness of these
parallels in gnostic materials which emanate from a
later date would seem to argue for the influence of
Christian writings upon the gnostics rather than vice
versa. Thus, although the Corinthian contrast could,
perhaps, be legitimately considered as proto-gnostic,
to use parallels drawn from later literature as a means
of illuminating the earlier situation remains a dubious
procedure.[124]

A second alternative has been advocated more recently by Birger Pearson who has proposed to explain
the sense of the contrast with reference to a background in Hellenistic Judaism, especilly as this is
represented in the writings of Philo.[125] Here, Pearson
argues, the Corinthian distinction is paralleled in em-
bryonic form, (if not in actual fact), by the conception of a 'divinely-created anthropological distinction'; a distinction between each person's 'higher nature', (πνεῦμα), and 'lower nature', (ψυχή; cf. Gen 2.7

117

LXX). A pattern of thinking is then developed from the framework of this distinction. Each human being is thought to have within him a "divinely-created capacity", a "pneumatikos nature", which, when it has been properly "cultivated through wisdom", enables that person to "arise above the sense-perceptive level of the earthly soul and its passions", and "receive impressions from the heavenly sphere".[126] According to Pearson, this is the pattern of thinking that forms the background to the theology and religious practice of Paul's Corinthian opponents and accounts for their distinctive self-designations.

Pearson's proposal does manage to avoid the chronological difficulties associated with the gnostic hypothesis.[127] But the argument, at least in the form in which he has presented it, rests upon several questionable contentions. For one thing, the specific terminological contrast between the πνευματικός and the ψυχικός does not occur in Philo, or in any of the other literature of Hellenistic Judaism.[128] Moreover, no fundamental distinction is drawn between πνεῦμα and ψυχή within the human constitution on the basis of which the adjectival usage might have developed. For while Philo and other Jewish authors did distinguish between a higher and a lower part of the human nature, it is to do violence to the evidence to maintain that this distinction was consistently framed among Hellenistic Jews in terms of a priority of πνεῦμα over ψυχή.[129] The distinction seems instead to have been drawn between a 'rational' part of the soul whose essence, or substance, (οὐσία), was πνεῦμα, and a 'bodily' part of the soul whose essence was 'blood', or the 'flesh'.[130] Thus the 'higher' soul could be, and was in fact, designated and described using several apparently interchangeable terms including νοῦς, and διάνοια, as well as πνεῦμα and λογική, or νοέρα ψυχή.[131] There is no indication, therefore, that πνεῦμα was always preferred over these other terms and consistently contrasted with ψυχή in the Jewish milieu.

However, if one is prepared to bear these modifications in mind, then Pearson's analogy does indeed seem to describe a pattern of thinking that is characteristic, at least in general terms, of the Philonic literature, and one which might be potentially useful in understanding the context into which the Corinthians' self-designations fit.[132] But before we can give attention to possible parallels between this pattern and the Corinthian situation, we should outline the

118

whole pattern again more thoroughly.133

Within the pattern, three distinct levels, or stages emerge. The first is typical of all, for all persons possess a spiritual element within the soul that enables them to receive and comprehend divine truth. But, as all individuals also have a bodily element within the soul that is especially susceptible to the pulls and passions of the flesh, the higher soul must first be freed from such hindrances and cultivated through a life dedicated to the pursuit of wisdom. Those who undertake the study and practice of wisdom, however, pass on to a second level in which the attempt is made to purify and actualize the created potential. A third stage is achieved by a still more select group who rise, through the pursuit of wisdom, to experiences of spiritual illuminatin, higher wisdom, and communion with God.

Now within the framework of this pattern, whose goal may be convienently epitomized as the reception of spiritual wisdom, it is apparent that anthropological considerations do play a part. For the higher soul does indeed provide the foundation for individual sapiential perception, and Pearson's work has served to point to the validity of this observation. But a much more important part is played at the middle stage of the pattern by wisdom, and Pearson has given this far too little attention.134 The reception of the higher, or spiritual wisdom is only partly dependent upon one's created capacity to receive it. It is also equally, if not more dependent upon one's ability to subdue the fleshly passions, and upon the cultivation of one's created capacity, and both of these objectives are achieved, according to the sources, through progress in the study and practice of wisdom. Thus, only the one who has attained to the second level and the possession of its wisdom can hope to pass on to the third, on to the custody of a still higher, spiritual wisdom.

Moreover, as Pearson appears to recognize, it is solely at the third level, after one has attained to the higher wisdom, that titles such as τέλειος and σοφός become appropriate, and appear to have actually been utilized.135 For properly they describe in an exclusive manner the individual who has had an experience of spiritual illumination and come into the possession of a higher, spiritual wisdom; the one who has entered into experiences of communion with God.136 The distinction between individuals which is represented by the τέλειος-νήπιος and the σοφός-μορός contrast is, therefore, a distinction between the one who possesses the capability for spiritual wisdom and the one who has actually attained to such wisdom; a distinction between ability and achievement, between capacity and realization.[137]

Now within 1 Co 1-3, there are certainly definite overtones of a pattern of thought quite similar to the one that we have just described; overtones which seem, furthermore, to be consistently attributable to Paul's Corinthian opponents. Thus, for example, something very much like the first stage of the pattern appears, at least, to underlie Paul's use of the 'like-by-like' analogy in 1 Co 2.11, and his polemical denial in 1 Co 2.12.[138] However, there is also a marked resemblance between the second stage of the pattern and the stress on wisdom that is characteristic of much of the material from 1 Co 1-3. Finally, consideration should be given to the fact that Paul's opponents also appear to have made distinctions between themselves and the rest of Corinthian congregation in precisely those terms which were used to designate persons who had reached the highest stage within the pattern; that is, they called themselves τέλειοι and σοφοί , and contrasted themselves with the νήπιοι and the μοροί. All of this evidence argues forcefully and persuasively, in our opinion, for a correspondence between the theological perspective of Paul's Corinthian adversaries and the pattern of sapiential thought outlined above. But the final piece of the puzzle is still missing. For up to this point we have still been unable to suggest a background which could account for the Corinthians' distinctive πνευματικός-ψυχικός contrast.

Here, however, Richard Horsley's recent research is quite suggestive.[139] Horsley has taken up Pearson's proposal about a pattern of thinking in Philo and other wisdom writers, and attempted, within that context, to provide a third explanation as to the origins of the πνευματικός-ψυχικός language. He does so by indicating that the terms of this distinction could have been developed by the Corinthians themselves out of the pneumatology of the pattern, and in parallel to the attested terminological antitheses associated with the pattern.

Horsley begins, however, by rejecting Pearson's notion that the distinction could have been derived the anthropological presumptions of the pattern. For the

120

distinction which exists at the basis of the pattern, between two parts or portions of the soul, will not of itself serve to explain a distinction between two kinds or classes of men.[140] He then recommends that consideration be given, instead, to the terms that are commonly used in the wisdom sources to describe this sort of relative, or qualitative distinction between persons of different levels of religious experience, status, or achievement.[141] For the terminological contrasts τέλειος-νήπιος and σοφός-μόρός, (contrasts which occur in both the wisdom literature and in 1 Corinthians), are, as has been noted, functionally and logically analagous to the πνευματικός-ψυχικός distinction.[142] Thus far then, Horsley's work confirms the conclusions that we have already reached concerning the background of the πνευματικός-ψυχικός contrast.

But what accounts for the expression of this sort of qualitative distinction in the particular terms of the πνευματικός-ψυχικός antithesis? Horsley suggests, (but really does no more than hint), that the answer to this question might lie within the pattern itself; in the idea of the Spirit as the source of the soul's illumination.[143] He notices, for instance, that Philo consistently interprets Genesis 2.7 in such a way as to show;

> "the purpose, or function of the Spirit with regard to the soul, or mind: the Spirit makes possible the mind's knowledge of the divine".[144]

And, he suggests, in the light of this observation;

> "that Hellenistic Jews, and/or Christians, influenced by this background could have spoken of those who possessed the Spirit and the power of spiritual discernment as πνευματικοί, and compared such persons with those who lacked the Spirit and its power calling them ψυχικοί".[145]

The distinction would have originated, then, to express the contrast between persons who claimed to have had an experience of spiritual illumination, and those who had not; between those who claimed the Spirit as the source of their sapiential perception, and those whose discernment remained that of the unaided mind or soul. Finally, Horsley brings these ideas to bear directly upon the Corinthian situation and concludes.

"In 1 Co 2.6-16, the distinction between
the spiritual man and the psychic man is
connected with the role of the Spirit in
spiritual discernment. ψυχικός characterizes the man who was not received the
things of the Spirit of God. These things
are foolishness to him because they are
spiritually apprehended. πνευματικός, on
the other hand, characterizes the man who
possesses the things given by the Spirit,
the man who knows the πνευματικά because he
has been enabled to discern them spiritually."146

What Horsley has only suggested, however, is confirmed by our own investigation of the relationship between wisdom and spirit in Jewish sapiential literature
of the Hellenistic-Roman period. Thus, in the first
part of this work, we have been able to draw upon substantial evidence to indicate that the Spirit was consistently seen as the source of a higher wisdom in Jewish sapiential circles.147 Moreover, our studies have
served to highlight the widespread nature and the importance of this claim within the materials. For each
of the sources that we have examined predicates wisdom
in some way upon the calim to an experience of spiritual inspiration or illumination. We conclude, therefore, that Horsley's analysis of the conceptual background of the πνευματικός-ψυχικός contrast is largely
convincing and very much in line with the findings of
our own research. However, at least one major criticism of his work does need to be voiced. For if Pearson's efforts towards explaining the Corinthian situation tended to concentrate attention too much upon the
significance of the anthropological basis of the pattern, then Horsley's, by way of correction, appears to
have overcompensated by focusing almost exclusively upon the culmination of the pattern. Both Horsley and
Pearson, therefore, have, in our opinion, given insuf-
ficient attention to the middle stage of the pattern,
for both of them have neglected to notice the extent to
which the phenomenon of Jewish wisdom defines wisdom
with reference to the Torah.

But if one examines Philo's writings, (which provide, by all accounts, the most comprehensive evidence
for the pattern of thinking that we have been describing), then one soon discovers that, for him, the experience of spiritual illumination and the gaining of
higher wisdom grow directly out of study and meditation

122

in the Torah. Indeed, as we have shown, for Philo, it is only the one who reads, practices, and reflects upon the wisdom of the Torah who may expect to a) experience consistent moments of spiritual illuminaiton, b) attain to the allegorical, or 'spiritual' meaning, the 'higher wisdom', and c) enter into a life of spiritual communion with God.[148] In Philonic literature, then, as elsewhere in the sapiential Judaism of that era, the gift of spiritual insight is bestowed only upon those who have trained themselves in the study of the Torah. For these:

> "the study of the Torah was not only done to learn proper conduct and action, it was also an act of worship which brought the student closer to God; the study of the Torah was a holy duty, the fulfillment of which became a religious experience".[149]

Thus, the quest for wisdom in Philo and in other Jewish sapiential sources should be set firmly within the context of Judaism.[150] These writings are not presenting an alternative mystical religion in which salvation is tied to the attainment of wisdom, but instead only a different means by which the benefits of the covenant may be fully and completely realized.[151] Perfection, understood in terms of a life guided and directed by higher wisdom and the experience of communion with God that it mediates, may be achieved through study and meditation in the wisdom of the Torah, with the help of the Spirit that comes to the one who has prepared himself to receive such inspiration. This pattern of religion is the distinctive contribution of the later Jewish wisdom literature, but it falls firmly within the sphere of Judaism.

We began by enquiring about the Corinthians' understanding of the meaning of the πνευματικός-ψυχικός contrast. In the course of our investigation into that question, however, we have found a pattern of religion that utilizes much of the terminology that appears to occur in 1 Co 1-3 with reference to the positions of Paul's opponents. We have already suggested some of the ways in which that pattern enables us to integrate the Pauline references to the Corinthian position into a coherent and consistent whole,[152] but it now seems appropriate to attempt to reconstruct the situation more fully in a tentative but still probable way based upon the evidence that has been collected in the course of our analysis into the πνευματικός-ψυχικός distinction.

Thus, it seems likely, we submit, that the pattern of religion at Corinth resembled the pattern of sapiential achievement or attainment associated generally with the quest for wisdom in later Jewish wisdom circles. More particularly, however, it seems to have approximated most closely to the general contours of Hellenistic-Jewish wisdom as represented in Philo.[153] At Corinth, therefore, the experience of the Spirit and the possession of spiritual wisdom was apparently associated by a certain faction of the church with the study and keeping of the Torah, the divine wisdom. Thus also, we suggest, that the issue at Corinth was not one of salvation as has often been proposed,[154] but instead the double issue of perfection and guidance. How does one go on in the Christian experience so as to receive all of the benefits of the new covenant, (i.e. the continuing experience of spiritual insight, close communion with God, and guidance as to the divine will in practical and ethical matters)?[155] The Corinthian pneumatics would have said, presumably, that in order to progress to perfection as a Christian, (perfection defined in the three-fold terms that have been outlined above), one must read and study, practice and meditate upon Torah, the wisdom of God. For God has given each person a higher soul that will quickly respond to such cultivation, enabling the individual who has been purified through his study to receive continual spiritual wisdom. This, in turn, the pneumatics would have argued, was the only way to assure oneself of a life of full communion with God.

It is convincing, then, to believe that it was the search for wisdom and guidance in living the christian life that led to the divisions at Corinth. The Corinthian pneumatics claimed to have come into the possession of such wisdom and guidance, and they thought of themselves, accordingly, as persons living on a higher spiritual plane.[156] For them, the πνευματικός was the individual who had moved on to this higher level, attaining to a regular experience of spiritual illumination. This person, then, was contrasted for them with the individual who made no such claim, and so, in the opinion of the pneumatics, relied for wisdom simply upon the unaided ψυχή.[157] Thus, we have come at last to an answer to our original question about the meaning of the πνευματικός-ψυχικός contrast in its Corinthian context. With this background in mind, therefore, we can now turn back to our analysis of the nature and substance of the Pauline response in 1 Co 2.14-3.4.

As we have already intimated, Paul's reply to the Corinthians appears to be divided into two parts. We submit that in the first, (1 Co 2.14-16), the attempt is to redefine the πνευματικός-ψυχικός antithesis so as to change the nature of the distinction from a qualitative distinction among believers, into an absolute distinction between Christian and pagan. Then, in the second, (1 Co 3.1-4), Paul reintroduces the notion of a qualitative distinction but changes the terminology slightly so that the distinction as Paul uses it is clearly seen to be a distinction between mature and immature, a distinction between the πνευματικός, and the νήπιος ἐν χριστῷ. It remains now to present the exegesis to support these contentions.

In 1 Co 2.14, Paul makes a double statement about the ψυχικός; first, he does not receive, or accept, (δέχεται), the 'things' of the Spirit, and second, he is not able to know, or comprehend them, (οὐ δύναται γνῶναι). In both cases, however, Paul's denials have a decidedly polemical character, since the Corinthians, if we have assessed them correctly, would not have denied, as Paul does here, the willingness and capability of the ψυχικός to attain to the revelation of the Spirit. For, if our analysis is accurate, their own thinking was based upon the foundational axiom that every person was capable of receiving divine wisdom because God had placed within each a portion of his own Spirit. Now it may certainly be conceded that the Corinthians could have believed in addition, (and probably did), in the need for the nurture and purification of the divine Spirit within through Torah-study before one could attain to spiritual wisdom. However, the Corinthian pneumatics would not have refused to affirm a belief in the capacity of the ψυχικός to recognize and advance in the knowledge of God's revealed wisdom even to the point of attaining to spiritual inspiration and wisdom, and so becoming πνευματικός.

But this kind of a belief in gradual progress towards the possession of spiritual wisdom is preccisely what Paul's statements appear calculated to deny. For if, as the apostle alleges, the ψυχικός is unable to comprehend the 'things' of the Spirit, then his deficiency is much more profound than the Corinthian develomental schema allows. His is not merely a relative

125

deficiency in relation to the achievement of others, but instead it is one of principle and nature.[158] In 1 Co 2.14ff. then, Paul changes the very essence of the Corinthian contrast between the πνευματικός and the ψυχικός, for according to the Pauline understanding, the distinction between the πνευματικός and the ψυχικός is not relative, but absolute. Accordingly, Hans Conzelmann has correctly grasped the underlying question in 1 Co 2.14; "Are the psychics unbelievers, or a lower class of Christians?".[159] The answer that is implied by Paul in 1 Co 2.12ff. is that all Christians are πνευματικοί in that all have received the Spirit and the spiritual wisdom contained in the kerygma quite apart from any considerations of attainment or achievement; (cf. 1 Co 2.12, 13).[160] The ψυχικός designation is only appropriate in Paul's mind, therefore, for unbelievers, (1 Co 2.14), for those who do not possess any share in the spirit or in all of the 'things' that are spiritually discerned' (πνευματικῶς ἀνακρίνεται).

In this last phrase of 1 Co 2.14, however, we encounter the first of three occurrences of the verb ἀνακρίνω, a term which links together the redefinition of ψυχικός in verse 14 with statements about the πνευματικός in verse 15. Consistently difficult to translate, ἀκακρίνω is especially problematical in 1 Co 2.15. The particular problem is with the assertion of 1 Co 2.15a; αὐτος, (i.e. the πνευματικός of 2.15a), δὲ ὑπ οὐδενος ἀνακρίνεται. Does Paul mean to suggest that the πνευματικός is above criticism of any sort? This seems unlikely, especially in view of later Pauline comments in 1 Co 14.29 and 32 about the need to test and approve the claim to inspiration. But if an absolute sense is not what is intended here, then how are we to understand Paul's meaning?

One suggestion would attempt to resolve the problem by referring οὐδενός in 1 Co 2.15b back to ψυχικός in 2.14a, so that Paul is said to affirm that the πνευματικός is not open to the investigation or judgement of the ψυχικός.[161] But, as C.K. Barrett has correctly objected: "this is not what Paul says; he says that the spiritual man is not investigated or appraised by anyone".[162] He then goes on to suggest an attractive alternative which is to interpret ἀνακρίνεται in 1 Co 2.15c in the light of 1 Co 4.3-4.[163]

In connection with this suggestion, it is particularly interesting to make some further observations with regards to the use of ἀνακρίνεται in 1 Co 2.15.

First of all, we wish to note that the verb ἀνακρίνω
appears only in 1 Corinthians among all of the Pauline
epistles.[164] From this we may infer that the word was
probably another of those which was in common use in
Corinth among Paul's adversaries, and the Paul has
picked it up here in order to use it, as he has used
other Corinthian terminology throughout this passage,
in his own way. In light of this inference, though, it
is important to notice that the word may be used in at
least two distinct senses.[165] In a technical sense, it
refers to a judicial interrogation,[166] but in a more
general sense, to any kind of inquiry, or examination
which leads one to the formulation of a judgement.[167]
Hence, it seems possible to take the uses of ἀνακρίνω
in 1 Co 2.15a and b in two different ways. In 1 Co 2.-
15a, Paul asserts that the πνευματικός has a general
ability to examine the 'things' of the Spirit's revelation, (τὰ πάντα), and that he has this ability, moreover, in direct contrast to the ψυχικός who is unable
to discover them. But in 1 Co 2.15b, it seems likely
to suggest that Paul has employed ἀνακρίνω in its more
technical, judicial sense so as to bring this clause
into relationship with his apologetic self-defense in 1
Co 4.3 and 9.3. As a πνευματικός , Paul is ultimately
to be held up to the judgement of the Lord. He is
therefore unwilling to subject himself to the presumptive personal judgement of the Corinthians, (1 Co 4.3),
nor even to self-judgement in advance, (1 Co 4.3-4),
but only to the ἀνακρίσις of the Lord, (1 Co 4.4-5).

But doesn't this solution bring 1 Co 2.15 back into conflict with Paul's later statements which exhort
the Corinthians to exercise discernment in their evaluation of persons manifesting spirtual gifts? Perhaps
not, particularly if Paul distinguishes, as he
seems to do at this point, between an evaluation of the
manifestation of the Spirit, and an evaluation of the
πνευματικός. For, as James Dunn has indicated, while
the πνευματικά are open in Paul's mind to evaluation
and scrutiny, the πνευματικός is not.

> "The charisma of evaluation does not in-
> clude the passing of opinions about this or
> that man's worth or status; it is confined
> to the evaluation of particular charismata
> on the occasion of their manifestation."[168]

The Corinthian pneumatics, however, from all indications, appear to have been making just this sort of

judgement about the status and standing of their fellow
believers, (and probably also about the worth of Paul
in comparison to their other teachers; cf. 1 Co 1.12,
3.4, 21, 22, 4.6). Indeed, in the context of their own
belief structure, it was perfectly natural for them to
make such evaluations, for the πνευματικός was marked
out for them by the possession of wisdom and eloquence.[169] Paul's critique in 1 Co 2.15 strikes, however, at the very heart of their presumptive judgemen-
talism by polemically asserting, over against them,
that a person's worth and spiritual status cannot be
finally evaluated or judged by anyone except the Lord
himself, and certainly not by the Corinthians on the
basis of a narrow set of sapiential criteria.

Paul turns once more now to a scriptural citation
to conclude his argument. He does so, (as his previous
use of scripture has made plain), to prove to the Corinthians that their behaviour in this matter is inconsistent with the scriptural standards they claim to ad-
mire and uphold. For scripture itself informs us, according to the Pauline citation, that, as no-one knows
the mind of the Lord, no-one may, therefore, presume to
instruct, or evaluate him.[170] But, as πνευματικοί, we
have the mind of the Lord himself, the mind of Christ.
Hence, for Paul, the parallel conclusion is surely implied: no-one should consequently presume to judge us
either.[171] Paul's argument, therefore, rests upon the
radical identification that he draws between the νοῦν
κυρίου in 1 Co 2.16a, and the νοῦν χριστοῦ in 2.16b.[172]
If the equivalence exists, then the result will follow,
and for the apostle, it certainly does.

But in 1 Co 3.1-4, it looks as if Paul has changed
his mind, for here he seems not only to set forth an
opinion about the state of the Corinthians, (both as
they were, and as they are), in apparent opposition to
1 Co 2.15-16, but also to work, after all, with some
sort of relative definition for the term πνευματικός,
for he distinguishes the πνευματικός from the νήπιος ἐν
χριστῷ in an ostensible contrast to the absolute and
inclusive definition that he gave to the term in the
context of his discussion of the πνευματικός-ψυχικός
antithesis in 1 Co 2.14. However, if we are correct,
then both of these tensions can be resolved by giving
attention to the fact that in 1 Co 3.1-4, Paul's remarks are framed in the context of a discussion originated by the apostle about Christian maturity, while in
1 Co 2.14-16 his comments are made within the framework
of a debate sparked off by the Corinthians about

128

Christian spirituality and status. Accordingly, Paul can deny in 1 Co 2.14-16 that anyone should pass judgements about a person's experience, or possession of the Spirit as the Corinthians apparently were doing by contrasting the πνευματικός with the ψυχικός. But he can also affirm in 1 Co 3.1-4 that a legitimate distinction can be drawn between those who have come to maturity in the Spirit, and those who remain in their spiritual infancy.[173] So the Pauline distinction, unlike its Corinthian counterpart, does not imply a distinction with respect to the possession of the Spirit. Instead, operating within the sphere of a belief in the general reception of the Spirit by all Christians, (cf. 1 Co 2.12), Paul's distinction contrasts the more mature πνευματικός not simply with the νήπιος, but with the νήπιος ἐν χριστῷ, with those, that is, who have recieved the Spirit but have only begun to develop in terms of Christian experience and understanding.[174]

Obviously, it was to this latter group that the Corinthians belonged at the time of Paul's initial visit, and so he was not able, (οὐκ ἠδυνήθην), to share with them, (λαλῆσαι; cp. 1 Co 2.6, 13), all of the implications of God's act in Christ, or disclose to them the further dimensions of the new christological wisdom. Instead, he could only begin to reveal to them the meaning and significance of the Christ-event in his kerygmatic preaching, 'feeding' them with the wisdom that was appropriate to those who had just received the Spirit, and not burdening them with detailed teaching about the further aspects and implications of God's new wisdom; (1 Co 3.1-2).

All of this, however, sounds more than a little like an apologetic self-defense inspired, perhaps, by Corinthian criticism about the deficiencies of Paul's previous ministry. Nevertheless, in 1 Co 3.2b, the tables are turned on the critics. With the words, ἀλλ' οὐδε ἔτι νῦν δύνασθε, Paul shows them that the true deficiency lies with them, and not with him. The Corinthians are still not ready for further wisdom, for they have strayed from the guidance of the Spirit, and from growth in spiritual and christological wisdom. They have turned in Paul's absence back to the Torah, apart from reference to Christ, seeking guidance from its instruction, and maturity, (or perfection, as they seem to have preferred to call it), through the 'wisdom' of its teaching. That their imperfection remains, however, is revealed clearly enough to Paul by their continual infighting and squabbling over spiritual sta-

129

tus, for jealousy and strife between believers is not the fruit of the Spirit, but the fruit of the flesh; (1 Co 3.1, cp. Gal 5.19-21). The additional fact that some of the Corinthians were trying, apparently, to denigrate the value of Paul's preaching in comparison with the teaching of others on the basis of their own standards of wisdom and spirituality only confirms the apostle's suspicions about their lack of spiritual direction; (1 Co 3.4). Thus, Paul continues to address the Corinthians as σαρκίνοις and νήπιος ἐν χριστῷ, for despite the fact that some time has elapsed since he was among them there has been no growth. Far from maturing in the Spirit, the Corinthians have succeeded in demonstrating their immaturity through factional strife, and they have shown their lack of spiritual knowledge in returning to the Torah alone for wisdom, authority, and guidance.

Paul's two-fold polemic, however, may also be inverted to imply that he does recognize the existence of at least two valid criteria for the purpose of assessing genuine spiritual maturity. Such maturity involves both growth in the wisdom that is in continuity with the kerygma, (1 Co 3.1-2), and accompanying growth in conduct, love, and unity; (1 Co 3.3-4).[175] But, for Paul, once again in contrast to the Corinthians, these criteria are mutually validating. The Spirit's presence, understood both individually and corporately, should produce not only development in terms of wisdom as the Corinthians have emphasized, but also a lifestyle that is in conformity with Christ; one that fosters love and unity within the body, as they have so evidently neglected.

In 1 Co 3.1-4 then, Paul brings his discussion of the source of wisdom to a conclusion by attempting to reclaim, through redefinition, the Corinthian designation πνευματικός as a designation for the man who is maturing under the direction of the Spirit. As such, however, 1 Co 3.1-4 should be recognized as the natural and integral counterpart to 1 Co 2.14-16. There Paul affirms, over against the Corinthians, that no Christian may be called ψυχικός. For inasmuch as every Christian possesses the Spirit and comprehends the spiritual wisdom contained within the kerygma, that one is πνευματικός. But in 1 Co 3.1-4, Paul shows up the one-sidedness of a purely sapiential criterion, by affirming that Christians become πνευματικοί, (that is, mature), as they reject the deeds and understanding of the flesh, and pursue the control and enlightenment of

the Spirit.[176]   Being 'spiritual', then, is not just a
matter of wisdom, but also of conduct and lifestyle,
and the Corinthians' conduct under the regulation of
the Torah, their perfectionistic factionalism, clearly
demonstrates that they are still νήπιοι, but νήπιοι ἐν
χριστῷ.

In the last analysis, therefore, the Pauline redefinition of the term πνευματικός reveals to us that
the 'we' of 1 Co 2.10-3.4 is never exclusive. While
Paul recognizes differences of maturity among believers, he consistently refuses to give these distinctions
a divisive significance. Indeed, despite his claim to
be πνευματικός, then, he has more than a little in common with these wayward Corinthians ἐν χριστῷ; in the
common possession of the Spirit, and the common acceptance of the kerygma. His 'we', therefore, serves to
show them the spiritual unity which he shares with them
and which they should share with each other. But it
also reveals the spiritual diversity which separates
Paul from his opponents. The Corinthians have gone
wrong by departing from their spiritual and kerygmatic
heritage in their quest for perfection through the wisdom of the Torah. They have turned away from progress
and maturity in the christological wisdom of the
Spirit, and, as a consequence, they cannot be included
with Paul among those who have gone on to share more
fully in a spiritual understanding of God's wisdom in
Christ which is ever increasing in its depth and extent.

5.4 Wisdom: Purpose and Function, and Status, (1 Co
      3.5-17)

In 1 Co 3.5-17, Paul leads his readers through a
series of three successive illustrations, all closely
inter-related to one another.[177] Individually and col-
lectively these three metaphors yield a richly colored
portrait of the nature and character of the Christian
community. But the primary purpose of Paul's figura-
tive language within its context is probably not to be
defined, or only indirectly to be defined with reference to ecclesiology. For, in their present literary
and historical setting, all three images are probably
intended to address issues that have been raised by
Paul's description of the Corinthian factionalism in 1
Co 3.3-4.[178]

131

In accordance with this, a concern for unity is apparent within each of the three metaphors in reply to the ζῆλος καὶ ἔρις of those who say, ἐγω εἰμι Παύλου , or εγω Ἀπολλῶς; (cf. 1 Co 3.4). In 1 Co 3.5-9, this concern for unity surfaces under the figure of the θεοῦ γεώργιον in regards to Paul's view of the relationship that exists between himself and Apollos. The relationship is one of equality, (ἕν εἰσιν; 1 Co 3.8), despite Paul's recognition of some distinction. In 1 Co 3.10-15, the interest in unity is discernible beneath the representation of the σοφὸς ἀρχιτέκτων, and the ἄλλος ἐποικοδομεῖ, emerging with respect to the need for correspondence and consistency between the teaching of the one who 'lays the foundation', and the instruction of the one who 'builds upon it'. Lastly, in 1 Co 3.5-17, the regard for unity is particularly evident in relation to the metaphor of the temple, for it is as a community, and not as individuals, that the Corinthians comprise the ναὸς θεοῦ.

Thus, taking our cue from Paul's response in 1 Co 3.5-17, it seems possible for us to talk about three areas, or three kinds of disunity within the community; a) there were disputes about the relative worth of Paul's ministry in comparison to that of others, notably Apollos; b) there was at least potential disagreement, in Paul's estimation, between his original teaching and the sort of instruction that was currently being given out by another; and c) there was division as to the value of the individual, or group, relative to the community, or the church as a whole. These various kinds of disunity within the Corinthian fellowship would tend to imply that more than one factor had contributed to the discord. However, on the basis of our own study to this point, it seems plausible to suggest that one element may have predominated in fostering the complex of conflicts and arguments that appear to lie behind 1 Co 3.5-17; namely, the respect among segments of the Corinthian community for σοφία and the σοφός.

In 1 Co 3.5-9, Paul takes up the metaphor of the field, or the vineyard, a figure long utilized in Jewish writings to describe Israel as the community of God's planting.[179] Paul's own use of this word-picture, however, gives only a secondary emphasis to the communal aspects of the metaphor. He chooses instead to focus attention upon another aspect of the horticultural image, specifically upon the role played

132

by ὁ φυτεύων, and ὁ ποτίζων as laborers in the γεώργιον θεοῦ. His intent in doing so is marked out by his comments in 1 Co 3.5 and 8. Paul wishes to demonstrate the essential equality between Apollos and himself as συνεργοί in God's field.[180]

As we have already indicated, the background to Paul's emphasis on equality between himself and Apollos is probably to be found in disagreement among the Corinthians as to the worth of Paul's minsitry in comparison to the subsequent mission of Apollos. Connecting this dispute with the preceding context, it seems reasonable to assume that a stress on wisdom had played a large part in creating this situation. From Paul's statements elsewhere, (cf. 1 Co 2.1-5, 3.1-2), we can infer that some of the Corinthians felt that Paul was lacking in wisdom and eloquence, and it is not difficult to suppose that Apollos could have been viewed by such people as Paul's superior in these areas, particularly if the portrait of Apollos in Acts 18.24-28 is thought to be a reliable one.[181]

Paul, however, adamantly refuses to treat the issue in terms of inferiority or superiority, for both he and Apollos are united as διάκονοι in God's employ. Their value is in reality, therefore, incomparable in relation to ὁ αὐξάνων θεός.[182] If then, there has been any growth among the Corinthians, it is to be attributed to God, and not to one or another of the community's teachers.[183]

On the other hand, 1 Co 3.5-9 does point to a recognition on Paul's part of some distinction between himself and Apollos. This distinction is normally understood in functional terms following closely the presumed 'allegorical' language of the agricultural metaphor. Paul 'planted', (i.e. evangelized), and Appollos 'watered', (i.e. taught the Corinthian converts). But C.K. Barrett and Hans Conzelmann, following Johannes Weiss, have correctly pointed to the danger of pressing Paul's metaphor exclusively in an allegorical direction. For, it is apparent from 1 Co 3.5 that Apollos had also been engaged successfully in evangelism at Corinth, and it is inherently probable, moreover, that Paul had given his own converts some instruction.[184] The distinction that Paul has in mind, therefore, is probably chronological as much as functional. Paul was the first to work in Corinth, while Apollos came later on into the field that Paul had initially cultivated stimulating further growth both in terms of expansion,

133

and in terms of edification.[185] Such distinctions, in Paul's opinion, should only serve to remind the Corinthians that neither he nor Apollos have been responsible for the overall development of the Christian community at Corinth. It is God who has been the consistent cause of growth. Accordingly, it follows that the loyalty and devotion of the Corinthian factions has been misplaced; it belongs to God, who has 'enriched' the community through a succession of able teachers; (cf. 1 Co 1.5).

In 1 Co 3.9b, Paul passes over from his first figure to a second, from the image of the community as God's planting to the metaphor of the congregation as God's building. The transition is a natural one, if somewhat abrupt, for the two images are routinely conjoined in a wide variety of Jewish and Greek literature.[186] But the change is significant, for with it Paul's thought shifts to another aspect of the situation in Corinth, an aspect that becomes identifiable especially in 1 Co 3.10b-11. Here Paul warns his readers of a requirement for consistency in relation to growth. There must be correspondence between the original Pauline preaching which 'laid the foundation' of God's building at Corinth, and any subsequent instruction that might attempt to 'build' upon the Pauline kerygma.[187]

It is not difficult to attribute the need for this metaphorical admonition once more to the Corinthians' passion for wisdom. Indeed, in the light of 1 Co 1.17, it seems as though the Corinthian wisdom was poised to displace the kerygma, at least in the practical terms of its relevance and authority within the community. For Paul, however, this situation only reveals the true ignorance of the Corinthians as to the nature of θεοῦ σοφία. The kerygma is, in fact, the epitome of divine wisdom because its content is the proclamation of the crucified Christ who is the new locus of God's wisdom; (cf. 1 Co 1.24, 30, 2.7). Thus, in 1 Co 3.10-11, the kerygma, as it was preached by Paul in Corinth, is viewed as forming a standard by which all subsequent wisdom should be evaluated.[188]

In 1 Co 3.12-15, Paul drives home his point by bringing the situation at Corinth into eschatological perspective. Ultimately, God's building at Corinth will be subjected to the apocalyptic fire of divine judgement.[189] At that time, the 'work' of each one who has been active in the construction of the 'building' will become 'manifest' as to its value; for the 'day' will 'disclose' its true worth. If the 'work' of any individual 'remains' upon the foundation after the great conflagration, that person will receive commendation or 'reward'. But the 'work' that is separated from the foundation by this divine test will be burnt away, and the builder who has erected the inadequate superstructure will himself not entirely escape the taint of his failure.[190]

Thus, 1 Co 3.12-15, like the earlier portion of the metaphor in 3.10-11, stresses a need for consistency in relation to the 'work' of teaching. The purpose of further instruction in wisdom is spelled out quite clearly. It is the edification, the οἰκοδομή, the 'building-up' of the community upon its foundation in Christ and kerygma.[191] Any wisdom that does not contribute to this function is worthless at best, and will, in the end, be revealed as such.[192]

The eschatological dimension seems to be chiefly responsible for carrying Paul's thought forward into 1 Co 3.16-17 where the 'building' of 1 Co 3.10-15 is given further definition and identified as the 'temple of God'. Here, however, Paul's image draws not only upon a rich and varied background in Jewish literature,[193] but also, apparently, upon previous Pauline teaching among the Corinthians; (cf. οὐκ οἴδατε; 1 Co 3.16).[194] The two uses of the second person plural, (ἐστε and ἐν ὑμῖν), point us towards Paul's emphasis, for they make it clear that the metaphor of the temple is applied in the first instance, to the community as a whole, and not to the individual.[195] Together the Corinthians comprise God's temple, (1 Co 3.16), therefore the unity of the congregation is not to be taken lightly. To rend the community into separate divisions would be to destroy God's temple and invite divine punishment; (1 Co 3.17).

The necessity for Paul's warning would seem to be best explained with reference to the behavior of the Corinthians. Their factions and party loyalties are discernible throughout 1 Corinthians 1-3, and this trait provides us with a cogent and reasonable justification for Paul's remarks. The Corinthians' divisiveness and bickering had not yet erupted into open schismatic separation between the factions, but that was a genuine possibility, and one that deeply concerned Paul.[196]

R.J. McKelvey has captured the essence of his reply.

> "Over against the splinter-groups in the
> church at Corinth, Paul sets the picture of
> the church as God's temple. His Jewish-
> Christian readers would not fail to see the
> point. God does not dwell in a multitude
> of temples. He is one, and there can only
> be one shrine which he can inhabit."[197]

Paul responds to the potential division of the congregation by reminding the Corinthians of the integrity of the community as the eschatological temple of God. Beyond the Pauline paraenesis, however, lies the stern warning of 1 Co 3.17. Promulgated in the form of the lex talionis, this verse functions as a solemn divine promise of destruction to the destroyer.[198] The unity of the community may not be lightly esteemed. The wisdom that does not build up the community is reprehensible, and its propagator shall be shamed, (1 Co 3.10-15), but the wisdom that succeeds in dividing the community must stand, along with its proponents, under the full force of divine judgement; (1 Co 3.17).[199]

Thus the temple imagery of 1 Co 3.16-17 functions within its context in unison with the previous Pauline metaphors of 1 Co 3.5-9 and 3.10-15. All three emphasize that the proper function of wisdom lies in the edification and upbuilding of the community. In 1 Co 3.5-9, this idea is presented positively, and even, perhaps, a bit idealistically in relation to the respective ministries of Paul and Apollos. 1 Co 3.10-15 exhibits the most eloquent presentation of Paul's thought, noting the necessity for consistency between the foundation of the kerygma and the structure of wisdom. The culmination of the Pauline imagery, however, is reached in 1 Co 3.16-17 where the community is revealed to be the eschatological temple of God, and the theme of edification is pursued in counterpoint to the divine warning.

5.5 Conclusion

Our analysis of the second half of the Pauline discourse may be concluded at this point, for in 1 Co 3.18-20 Paul may be seen to return to a reprise of the initial polemical theme statement of 1 Co 1.18-20 and to draw the discourse as a whole to its close by reiterating the thought with which it began.[200] In and

136

through his own activity, God has superseded ἡ σοφία
τοῦ κόσμου τούτου and transcended the ability of ὁ
σοφός 'τοῦ αἰῶνος τούτου to discern his plan. But in 1
Co 2.6-3.17, over against this thought, Paul sets forth
something of the character of the σοφία which has been
brought into being as a result of God's action. Its
essence is christological, and its central focus is on
the hidden significance of the cross; (1 Co 2.6-9). It
has not been made known solely to a select few who have
reached the culmination of a quest for religious perfection, but instead, through the Spirit, it has been
revealed to all Christian believers in the kerygma and
its full implications progressively revealed in the
same way to all who continue towards a spiritual maturity in Christ; (1 Co 2.10-3.4). Thus, in its true
role, wisdom should not operate in such a way as to divide the community, but rather it should serve to unite
it as the upbuilding of the whole depends upon the contribution of the knowledge of each; (1 Co 3.4-17).
Such exegesis means, however, that 1 Co 2.6-3.20 may be
persuasively interpreted against the same background as
1 Co 1.18-2.5.

137

CONCLUSION

It has been just over one hundred and fifty years since F.C. Baur first attempted to interpret the controversies reflected in Paul's first letter to the church at Corinth through the lens of 1 Co 1.12, reducing the four parties named within that verse to two: a group tied to the teaching of Paul and Apollos, (whom Baur understood as allies), and a "judaizing-party" aligned to Peter, and, in its own mind, even more to Christ.[1] Baur proposed in this way to account for the fact that in the rest of the epistle Paul does not go on to oppose a variety of different or divergent party opinions, but rather the single phenomenon of false wisdom and the challenge presented by its influence to the guidance and direction of the church.

At the time, and in the history of scholarship since, Baur's attempt to make 1 Corinthians conform to his own dialectical understanding of the whole of early church history drew searching criticism from those who were convinced that his interpretation of 1 Co 1.12 was incorrect. They argued that Baur had blurred the distinction between the internal problems of 1 Corinthians and the conflicts caused initially in Galatia, and perhaps later on in Corinth as well by the entrance of "judaizers" into the fellowship; (cf. Ga 5.1-12, 2 Co 11.12-15, 22ff.).

The weakness of Baur's dialectical theory applied without qualification or nuance to the interpretation of 1 Corinthians is glaringly and justly exposed by such criticism. Nevertheless his suggestion about possible jewish-christian influence upon the historical situation that provides the context for Paul's first letter to the church at Corinth has consistently attracted attention among certain scholars who, in a less sweeping but more discriminating and careful way, have pointed to indications within 1 Corinthinas and Acts of the influential presence of a jewish-christian element among the membership of the Corinthian church.[2] Furthermore, as a result of recent investigations by Birger Pearson and Richard Horsley into the jewish sapiential background of the non-Pauline language of 1 Co 1-3, a great amount of additional evidence has been collected to support a view which would attribute influence to a jewish-christian element within the Corinthian church and assign substantial significance to the traditions and expressions of hellenistic or diaspora Judaism in terms of their impact upon the life of the community.

Our own work has attempted to build upon such evidence, especially the recent contributions of Pearson and Horsley, and to carry their studies forward both in regards to the jewish background materials, and in regards to the interpretation of 1 Corinthians. Our method in both cases has been to broaden the focus of investigation and to test our hypotheses on a much broader basis. Thus, in part one of this book, we were able, upon analysis, to establish significant areas of agreement in perspective between the wisdom literature of hellenistic Judaism, (which provided the basis for the work of Pearson and Horsley), and the sapiential thought of palestinian Judaism as represented by the the Book of Sirach and the Dead Sea Scrolls. In both hellenistic and palestinian Judaism we found that the content of wisdom is defined with respect to the Torah; there is discussion about levels of attainment with regard to the acquisition of wisdom; the mediation of wisdom at the highest level of sapiential achievement is consistently attributed to a spirit sent by God, or to God's own Spirit; and qualities such as eloquence and perfection are throughout our sources assigned to the person who has successfully attained to the wisdom and understanding brought by divine assistance. Such findings, we asserted, agreed with the broad conclusions of Martin Hengel concerning the lack of any rigid distinction between hellenistic and palestinian Judaism in the Greco-Roman period.

In the second half of our study, we were able to demonstrate how the broadened base of evidence, derived from the jewish wisdom traditions of the Greco-Roman period as a whole, both necessitates corrections to the earlier conclusions of Pearson and Horsley, and provides a perspective from which one may interpret not only the historical and conceptual background to the Corinthian terminology of 1 Co 1-3, but also Paul's response to the manifestation of wisdom at Corinth.

Such a response is begun, as we have shown, in 1 Co 1.18-3.20, a self-contained literary unit resembling in form a homily or discourse on wisdom divided antithetically into two parts. The first of these is 1 Co 1.18-2.5, where Paul criticizes the wisdom to which some of the Corinthians have committed themselves and the effects of such wisdom upon the community. From an eschatological conviction that in Christ the fullness of God's wisdom has become manifest, Paul asserts that the wisdom that belongs to and governs this present age

142

and this world, the partial wisdom of the "wise man", the "scribe", and the "interpreter", the wisdom of the Torah, has been transcended and superseded; (1 Co 1.18-25). In its judgement upon Christ, upon the signifi-cance of the cross, and upon the kerygma, Paul argues, its incompleteness and inadequacy have been clearly manifested. To rely solely upon its instruction for wisdom and guidance apart from any reference to the implications of the Christ-event for the meaning and application of the law in the age that has been inau-gurated by the coming of the messiah is therefore wrong and invites the divisions between individual jews and gentiles in the community that characterized their boastful lives before the time of their conversion to Christ; (1 Co 1.26-31). Particularly symptomatic of the problems being engendered by a respect for nomistic wisdom within the community, however, is not only divisiveness, but also the pre-eminent value being ac-corded to eloquence in relationship to the authentica-tion and evaluation of wisdom. The inadequacy of the criterion is, as Paul points out, exposed once more by the kerygma whose power depends not on eloquence, but upon the Spirit poured out upon the messengers of the messianic age; (1 Co 2.1-5). Thus, in his critique of the manifestation of wisdom at Corinth, Paul may be seen to concentrate on precisely those features which were earlier found to be characteristic of jewish wis-dom traditions in the Greco-Roman era: a nomistic em-phasis, a tendency to distinguish between individuals in regard to their possession of wisdom, and a stress upon eloquence as a quality of the person gifted by God to understand, interpret, and impart wise guidance and teaching.

However, in 1 Co 2.6-3.20, the second part of his discourse, the apostle's tone, as we noted, changes; (a change which we argued, is both understandable, and to be anticipated in light of the antithetical, negative to positive form of his discourse). Here Paul moves away from rebuke alone, and attempts to instruct the church in their understanding of the contents and mediation of the christological and eschatological "wisdom of God". The center of such wisdom, its core, lies in the meaning and significance of the crucifix-ion; (1 Co 2.6-9). It is this event that has begun to unveil all of the formerly hidden contents of God's plan for his people within the age inaugurated by mes-siah's death and ressurection. Such wisdom, however, belongs in its totality only to the Spirit of God who

reveals it progressively, (beginning with the significance of the kerygma itself and working out from that
to the implications of the kerygma for the life of the
individual and the community), to those persons who
have passed from a purely natural existence into a
growing spiritual existence guided, directed, and fed
by the presence of the Spirit in their lives; (1 Co
2.10-3.4). Furthermore, Paul concludes, the mutual
sharing of spiritual wisdom within the community, no
matter its human source, will succeed in the upbuilding
of the church, the new temple of God, only if it is in
continuity with the kerygma, the foundation of eschatological wisdom; (1 Co 3.5-20). Once again then, in
his teaching, Paul may be seen to formulate his own
thoughts against the background of earlier jewish
sapiential traditions. In contrast to a nomistic emphasis, Paul stresses the christological and eschatological nature of "the wisdom of God". In contrast to a
relative distinction between the spiritual capacity of
each created individual and the spirituality attained
by those who cultivate their capacity through the study
of the law, Paul sets an absolute distinction between
the "natural man" and the person who has received the
Spirit of God and the wisdom which the Spirit brings.
In contrast to the divisions produced by the quest
among the Corinthians to discover the teacher most advanced in wisdom and the eloquence they supposed would
accompany him, Paul presents a picture of himself
together with the rest of the Corinthians' teachers
laboring together to reveal to the community the fullness of the Spirit's wisdom in order that the community
might be built up as the eschatological temple of God.
Thus the didactic elements of Paul's discourse also
become coherent and powerful when interpreted as a
response to the principal features of sapiential
Judaism.

Having now briefly summarized the results of our
research, some possible implications growing out of our
investigation and its outcome may also be noted.
Primarily such implications would appear to fall into
three broad categories. First of all, if our conclusions about the background and interpretation of 1
Co 1.18-3.20 are correct then some important implications about the understanding of the rest of the letter
in terms of its structure and its content would seem to
follow.

Consistently in the past these opening chapters of
1 Corinthians have proved difficult for many to relate

144

closely to the more concrete ethical and practical problems addressed by the following chapters of the letter. The tendency, therefore, has been to consider wisdom as simply one of the many issues which had proved divisive within the Corinthian community. On these premises, there would seem to be no particular reason for the placement of the wisdom issue at the outset of the epistle. However, our analysis tends in a different direction. For if Paul in 1 Co 1.18-3.20 is indeed attempting to critique the wisdom that formerly guided the ethical and practical behavior of those within the Corinthian church who had been closely associated with Judaism and the synagogue and set in its place a new understanding of the contents of divine wisdom, a new frame of reference for christian conduct, then there are strong reasons for the placement of the discourse on wisdom at the beginning of the letter and strong reasons for thinking that the rest of the problems manifest within the letter are most adequately interpreted with reference to the background and and teaching contained in 1 Co 1.18-3.20. The central issue of the letter would be the one highlighted within this opening section, namely, the issue of deciding upon the locus, content, source and purpose of the wisdom which would guide the community and the individuals within it into proper sorts of christian behavior. What sort of wisdom was to govern their morality, their response to food that had been dedicated to idols, the conduct of their worship, and the shape of their hope for the resurrection? Where was such wisdom to be found, and who was its most authoritative teacher? Such questions logically and in a historically plausible way would seem to be able to demonstrate how the contents of the rest of the letter, the problems at Corinth and the Pauline response, might grow quite naturally out of an initial emphaiss on wisdom within the community. Our research would imply that a large part of that emphasis on wisdom was due to the residual but highly influential presence of jewish wisdom traditions among certain segments of the community.

A second implication arising out of our analysis concerns the relationship between 1 and 2 Corinthians. Is it possible to relate the two more closely together than is the custom at present by taking greater account of the stress upon jewish sapiential traditions at Corinth uncovered as the background to 1 Co 1.18-3.20 by our study? Perhaps after all there is some connection between the internal struggles of 1 Corinthians and the external agitators who entered the church sometime after the writing of that letter and became the opponents whom Paul so bitterly and yet carefully attacks in 2 Corinthians 10-13. Our research would seem to indicate that much of the ground might have been prepared for the arrival of Paul's opponents in Corinth and their impact upon the community by the influence of jewish wisdom traditions upon significant portions of the church. For if indeed they came as individuals possessing great personal presence and powerful speech (cf. 2 Co 10.9, 11.6), comparing themselves actively and favorably with other teachers like themselves (cf. 2 Co 10.12, 11.12), in terms of wisdom and foolishness (cf. 2 Co 10.16, 19), as Hebrews, Israelites, and descendants of Abraham (2 Co 11.22), then they entered a community already susceptible to their claims to be "superlative apostles" on the basis of such criteria as has been shown in our investigation of 1 Co 1.18-3.20, and to a christian community prepared to that extent to give credence to the "different gospel" which they preached.

A third and final implication of our analysis of the wisdom discourse in 1 Co 1.18-3.20 pertains to the attitude revealed within the discourse to the Torah, the law and wisdom of Judaism. The thorny question of Paul's attitude towards the law has, of course, provoked an enormous amount of research and writing in the past which shows little or no sign of abating over the last few years. Indeed in the light of E.P. Sanders' recent works, _Paul and Palestinian Judaism_, and _Paul, the Law and the Jewish People_, the quest for a realistic appraisal of Paul's view of the law and its continuing significance for the christian community may be said to have received a considerable and crucially important new impetus. For Sanders' presentation of the place of the law within the religious pattern of jewish covenantal nomism with its dual concern for "getting" and "staying" in the covenant has set forth a much more realistic and accurate basis for purposes of comparison between Pauline Christianity and Early Post-Biblical Judaism than those employed by scholars in the past. In the light of the size and scope of the issue we would not wish to suggest that our research does any more than hint at a part of the solution to this persistently difficult problem. But our study does indicate that in terms of maintaining one's place within the covenant of grace established as a result of the Christ-event, Paul was firmly opposed to the attempt to maintain covenantal righteousness through adherence to the widom, guidance, direction, and stipulations of the

146

law of Judaism.

His argument, as we have seen, critiques those who
by their allegiance to the law in their search for wisdom and guidance fail, in his estimation, to recognize
that the wisdom of the law, together with the pattern
of religion characteristic of sapiential Judaism and
its attempt to maintain and deepen individual covenantal righteousness, has been decisively transcended and
superseded by the new christocentric wisdom of God and
the abiding presence of the Spirit who progressively
communicates God's wisdom to each individual Christian.
The inadequacy and incompleteness of the former wisdom
of the law has been decisively demonstrated by the
crucifixion and the ignorance of the rulers. In matters of christian conduct therefore and the maintenance
of our relationship with God through Christ we can no
longer, Paul argues, turn back solely and simply to the
law as the standard for wisdom, counsel, and action.
For the law as the pre-eminent locus of divine wisdom
belongs to a world and an age that is passing away. It
has been transcended by the eschatological wisdom of
God that has broken into the world in and through the
Christ-event. Thus for guidance and direction based
upon this new eschatological wisdom we must look initially not to the old written code, but to the Spirit
who can make plain to the christian community through
its teachers the implications of the Christ-event that
alter the former wisdom and provide a fresh path for
the new community of God's people. It is the law by
itself then, apart from reference to the Christ-event
and the interpretation of that event through the
Spirit, that Paul rejects as an appropriate standard
for wisdom, or for the maintenance of christian covenantal righteousness. This much seems clear from 1 Co
1.18-3.20. But Paul's argument leaves the door open,
at least potentially, to a continuing place for those
aspects of the law that have the potential to be interpreted in ways consistent with Paul's own christological and eschatological wisdom.

How this perspective might enable one to gain a
more comprehensive and accurate view of Paul's attitude
to the law, of course, remains to be seen, and the same
is the case in regards to the further investigations
called for by the implications of our research discussed above. However, such almost always is the case as a
new perspective raises a number of new and interesting
questions. If our work has provided a firm basis from
which to begin to pursue the resolution of some of

147

these questions we shall rest content - at least for
the moment.

FOOTNOTES

The form of the footnotes follows, in general, the guidelines established by the Society for Biblical Literature and outlined in an article entitled, "Instruction to Contributors" which appeared on pages 83-97 in The Society for Biblical Literature: Members Handbook, compiled by G. Macrae, (Missoula: Scholars, 1980).

A major exception to these guidelines, however, is to be found in my references to articles in scholarly journals where volume and page numbers are given first, (separated by a period), and then the year in which the volume appeared.

Abbreviations follow this guide as well, or alternatively, have been adopted from Sigfried Schwertner's, International Glossary of Abbreviations for Theology and Related Subjects, (Berlin: Walter de Gruyter, 1974).

Commentaries on First Corinthians have been cited throughout the footnotes solely by name and page number. Complete publication data may be found in the bibliography.

1. This article, originally delivered by Barrett to the University of Manchester as the T.W. Manson Memorial Lecture in 1963, was published the following year in BJRL 46.269-297.

2. So C.K. Barrett, "Christianity at Corinth", 275-276.

3. Examples of Paul's polemic in 1 Co 1-4 may be seen in 1 Co 1.26, 2.1, 4; and 3.18. (No punctuation follows the abbreviations of primary source materials in this work following the guidelines established and outlined at the head of the footnotes.)

4. For the most recent confirmation of the validity of this methodology and of its results see J. Painter, "Paul and the πνευματικοί at Corinth", 237-250 in Paul and Paulinism, eds. M.D. Hooker and S.G. Wilson, (London: SPCK, 1982).

5. The following comments do not purport to represent an attempt to provide more than a highly selective review of the history of scholarship on this issue. A more complete picture may be gained from any of the following works: R. Baumann, Mitte und Norm des Christlichen, (Munster: Aschendorff, 19-68); E.E. Ellis, Prophecy and Hermeneutic in Early Christianity, (Grand Rapids: Eerdmans, 1978); J. C. Hurd, The Origin of 1 Corinthians, (London: SPCK, 1965); U. Wilckens, Weisheit und Torheit, (Tubingen: J.C.B. Mohr, 1959); M. Winter, Pneumatiker und Psychiker in Korinth, (Marburg: N.G. Elwert, 1975).

6. See, for example, Grosheide, 41; Lightfoot, 157; Edwards, 47; and A. Robertson -A. Plummer; 15, 33.

7. The proposal originated, of course, with W. Lutgert. See Freiheitspredigt und Schwarmgeister in Korinth, (Gutersloh: C. Bertelsmann, 1908). It has been defended more recently, however, by U. Wilckens, W. Schmithals, and M. Winter.

8. See E.M. Yamauchi, Pre-Christian Gnosticism, (London: Tyndale, 1973); A.D. Nock, "Gnosticism",

HTR 57.255-279; and R. McL. Wilson, Gnosis and the
New Testament, (Oxford: Blackwell, 1968).

9. So R. McL. Wilson, Gnosis and the New Testament,
    52. See also idem. "How Gnostic were the Corin-
    thians", NTS 19.65-74 (1972).

10. See B.A. Pearson, The Pneumatikos-Psychikos Ter-
    minology in 1 Corinthians, (Missoula: Scholars,
    1973); and R.A. Horsley, Paul and the Pneumatikoi,
    (a dissertation completed at Harvard University in
    1970).

11. See B.A. Pearson, The Pneumatikos-Psychikos Ter-
    minology; 1-6, 82-86. The most therefore that can
    be said is that Corinthian thought reflects some
    of the terminology and part of the phraseology la-
    ter used within Gnosticism.
    See J.D.G. Dunn, Unity and Diversity in the New
    Testament, (Philadelphia: Westminister, 1977).

12. It would be superfluous to reduplicate the work of
    Horsley and Pearson in any detail. It may, how-
    ever, be useful for the reader to compare quickly
    1 Co 3.1ff. and De Agricultura 9, or De Migratione
    28, 46 in order to gage the value of the argument
    that may be presented in relation to virtually all
    of the non-Pauline terminology in 1 Co 1-4.

1. There is a broad consensus among scholars with respect to the likely date of ben Sira's composition. See G.W.E. Nickelsburg, Jewish Literature between the Bible and the Mishnah, (London: SCM, 1981), 64; R.H. Pfeiffer, A History of New Testament Times, (New York: Harper and Brothers, 1949), 364-367; M. Hengel, Judaism and Hellenism, (London: SCM, 1974 - 2 vols.), 1.131; and E. Jacob, "Wisdom and Religion in Sirach", 247-260 in Israelite Wisdom, eds. J.G. Gammie, W.A. Brugemann, W.L. Humphreys, and J.M. Ward, (Missoula: Scholars, 1978), 251. All of these writers present arguments from internal and external evidence to support a date between 198 and 175 BCE. The more precise figure of 180 BCE is adopted following R.H. Pfeiffer.
The same sources provide further evidence to indicate that the transportation of ben Sira's work to Alexandria probably occurred c. 132 BCE. Its' translation into Greek will have been slightly later, about 117 BCE. The provenance of the original composition is clear from Sir 50.27.

2. The proper form of the author's name, and it's significance is discussed by M. Hengel, Judaism and Hellenism, 1.131, and R.H. Pfeiffer, History, 352. I shall make use of both the Hebrew nomenclature and the Greek, the former mostly with reference to the author, the latter primarily with reference to the book. The comparative form of the name in Greek and Hebrew raises, however, the question of language and text. The matter is still in a state of flux, but much less so following the discovery of fragments of Sirach at Masada and Qumran. These discoveries, in conjunction with earlier finds from the Cairo Geniza, have considerably advanced the establishment of an accurate Hebrew text. However, in view of the many significant lacunae which remain in that text despite the recent discoveries, the Greek text has been adopted as the primary basis for the current study, though I have attempted to compare the Greek with the Hebrew where that is possible. For a discussion of the issues involved in the establishment of the Hebrew text, see A.A. di Lella, The Hebrew Text of Sirach, (The Hague: Mouton and

Notes to page 9

Co., 1966). The Greek text utilized is that of J.
Ziegler, <u>Sapientia Iesu Filii Sirach</u>, (Göttingen:
Vandenhoeck and Ruprecht, 1965). English translations follow <u>The Oxford Annotated Apocrypha</u> - <u>Re-
vised Standard Version</u>, ed. B.M. Metzger, (New
York: Oxford University Press, 1977 - second edition), unless otherwise noted. A detailed text-
critical study of Sir 1.1-27, 4.11-19, 6.18-37,
14.20-15.10, 19.20-24, 20.27-31, 21.12-28, 24.1-
34, 39.1-16; 38.24-39.14, and 51.13-30 has been
made by O. Rickenbacher in which account has been
taken of Hebrew, the Greek and the Syriac texts.
See <u>Weisheitsperikopen bei Ben Sira</u>, (Freiburg:
Universitats Verlag, 1973).

3.   So Sir 50.27. The close association of συνέσεως,
(שכל), ἐπιστήμης, (משל), and σοφίαν, (בנה), within
the context of this one verse is notable.

4.   One may compare, for instance, the goal stated in
Prov 1.2.

5.   So J.L. Crenshaw, <u>Old Testament Wisdom</u>, (London:
SCM, 1982), 149. See also J. Fichtner, <u>Die Altorientalische Weisheit in ihrer Israelitisch-
Jüdischen Auspragung</u>, (Geissen: Verlag von Alfred
Töpelmann, 1933); and J. Marböck, <u>Weisheit im Wan-
del</u>, (Bonn: Peter Hanstein Verlag, 1971).
Against G. von Rad, <u>Wisdom in Israel</u>, (London:
SCM, 1972), 240-262, who argues that ben Sira's
concern for the law does not, in fact, mark any
change in the theological perspective of Jewish
wisdom.

6.   The presence of traditional wisdom in Sirach, and
the relationship of such wisdom to nomistic wisdom
is discussed by J.L. Crenshaw, <u>Old Testament Wis-
dom</u>, 149-173; J. Fichtner, <u>Die Altorientalische
Weisheit</u>; 49, 92-95; P.S. Fiddes, <u>The Hiddenness
of Wisdom in the Old Testament and Later Judaism</u>,,
(an unpublished doctoral thesis completed at Oxford University in 1976); 268-280, 344-346; J.C.
Rylaarsdam, <u>Revelation in Jewish Wisdom Literature</u>
(Chicago: University of Chicago, 1974 = 1946
edition), 18-46; E.P. Sanders, <u>Paul and Palestinian Judaism</u>, (Philadelphia: Fortress, 1977), 329-

156

333; G. von Rad, Wisdom in Israel, 240-262; and J. Marbock "Gesetz und Weisheit. Zum Verstandnis des Gesetzes bei Jesus Sira", BZ 20.1-21 (1976).

7. See P.E. Bonnard, La Saesse: En Personne Annoncée et venue, Jésus Christ, (Paris: Les Éditions du Cerf, 1966), 55; J. Fichtner, Die Altorientalische Weisheit, 92-93, M. Küchler, Frühjüdische Weisheitstraditionen, (Freibourg: Universitätsverlag, 1979), 38-39; A. Sauer, "Wisdom and Law in Old Testament Wisdom Literature", CTM 43.600-609 (19-72), 607; G.T. Sheppard, "Wisdom and Torah: The Interpretation of Deuteronomy underlying Sirach 24.23", 166-176 in Biblical and Near Eastern Studies, ed. G.A. Tuttle, (Grand Rapids: Eerdmans, 1978); idem., Wisdom as a Hermeneutical Construct, (Berlin: Walter de Gruyter, 1980); E. Zenger, "Die Späte Weisheit und das Gesetz", 43-56 in Literatur und Religion des Frühjüdentums, eds. J. Maier, J. Schreiner, (Wurzburg: Echter Verlag, 1973), 50.

8. See M. Hengel, Judaism and Hellenism, 1.131-132, 135.

9. J. Haspecker in Gottesfurcht bei Jesus Sirach, (Rome: Paplisches Bibelinstitut, 1967), has argued that the central theme of Sirach does not actually revolve around the identification of wisdom and law, but rather around the development of the fear of God motif. His work has been perceptively critiqued, however, by E.P. Sanders, (Paul, 332), who contends that, "the argument of the book, and in that sense its theme seems to lie in the dialectic between wisdom and law". See also H. Stadelmann, Ben Sira als Schrifgelehrter, (Tubingen: J.C.B. Mohr/Paul Siebeck, 1980), 222.

10. A considerable attempt has been made by scholarship to discover a historical background to the emphasis upon nomistic wisdom in Sirach, particularly in terms of the attitude of ben Sira vis-a-vis Hellenism. On the one hand, it is asserted that ben Sira's affirmations concerning wisdom and the law were formed in the face of a growing threat from Hellenistic liberalism. See V. Tcher-

ikover, <u>Hellenistic Civilization and the Jews</u>, (New York: Atheneum, 1979=1959 edition), 142-151; M. Hengel, <u>Judaism and Hellenism</u>, l. 131-152; A.A. di Lella, "Conservative and Progressive Theology: Sirach and Wisdom", <u>CBQ</u> 28.139-154 (1966). Compare Sir 33.2, 3 with Sir 41.8. More recently, however, scholarship has pointed to the possibility of apologetic rather than polemical motivations in relation to ben Sira's concepts of wisdom and law, and to the positive presence of Greek influence within Sirach. See J.L. Crenshaw, <u>Old Testament Wisdom</u>, 159; E. Lohse, <u>The New Testament Environment</u>, (London: SCM, 1976); 126, 132; S. Sandmel, <u>Judaism and Christian Beginnings</u>, (New York: Oxford University Press, 1978), 230; and H. Stadelmann, <u>Schriftgelehrter</u>, 226-228. For argument in favor of seeing Greek influence behind ben Sira, see Th. Middendorp, <u>Die Stellung Jesu ben Siras zwischen Judentum und Hellenismus</u>, (Leiden: E.J. Brill, 1973). Argument against an over-emphasis upon these parallels is presented, however, by M. Hengel in a review entitled, "Besprechung von Th. Middendorp, Die Stellung Jesu ben Siras zwischen Judentum und Hellenismus", <u>JSJ</u> 5. 83-87 (1974).
To attempt to decide between these alternatives is surely to pose a false dilemma, however, and we may best understand ben Sira's nomistic wisdom as an attempt to defend the value of the Torah among the Jews, <u>and</u> as an attempt to demonstrate the uniqueness of the Jewish law to the Greeks.

11. The influence of the Torah-wisdom link upon subsequent Jewish authors is explored in chapters 2 and 3. See also J.G. Snaith, "The Importance of Ecclesiasticus (The Wisdom of ben Sira)", <u>Exp Tim</u> 75.66-69 (1963/64).

12. This is implied, for example, in the invitations issued by personified wisdom in Prov 1.20-23, 8.1-6, 32-36: compare Prov 1.2-6, 2.1-5, 3.13, 4.1-9, etc. It is important to add, however, that there was also a frank and explicit recognition of certain limitations with respect to human attempts at investigation and understanding. See P.S. Fiddes, <u>The Hiddeness of Wisdom</u>, <u>passim</u>. This sense of limitation comes through clearly in both

Job and Ecclesiastes. The relation between the skepticism of these books and the more confident outlook of other sapiential literature is explored by Fiddes and by M. Hengel, <u>Judaism and Hellenism</u>, 1.115-130. On the basis of their analyses, it seems most probable to view the relationship between wisdom and law in ben Sira as a positive response to an over-emphasis upon the limitations of wisdom in later biblical wisdom, and as a negative response to the claims made on behalf of a universal wisdom within Hellenistic culture.

13. See J. Marböck, <u>Weisheit im Wandel</u>, and, "Gesetz und Weisheit".

14. This conclusion is represented in both book, (<u>ibid</u>. 30-34, 61-63, 131), and article, (<u>ibid</u>. 8-11). Compare also Sir 18.28; 39.1. Contrast Sir 36.1-17 and Bar 3.28.

15. See E.P. Sanders, <u>Paul</u>, 331-333. Our comments are largely dependent upon Sander's perceptive critique.

16. See above n. 10.

17. Several passages stress the essential interrelatedness of these two themes, (e.g. Sir 1.26-29, 15.1; 19.20-23). The weakness of J. Haspecker's otherwise excellent book, <u>Gottesfurcht bei Jesus Sirach</u>, lies in Haspecker's attempt to subordinate the wisdom-law link to the fear of God motif, when the two are, in fact, complimentary themes. The fear of the Lord is the attitude, and the observance of the law the corresponding action.

18. So also E.P. Sanders, <u>Paul</u>, 332; "the wisdom which has a possession among every nation (24.6) <u>truly and fully</u> resides in Israel (24.12), and is the equivalent of the 'law which Moses commanded us' (24.23)". Compare J. Marböck, "Gesetz und Weisheit", 8-9; W. Eichrodt, <u>Theology of the Old Testament</u>, (London: SCM, 1972 - 2 volumes), 2.90; M. Küchler, <u>Früjüdische Weisheitstraditionen</u>, 43; J.C. Rylaarsdam, <u>Revelation in Jewish Wisdom</u>, 31-34; G.T. Sheppard, "Wisdom and Torah", 171-175;

E.G. Bauckmann, "Die Proverbien und die Sprüche des Jesus Sirach", ZAW 72.33-63 (1960), 55; J.D.G. Dunn, Christology in the Making, (London: SCM, 1980); 170-176, 210; G. Maier, Mensch und Freier Wille, (Tübingen: J.C.B. Mohr/P. Siebeck, 1971).

19. To the references in the text should be added Sir 19.20, 23-24, 21.11; 34.8; 39.1, 8, and the evidence of the Prologue.

20. Parallels to the first half of Sir 29.9a may be found in Job 29.12, and in Prov 14.21, 19.17; 22.-9; 28.27, 21.20.

21. As to the canonical status of the law, the prophets, and the writings in the time of ben Sira, see G.T. Sheppard, Wisdom as a Hermeneutical Construct, 13-16. The remainder of Sheppard's book is devoted to an extended proof of ben Sira's reliance upon the law as a source of wisdom; "the writer will attempt to defend the thesis that at a certain period in the development of Old Testament literature, wisdom became a theological category associated with an understanding of canon which formed a perspective from which to interpret Torah and prophetic traditions". Ibid., 13.

22. Thus Jewish history becomes the vehicle for the disclosure of wisdom. See M. Hengel, Judaism and Hellenism, 131. The Book of Wisdom also contains a passage which is representative of this genre, (Wisd 10.1-11.1), but is, of course, demonstrably later than Sirach.

23. See J.L. Crenshaw, Old Testament Wisdom, 150.

24. So R.H. Pfeiffer, History, 383. See also G.F. Moore, Judaism in the First Centuries of the Christian Era, (Cambridge Mass.: Harvard University, 1927), 37-47; J.L. Koole, "Die Bibel des ben Sira", OTS 14.374-396 (1965). According to Pfeiffer and Moore, ben Sira also shows a knowledge of the developing oral traditions of Torah interpretation which were later to find literary form in rabbinical materials. See Sir 39.2-3 and see below p.17.

25. The significance and interpretation of Sir 39.1 and 49.10 is discussed in G.T. Sheppard, <u>Wisdom as a Hermeneutical Construct</u> 13-16. See also W. Roth, "On the Gnomic Discursive Wisdom of Jesus ben Sirach", <u>Semeia</u> 17.59-79 (1980), 62.

26. The quest for wisdom, a traditional motif in the older wisdom literature, (cf. Ecc 1.13, 7.23-25, Prov 1.28, 2.4, Job 28.12, 20), is approved by ben Sira in Sir 4.11, 6.18, 27, 14.22, 18.28; 33.17; 51.13.

27. Numerous examples of the prior use of the cognate משׂר may be found in Proverbs; (cf. 1.2, 3, 7, 8, 4.1, 13, 5.12, 25, etc.).

28. Compare Sir 1.27, 6.18, 8.8; 24.32; 50.27; 51.16.

29. See M. Hengel, <u>Judaism and Hellenism</u>, 1.135; "here we come up against an inner transformation of the old institution of the soper ... the 'wisdom teacher' becomes the man 'learned in the scriptures', in that his activity is concentrated more and more on the holy scriptures of Israel". See Sir 38.24; 39.1. See also M. Küchler, <u>Frühjü-dische Weisheitstraditionen</u>, 41; J.C. Rylaarsdam, <u>Revelation in Jewish Wisdom</u>, 32; H. Stadelmann, <u>Schriftgelehrter</u>, 216-270; E. Zenger, "Die Spate Weisheit", 55: J. Hadot, <u>Penchant Mauvais et Volonté Libre dans la Sagesse de Ben Sira</u>, (Brussels: Presses Universitaires, 1970), 75-90.

30. On the apologetic value of ben Sira's composition see above n. 10. According to M. Hengel, <u>Judaism and Hellenism</u>, 1.131; "we may see this work as a testimony to the influence of Palestinian piety on the Jewish Diaspora in Egypt in the Hasmonean period". On the relationship between Prologue and Body in Sirach see also H.J. Cadbury, "The Grandson of ben Sira", <u>HTR</u> 48.219-225 (1955).

31. Talk of progress in relationship to wisdom like that evident in the Prologue is also found in Sir 51.17, and there is talk of perfection in wisdom in Sir 24.28 and 34.8.

32. Though this possibility cannot be established as more than a possibility, the prominence accorded to the concept in Sirach (cf. 4.18, 14.21; 39.6), in comparison to the relatively rare occurrence of the motif in the Old Testament literature (cf. Job 11.6, Amos 3.7), does seem to support the contention that ben Sira has rehabilitated and redefined earlier vague talk of wisdom's secrets in connection with his concept of nomistic wisdom.

33. Reading αὐτοῦ in Sir 39.7 with reference to κυρίῳ in 39.6. Against R. Smend, Die Weisheit des Jesus Sirach Erklärt, (Berlin: Verlag von Georg Reiner, 1906 - 2 vols.), 2.355. So also H. Stadelmann, Schriftgelehrter, 235 and 241.

34. Compare also with these two passages Sir 6.37 quoted above.

35. Also interesting in this regard is Sir 15.3 where personified wisdom, (i.e. the law, 15.1), is said to dispense wisdom; "She will feed him, (i.e. the one who fears the Lord and holds to the law, 15.-1), with the bread of understanding, and give him the water of wisdom to drink".

36. So G.T. Sheppard, Wisdom as a Hermeneutical Construct, 68.

37. Unfortunately, the text is completely lacking in the Hebrew manuscripts, and so our investigation, of necessity, is dependent here upon the Greek, though notice of the Syraic text has also been taken by way of O. Rickenbacker, Weisheitsperikopen, 176-196, and R. Smend, Weisheit Erklärt, 2.352-353.

38. A detailed exegetical study of these verses may be found in J. Marböck, "Sir 38.24-39.11: Der Schriftgelehrte Weise", 293-316 in La Sagesse de L'Ancien Testament, ed. M. Gilbert, (Leuven: Presses Université, 1979); and in H. Stadelmann, Schriftgelehrter, 216-270.

39. See J. Marböck, "Der Schriftgelehrte Weise", 296-301. J. Hadot in Penchant Mauvais, 75-90 provides

comment upon ben Sira's description of himself as the last of the traditional wise men, (cf. Sir 33.16), and the first of the scribal sages; (cf. Sir 38.24). See also M. Hengel, Judaism and Hellenism, 1.135, and G. von Rad, Wisdom in Israel, 242.

40. In defense of this interpretation of Sir 39.1b and c, see G.T. Sheppard, Wisdom as a Hermeneutical Construct, 14; W. Roth, "Gnomic Discursive Wisdom", 62; H. Stadelmann, Schriftgelehrter, 221-222; J.L. Crenshaw, Old Testament Wisdom, 35; and J.G. Snaith, Ecclesiasticus, (Cambridge: Cambridge University, 1974), 191.

41. See G. Von Rad, Wisdom in Israel, 261, and H. Stadelmann, Schriftgelehrter, 225.

42. So W. Roth, "Gnomic Discursive Wisdom", 63-64, following R. Smend, Weisheit Erklärt, 2.353. So also J.G. Snaith, Ecclesiasticus, 192.

43. Ben Sira seems to recognize the existence of such oral traditions in Sir 8.8-9, 18.29, and 21.15.

44. W. Roth, "Gnomic Discursive Wisdom", 63-64 sees in these verses a summary of ben Sira's "hermeneutical-pedagogic theory". "Sirach 39.2 describes in synthetic parallelism the first, the learning stage ... The second couplet (39.3) deals with the second, the research stage." This, though, is probably to read into the text more information than the author intended to supply.

45. Interpreting the γάρ in Sir 39.4d causally. See W. Roth, "Gnomic Discursive Wisdom", 64. This idea also accords with Stoic advice and praxis as is shown by Th. Middendorp, Die Stellung Jesus Ben Siras; 166, 180. On other facets of Stoicism which find a place in Sirach, see R. Pautrel, "Ben Sira et le Stoïcisme", RSR 51.535-549 (1963).

46. See J. Marböck, "Der Schriftgelehrte Weise", 304-306.

47. Ben Sira here echoes the consensus of previous sapiential literature. Wisdom is to be earnestly

sought, and every effort is to be made to obtain
it, (see above n. 26), yet wisdom is also the gift
of God and does not come to one except through divine favor, (cf. Prov 2.6, Eccl 2.26, 12.11, Job
11.6; 26.6, 10; 32.8, 18-20; cp. also Gen 41.16,
38, Ex 28.3; 31.3; 35.35; 36.1, 2, Ps 32.8, Isa
50.4, Dan 1.17, 2.21). For further discussion on
this point, see J.C. Rylaarsdam, Revelation in
Jewish Wisdom; P. van Imschoot, "Sagesse et Ésprit
dans L'Ancien Testament", RB 47.23-53 (1938); G.
von Rad, Wisdom in Israel; J.W. Montgomery, "Wisdom as a Gift", Int 16.43-64 (1962).

48. See Sir 1.1, 26, 6.37, 15.18; 24.3, 9; 43.33; 51.-
13, 17.

49. Wisdom comes in response to prayer in Sir 51.13
as well. For related references and further discussion see J. Marböck, "Der Schriftgelehrte
Weise", 305-306.

50. On pneuma as the natural seat of the intellect,
see F. Baumgartel, "Spirit in the Old Testament",
TDNT 6. 359-368, especially p. 361 (b).

51. So also H. Stadelmann, Schriftgelehrter, 232-3.

52. "So ist das pneuma suneseos nicht einfach allge-
meines Berufscharakteristikum des Gelehrten, ges-
chweige denn allgemeine Schopfungsgabe, sondern -
wie Maier es ausdruckt -'gelegentliches donum sup-
eradditum'." So H. Stadelmann, Schriftgelehrter,
234, following G. Maier, Mensch und Freier Wille,
37.

53. Compare Sir 48.24 where Isaiah's prophecy is said
to have come πνεύματι μεγάλῳ. The reference here,
though anarthrous like that in 39.6, can hardly be
anything other than a circumlocution for the Spirit of God, the source of all true prophecy.
Given the Septuagintal parallels cited, Sir 39.6
may also, perhaps, be interpreted similarly. But
in any event the connection in both 39.6 and 48.24
between the 'spirits' and God is quite strong
rendering each expression definite to that extent.

54. See   H. Stadelmann, Schriftgelehrter, 232-247; G.
    Maier, Mensch und Freier Wille, 37.   Compare V.
    Englezakis, New and Old in God's Revelation, (an
    unpublished doctoral thesis completed at Cambridge
    University in   1975), 112-127; M.   Hengel, Judaism
    and Hellenism, 1.134-136; M. Küchler, Frühjüdische
    Weisheitstraditionen, 40-43; E. Zenger, "Die Späte
    Weisheit", 55; S. Sandmel, Judaism and Christian
    Beginnings, 79; D.J. Harrington, "The Wisdom of
    the   Scribe according to Ben Sira", 181-188 in
    Ideal Figures in Judaism, eds. G.W.E. Nickelsburg
    and J.J. Collins, (Chico: Scholars, 1980); and J.
    Marböck "Der Schriftgelehrte Weise", 307-311.

55. So also H. Stadelmann, Schriftgelehrter, 234-235.

56. Compare Sir 1.10 and 17.6-7.   For further discus-
    sion see H. Stadelmann, Schriftgelehrter, 234.
    According to Stadelmann, all of these three pas-
    sages intend to show that "jeden Menschen eignet
    von der Shöpfung her Denkkraft und ein Kritisches
    Erkennungspotential; ...".   Similarly G. Maier,
    Mensch und Freier Wille, 61-83; and J.C. Rylaars-
    dam, Revelation in Jewish Wisdom, 65.

57. Compare Sir 1.10 and 14; 15.1 and 7; 19.20.   See
    H. Stadelmann, Schriftgelehrter, 234-235.

58. See above n. 50. Compare Sir 6.22, "for wisdom is
    like her name and is not manifest to many".

59. J. Marbock, "Der Schriftgelehrte Weise", 308, and
    H. Stadelmann, Schriftgelehrter, 235-240, also
    present useful parallels and further discussion.
    For a complete treatment on this subject see P.
    van Imschoot, "Sagesse et Esprit", or J.C. Ry-
    laarsdam, Revelation in Jewish Wisdom, 99-118.

60. So M. Hengel, Judaism and Hellenism, 1.135.   See
    also above n. 50.   The Old Testament references
    may have led ben Sira towards an interpretative
    role for the spirit in relation to wisdom, (cf.
    especially Ex 31.3 and Job 32.8), but the primary
    factor was still quite clearly the nomistic empha-
    sis.

61. Do these words constitute a possible reference to the sage's authority to add to, or supplement existing, or recognized oral traditions? Compare Sir 39.2-3 with the materials cited in n. 42 and 43 above. See also H. Stadelmann, <u>Schriftgelehrter</u>, 241.

62. See above, pp 14-15 for further discussion on this point.

63. On the meaning and significance of παιδεία, or instruction in Sirach, see above pp. 12-15

64. The vague content of these two phrases defies a precise relationship between their praise and the sage's role as an interpreter of scripture. Yet the description of the sage as a man of understanding, and the fact of Israel's commendation would appear in context to speak of this connection in an implicit way. See also n. 69 below.

65. See P. van Imschoot, "Sagesse et Esprit", 35.

66. A full history of scholarship on this issue is provided by H. Stadelmann, <u>Schriftgelehrter</u>, 177-188. See also J. Marböck, <u>Weisheit im Wandel</u>, 80; idem. "Der Schriftgelehrte Weise", 308-311; G. Maier, <u>Mensch und Freier Wille</u>, 37-42; J. Hadot, <u>Penchant Mauvais</u>, 77-81; M. Hengel, <u>Judaism and Hellenism</u> 1.134-136; and O. Rickenbacker, <u>Weisheitsperikopen</u>, 169-171.

67. As is done, for example, by R. Smend, <u>Weisheit Erklärt</u>, 2.224, on the basis of the Syriac.

68. So H. Stadelmann, <u>Schriftgelehrter</u>, 259-266; G. Maier, <u>Mensch und Freier Wille</u>, 37-42. See also below n. 65. The parallels between Sir 24.32a and 33a also support this interpretaion as is noted by Stadelmann.

69. So J. Marböck, <u>Weisheit im Wandel</u>, 80. See also idem, "Der Schriftgelehrte Weise", 308-311.

70. See Sir 6.8; 9.14-15, 10.25, 18.27, 20.5, 7, 13; 21.13; 37.23, 24, 26.

71. There is an alternation in Sirach between the speeches of personified wisdom, and other passages which speak of wisdom in a more objective way. Thus ben Sira can speak either of Lady wisdom's gifts, personifying wisdom as the giver, or of the benefits associated with the sage's possession of wisdom with equal facility.

72. See Sir 1.18; 21.11; 39.7; 50.27.

73. See Sir 25.5; 39.6, 9; 50.27; 51,20. Particular notice should be paid to a comparison of Sir 15.3 and 24.25, for understanding is associated in the first verse with Lady wisdom, and in the second with wisdom personified in the law.

74. See Sir 4.18, 14.21; 39.7. Compare also wisdom's association with light in Sir 24.27.

75. See Sir 4.12, 19, 15.5; 37.24; 51.15.

76. See Sir 1.19, 4.11, 13, 11.1; 14.27, 15.5; 39.9; 44.15.

77. See above p. 19. See also Sir 1.14, 25; 27.11, and especially 43.33.

78. Besides the texts quoted see Sir 1.25, 4.19; 21.-15, 18; and 27.11. In a number of these passages, ben Sira seems to draw a distinction between foolish ones, (ἄνθρωποι ἀσυνέτοι), and sinful ones, (ἄνδρες ἁμαρτολοί), in similar fasion to Sir 15.7.

79. See Sir 4.17, 6.19-21; 23.2.

80. So Sir 24.22.

81. See also Sir 4.23, 15.5; 21.16-17; 37.20-23; 51.-21, 22. Prior associations between wisdom and speech are fairly common in earlier biblical wisdom literature. See Prov 10.13, 31; cp. 24.7 and 17.7. See also Ps 37.30 and 49.7. Finally, see Job 32.6-37.24.

1. In _Judaism and Hellenism_ 1.224, M. Hengel has called the early Essene theology, "the most impres-
sive theological contribution produced by Judaism
in the time 'between the Testaments'".

2. This dating is adopted following L. Rost, _Judaism
Outside the Hebrew Canon_, 155-190, and G.W.E.
Nickelsburg, _Jewish Literature_, 122-141. Both authors present further discussion and bibliographi-
cal references to support the placement of 1 QS,
CD, and 1 QH within this period. On the broader
question of the relationship of the literature to
the history of the sect, see also G. Vermes, _The
Dead Sea Scrolls: Qumran in Perspective_, (London:
Collins, 1977), 29-44; J.H. Charlesworth, "The
Origin and Subsequent History of the Authors of
the Dead Sea Scrolls: Four Transitional Phases
among the Qumran Essenes" _Rev Q_ 10.213-233 (1980);
and R. de Vaux, _Archaeology and the Dead Sea
Scrolls_, (London: Oxford University, 1973).

3. An identity between the Qumran community and the
Essenes may now be said to firmly established
among the majority of scholars. See M. Black - F.
Millar - G. Vermes, _The History of the Jewish People in the Age of Jesus Christ_, (Edinburgh: T & T
Clark, 1973 and 1979 -2 volumes), 2.583-585. See
also J.H. Charlesworth, "Origin and History", 216;
and G. Vermes, _The Dead Sea Scrolls_, 116-136.

4. See W. Foerster, "Der Heilige Geist im Spatjüdent-
um", _NTS_ 8.117-134 (1962); A.A. Anderson, "The Use
of 'Ruah' in 1 QS, 1 QH, and 1 QM", _JSS_ 7.293-303
(1962); F.F. Bruce, "Holy Spirit in the Qumran
Texts", _ALUOS_ 6.49-55 (1969); and G. Johnston,
"'Spirit' and 'Holy Spirit' in the Qumran Literature", 27-42 in _New Testament Sidelights_, Ed. H.K.
McArthur, (Hartford: Hartford Press, 1960).

5. Statistics vary slightly, but a safe estimation
would seem to allow for a combined total of about
20 occurrences. See M. Küchler, _Frühjüdische
Weisheitstraditionen_, 89; K.G. Kuhn, _Konkordanz zu
den Qumran-Texten_, (Göttingen: Vandenhoeck and

Rupprecht, 1960); idem., "Nachträge zu den Qumran-Texten", Rev Q 4.163-234 (1963/64); and G. Fohrer - U. Wilckens, "σοφία ...", TDNT 7.504-505.

6. Two complete and thorough studies that take into account all three of these factors are J.E. Worrell, Concepts of Wisdom in the Dead Sea Scrolls, (an unpublished doctoral dissertation completed at Claremont Graduate School in 1968), and M. Küchler, Frühjüdische Weisheitstraditionen, 88-114. See also F. Nötscher, Zur Theologischen Terminologie der Qumran-Texte, (Bonn: Peter Hanstein, 19-56); J. de Caevel, "La Conaissance dans les Hymnes d'Action de Grâces de Qumran", ETL 38.435-460 (19-62); A.M. Denis, Les Thèmes de Connaissance dans le Document de Damas, (Louvain: Desclées du Brouwer, 1967). A much more critical evaluation of the evidence is given by W.L. Lipscomb and J.A. Sanders in "Wisdom at Qumran", 277-285 in Israelite Wisdom, eds. J.G. Gammie et. al.

7. The translations used by permission unless otherwise noted are by G. Vermes, The Dead Sea Scrolls in English, (Harmondsworth: Penguin, 1975 - 2nd edition). The Hebrew text of E. Lohse, Die Texte aus Qumran, (München: Kösel, 1971), has everywhere been compared.

8. On the historical relation of 1 QS 3.13-4.26 to the context see P. Wernberg-Møller, "The Two Spirits in 1 QS 3.13-4.26", Rev Q 3.413-441 (1961).

9. See 1 QS 3.15, 4.3-6, 18, 22. Similar parallels occur elsewhere. Representative examples may be seen in 1 QS 2.2-4; 11.16-20, 1 QM 1.19, 35, 2.17-19. For discussion on this point see C. Romaniuk, "Le Thème de la Sagesse dans les Documents de Qumran", Rev Q 9.429-435 (1978); J.E. Worrell, Concepts of Wisdom, 181-237; H.W. Kuhn, Enderwartung und Gegenwärtiges Heil, (Göttingen: Vandenhoeck and Rupprecht, 1966), 140-166; F. Nötscher, Theologischen Terminologie, 38-78. M. Küchler, Frühjüdische Weisheitstraditionen, 89, provides a helpful chart showing the frequency of each of the synonyms in each of the documents.

Notes to pages 32-34

10. See M. Hengel, Judaism and Hellenism, 1.222.

11. On the essential identity of these two designations see G. Fohrer - U. Wilckens, "σοφία ...", 505; J.E. Worrell, Concepts of Wisdom, 150-154; C. Romaniuk, "Le Thème de la Sagesse", 433; M. Küchler, Frühjüdische Weisheitstraditionen, 90-92; and F. Nötscher, Theologischen Terminologie, 46.

12. The Text of 11 QPsª appears in The Psalms Scroll of Qumran cave 11, ed. J.A. Sanders, (Oxford: Clarendon, 1965), and it is quoted in translation from that source.

13. On the interpretation of 11 QPsª 18 see M. Küchler, Frühjüdische Weisheitstraditionen, 95, and J.E. Worrell, Concepts of Wisdom, 270-280.

14. See J.E. Worrell, Concepts of Wisdom; 181-186, 406.

15. This explanation is also supported by later rabbinical usage of the title חכם if the Hasidim are understood as rabbinic precursors. See G. Fohrer - U. Wilckens, "σοφία ...", 507.

16. See O. Betz, Offenbarung und Schriftforschung in der Qumransekte, (Tübingen: J.C.B. Mohr, 1960), 138. So also M. Hengel, Judaism and Hellenism, 1.223.

17. See above n. 6.

18. Relationships between Qumran and Sirach have previously been explored in several short articles. See J. Carmignac, "Les Rapports Entre L'Ecclesiastique et Qumran", Rev Q 3.209-218 (1961/62); H. Germann, "Jesus ben Siras Dankgebet und die Hodajoth", TZ 19.81-87 (1963); M.R. Lehmann, "Ben Sira and the Qumran Literature", Rev Q 3.103-116 (1961/62); J. Priest, "Ben Sira 45.25 in light of the Qumran Literature", Rev Q 17.111-118 (1964); and P. Winter, "Ben Sira and the Teaching of the Two Ways", VT 5.315-318 (1955).

19. For discussion on this question see F.M. Cross, *The Ancient Library of Qumran*, (London: Duckworth, 1958), 170-173. Our interpretation follows Cross in identifying the "Stave" with the Teacher of Righteousness, or a hasidic precursor of the Teacher, and the "men of wisdom" with the founders of the Qumran community. See also N. Wieder, "The Law-Interpreter of the Sect of the Dead Sea Scrolls", *JJS* 4.158-175 (1953).

20. See O. Betz, *Offenbarung und Schriftforschung*, 135-142; W.D. Davies, "'Knowledge' in the Dead Sea Scrolls and Matthew 11.25-30", 119-144 in *Christian Origins and Judaism* by W.D. Davies, (Philadelphia: Westminister, 1962), 126-127; M. Küchler, *Frühjüdische Weisheitstraditionen*, 95; J. de Caevel, "Connaissance Religieuse", 444-446; M. Mansoor, *The Thanksgiving Hymns*, (Leiden: E.J. Brill, 1961), 69-71; F. Nötscher, *Theologischen Terminologie*; 43-49, 163-168; H. Ringgren, *The Faith of Qumran*, (Philadelphia: Fortress, 1963), 114-119; and C. Romaniuk, "Le Thème de la Sagesse", 431. All of these scholars note the strong link between wisdom and law at Qumran.

21. So also J. Worrell, *Concepts of Wisdom*, 379-385.

22. Analagous wisdom terminology is also associated with the law. See CD 2.3, 1 QS 1.11-13, 6.9-10, 18, 9.17-20, 1 QH 4.7-10, 7.26, 10.4, 20, 29, 11.-9. To place an emphasis upon the need for the law's interpretation was, of course, not new, (cf. Sir 39.1-5). But in Sirach, the search for wisdom remains open to every student of the law. At Qumran, the possibility of acquiring wisdom, or becoming wise is effectively closed off from those who study the law outside the community and apart from its interpretations.

23. See O. Betz, *Offenbarung und Schriftforschung*, 36-38; R.E. Brown, *The Semitic Background of the Term "Mystery" in the New Testament*, (Philadelphia: Fortress, 1968); J.L. Coppens, "'Mystery' in the Theology of St. Paul and its Parallels at Qumran", 132-158 in *Paul and Qumran*, ed. J. Murphy O'Connor, (London: G. Chapman, 1968); F. Nöt-

scher, Theologischen Terminologie, 71-77; and B.
Rigaux, "Révélation des Mystères et Perfection a
Qumran et dans le Nouveau Testament", NTS 4.237-
262 (1957/58). Sirach also contains references to
"hidden things" (ἀπόκρυφων); see above pp. 9 and
17.

24. See M.P. Horgan, Pesharim: Qumran Interpretations
of Biblical Books, (Washington D.C.: Catholic
Biblical Association of America, 1979); F.F.
Bruce, Biblical Exegesis in the Qumran Texts,
(London: Tyndale, 1960); and G. Vermes, "The Qum-
ran Interpretation of Scripture in its Historical
Setting", ALUOS 6.85-97 (1966-68).

25. See M. Hengel, Judaism and Hellenism, 1.222-223.
"In the community the Torah and the Prophets are
interpreted in respect of the divine mysteries of
history and a perfect fulfillment of the divine
commandments, and are thus disclosed in their
deeper meaning ... Only in the community is the
Torah of God truly expounded and are its demands
really fulfilled." While wisdom at Qumran is related to apocalyptic conceptions of hidden wisdom,
then, it is also somewhat different since hidden
wisdom is fully present within the community. See
H.W. Kuhn, Endewartung und Gegenwärtiges Heil,
137-139; J.E. Worrell, Concepts of Wisdom, 351-
357; O. Betz, Offenbarung und Schriftforschung,
155-182.

26. So especially in 11 Q Ps^a 18.12-15, CD 6.4, 1 QM
10.10, etc., (cf. n. 22). See M. Mansoor, The
Thanksgiving Hymns, 69-71; and F. Nötscher, Theologischen Terminologie, 64-68. See also above n.
20.

27. So 1 QS 1.1-3, 8-10, 2.2-4, 3.9-10, 5.7-9, etc.
E.P. Sanders, Paul, 240-255, has argued that the
references to a 'new covenant' at Qumran should be
interpreted accordingly. The new covenant at Qumran is only new in the sense that it represents a
more complete understanding of the Mosaic covenant. See CD 3.12-13, 7.5, 1 QS 5.5; 15.9.

28. The blame for this state of affairs is placed
squarely upon the shoulders of those who interpret

the law to the people. See 1 QH 4.7-11, 5.26.

29. For further discussion see B. Rigaux, "Révélation des Mystères et Perfection à Qumran", 237-241; J.-P. du Plessis, TELEIOS, (Uitgave: J.H. Kok, 19-59),   104-111; A.R.C. Leaney, The Rule of Qumran and its Meaning, (London: SCM, 1966);   178, 190-197; M. Hengel, Judaism and Hellenism, 1.222; G. W.E. Nickelsburg, Jewish Literature, 134;   and M. Mansoor, The Thanksgiving Hymns, 103 n. 6.

30. This interpretation of 1 QS 8.1 is accepted following E.P. Sanders, Paul, 323-325.   Sanders perceptively critiques the alternative historicizing interpretation of A.R.C. Leaney which views 1 QS 8.1 with reference to the founding of the community, (The Rule of Qumran, 208-232).

31. See   P. du Plessis, TELEIOS, 104-111, and B. Rigaux, "Révélation des Mystères et Perfection à Qumran", 237-241. Compare chapter 1 n. 31.

32. There is particular controversy surrounding the identity of the 'spirit of truth' in this regard; (cf. 1 QS 3.13-4.26).   P. Wernberg-Møller, in an article entitled, "The Two Spirits in 1 QS 3.13-4.26", has argued that the two spirits should be understood anthropologically since both are said to "struggle in the hearts of men"; (1 QS 4.23, cp. 3.18 and 4.15).   Others, however, such as W. Foerster, in "Der Heilige Geist", have pointed to parallels between the spirit of truth in 1 QS and the קדש רוח in 1 QH; (cf. 1 QS 4.21). We find the arguments to be almost balanced, but the former to be slightly more persuasive.

33. Early studies of רוח in the Qumran literature sometimes tended to blur the contours of the problem by talking too glibly of a uniform concept of spirit.   The studies of F. Nötscher, however, served to show that an analysis of spirit at Qumran must deal more thoroughly with the relationship between God's holy Spirit, and the spirit of holiness within humanity, (cp. 1 QS 9.3, 1 QH 7.7, CD 5.11, 1QH 9.32).   See F. Nötscher, "Geist und Geister in den Texten von Qumran", 176-187 in Von Alten zum Neuen Testament by F. Nötscher, (Bonn;

P. Hanstein, 1962); idem., "Heligkeit in den Qumranschriften", Rev Q 2.315-344 (1959/60); idem.,
Theologischen Terminologie, 38-78. The concept of
spirit at Qumran must also, however, be related to
God, and here, A.A. Anderson, "The Use of 'Ruah'",
301-302; W. Foerster, "Der Heilige Geist", 129-
130; G. Johnston, "'Spirit' within the Qumran Literature", 33-34; and H. Ringgren, The Faith of
Qumran, have all shown that the Spirit of God at
Qumran is neither a person, nor a hypostasis, but
rather a way of speaking about God's activity.
Our integrative conclusion about the role of the
Spirit in regards to revelation at Qumran attempts
to reflect such analyses.

34. See 1 QS 2.3; 11.16-20; 1 QH 1.21, 7.26, 10.4-7;
11.4-10; 14.12, 13; 15.12. See also M. Mansoor,
The Thanksgiving Hymns, 70, and S. Holm-Nielsen,
Hodayot, 277-282.

35. Compare chapter 1 n. 47.

36. See 1 QH 2.13, 4.27, 28, 6.10-12, 8.16-18, etc.

37. So also E.L. Beavin, Ruah Hakodesh in some Early
Jewish Literature, (an unpublished doctoral dissertation completed at Vanderbilt University in
1961), 91-95; O. Betz, Offenbarung und Schriftforschung, 135-140; J.L. Coppens, "Le Don de L'Esprit
d'après les Textes de Qumran et le Quatrième Évangile", 209-223 in L'Évangile de Jean, ed. M.E.
Boismard, (Louvain: Desclée de Brouwer, 1958); M.
Hengel, Judaism and Hellenism; 1.222, 223, 229; S.
Holm-Nielsen, Hodayot, 288; H.W. Kuhn, Enderwartung und Gegenwärtiges Heil, 120-138; F. Nötscher,
Theologischen Terminologie, 42-43; B. Rigaux, "Révélation des Mystères et Perfection à Qumran",
244; C. Romaniuk, "Le Thème de la Sagesse", 430-
432; J.E. Worrell, Concepts of Wisdom, 176-180;
and others listed in n. 4 above.

38. It is important to notice, however, that the wisdom which the Spirit mediates is nothing other
than an understanding of the law. Qumran, therefore, like Sirach does not understand its leaders
as prophets but as teachers. See below p. 36.
See also F. Nötscher, Theologischen Terminologie,

43; O. Betz, <u>Offenbarung</u> und <u>Schriftforschung</u>,
138; W. Foerster, "Der Heilige Geist", 123-124.

39. The following argument is largely based upon O.
Betz, <u>Offenbarung</u> und <u>Schriftforschung</u>, 135-140;
H.W. Kuhn, <u>Enderwartung</u> und <u>Gegenwärtiges Heil</u>,
120-138; and F. Nötscher, "Heligkeit", <u>passim</u>.
See also P. Garnet, <u>Salvation and Atonement in the
Qumran Scrolls</u>, (Tübingen: J.C.B. Mohr, 1977),
and S. Holm-Nielsen, <u>Hodayot</u>; 274-277, 282-293.
Compare chapter 1 pp. 19, 24.

40. The notion of the human spirit exists, however,
without any thought, in all likelihood, of a dualism in human nature. See F. Nötscher, <u>Theologis-
chen Terminologie</u>, 96.

41. See especially S. Holm-Nielsen, <u>Hodayot</u>, 274-277.

42. So 1 QS 3.5-8. "Unclean, unclean shall he be for
as long as he scorns the ordinances of God and allows not himself to be taught by the community of
His council. For by the spirit of true counsel
concerning the ways of man shall all his sins be
atoned when he beholds the light of life. By the
Holy Spirit of the community in His truth shall he
be cleansed of all his sins, and by the spirit of
uprightness and humility shall all his iniquity be
atoned." (This translation follows A. Dupont-
Sommer, <u>The Essene Writings from Qumran</u>, Oxford:
Blackwell, 1961.) On the ranking of community
members see above, p. 41.

43. On the equation of the הנכמים and the משכלים at
Qumran see above n. 11. Members of this group appear to have been primarily responsible for the
sectarian literature. See J. Coppens, "'Mystery'
at Qumran", 137.

44. See 1 QS 1.1-2; 3.13, 4.22, 8.1, 12, 9.13, 17,
etc.

45. See also 1 QH 1.28-29, 7.11, 8.36. The form as
well as the content of their message is the gift
of God.

1. Our analysis of the purpose, provenance, and date
    of the Book of Wisdom follows the most recent dis-
    cussion of these questions by D. Winston in The
    Wisdom of Solomon, (New York: Doubleday, 1979).
    Winston bases his conclusions about the purpose
    and provenance of the book upon a widely accepted
    scholarly consensus; (cf. pp. 3, 12-15, 25, 63-
    64). As for the date of the work, Winston's opin-
    ion concurs in the main with that of S. Holmes in
    placing the book somewhere in the late Greek or
    early Roman era in Egypt; (c. 50 BCE - 50 CE).
    See S. Holmes, "The Wisdom of Solomon", 518-568 in
    The Apocyrpha and Pseudipigrapha of the Old Testa-
    ment, ed. R.H. Charles, (Oxford: Clarendon, 1913
    - 2 vols.), 1.520-521. However, less plausibly,
    Winston seeks to specify a more accurate date for
    the work, placing it, with some hesitance, in the
    reign of Gaius Caligula; (c. 37 - 41 CE). Our own
    study follows Holmes more closely assigning the
    first half of the book, (chapters 1-9), to the
    period c. 50 BCE - 30 BCE, and the second half to
    the years c. 30 BCE - 10 CE.

2. S. Sandmel, in the most recent introduction to
    Philo, Philo of Alexandria, (Oxford; Oxford Uni-
    versity, 1979), 3, dates Philo's life between 25
    BCE and 50 CE. So also E.R. Goodenough, An Intro-
    duction to Philo Judaeus, (Oxford: Basil Black-
    well, 1962 - 2nd edition), 2.

3. D. Winston, Wisdom of Solomon, 59-61, provides
    the most useful summary of these parallels, noting
    agreement in some 42 cases between the thought and
    the language of Wisdom and Philo. See also C.
    Larcher, Études sur le Livre de la Sagesse, (Par-
    is: J. Gabalda, 1969), 151-178, and J. Rieder,
    The Book of Wisdom, (New York: Harper and Bro-
    thers, 1957), 32-38. In light of the number and
    nature of these parallels, there is no need to
    gloss over the fact that isolated differences also
    exist; see Winston, ibid., 61-62, and Larcher,
    ibid. 159-161. Our argument, however, does not
    attempt to prove the dependence of Philo upon Wis-
    dom, or the reverse, but only seeks to demonstrate
    a substantial inter-relationship between the ex-
    pression and the conceptuality of both authors.

4.   See Wisd 6.12-20, 7.21-9.18.   For discussion see
     W.P. Berwick, The Way of Salvation in the Wisdom
     of Solomon, (a doctoral dissertation completed at
     Boston University Graduate School in 1957); E.R.
     Goodenough, By Light, Light, (Amsterdam: Philo
     Press, 1969=1935 edition), 268-276; R.A. Horsley,
     Paul and the Pneumatikoi, (a doctoral dissertation
     completed at Harvard University in 1970), 120-127.
     In Philo see Heres 96-98, Abr 68, Mig 39, Immut
     143, 160, Cong 13, 39; (abbreviations of Philo's
     treatises follow the system employed in Good-
     enough, ibid., xiii-xiv).   For discussion see S.
     Sandmel, Philo of Alexandria, 24-25, 83; H. Lewy,
     Philo, (Oxford: Phaidon, 1946), 1-24; H. Chad-
     wick, "Philo and the Beginnings of Christian
     Thought", 137-157 in The Cambridge History of
     Later Greek and Early Medieval Philosphy, ed. A.H.
     Armstrong, (Cambridge: Cambridge University, 19-
     70); J. Pascher, Der Königsweg zu wieder geburt
     und Vergottung bei Philon von Alexandreia, (Pader-
     born: Publisher Unknown, 1931); and E.R. Good-
     enough, ibid.

5.   Most commentators would wish to argue that the ad-
     dress to the kings or rulers in 6.9 and 21 should
     be understood and interpreted more generally in
     light of 6.20.   The author intends to address his
     work to all who desire wisdom and instruction.
     See D. Winston, The Wisdom of Solomon, 131-156;
     J.A.F. Gregg, The Wisdom of Solomon, (Cambridge:
     Cambridge University, 1922), 60-62; E.G. Clarke,
     The Wisdom of Solomon, (Cambridge: Cambridge Uni-
     versity, 1973), 44-48;   J. Geyer, The Wisdom of
     Solomon, (London: SCM, 1963), 78-79; J. Rieder,
     The Book of Wisdom, 104-106; and W.J. Deane, The
     Book of Wisdom, (Oxford: Clarendon, 1881), 142-
     143.

6.   So also those listed above in n. 4.

7.   We have no wish, consequently, to imply that Wis-
     dom is everywhere in agreement with Philo, and
     where no parallel is noted, it may be assumed by
     the reader that there is a difference between Wis-
     dom and Philo.   Our contention, however, is simply
     that there is enough material in common between
     both works to justify a combined study.

The full dimensions of the relationship between Wisdom and Philo is a question that remains to be settled.

8. Quotations from Philo in the sections that follow are derived with the permission of the publishers from the Loeb Classical Library edition of Philo's works by F.H. Colson and G.H. Whittaker, (Cambridge, Mass: Harvard, 1921-1962 - 10 vols.). Quaestiones et Solutiones in Genesin et Exodum has appeared as a two volume supplement by R. Marcus, (Cambridge, Mass: Harvard, 1969 and 1970). The text of The Wisdom of Solomon utilized in our study is Sapientia Salomonis, edited by J. Ziegler, (Göttingen: Vandenhoeck and Ruprecht, 1962). Translations follow The Oxford Annotated Apocrypha, ed. B.M. Metzger.

9. Confirmation of this claim may be obtained by consulting the scripture index to Philo's works compiled by J.W. Earp. It appears as volume 10 of the Loeb editions of Philo. The significance of Philo's emphasis upon the Pentateuch is discussed by E.R. Goodenough, By Light, Light, 78-78. Compare Wisd 10.1 -12.27.

10. So C. Larcher, Études sur Sagesse, 152. See also E. Starobinski-Safran, "La Lettre et L'Esprit chez Philon D'Alexandrie", RCJ 10.43-51 (1976). V. Nikiprowetsky, in "L'Exegèse de Philon D'Alexandrie", RHPR 53.309-329 (1973), and Le Commentaire de L'Ecriture chez Philon D'Alexandrie, (Leiden: E.J. Brill, 1977), has demonstrated forcefully how many interpretations of Philo fail to give sufficient weight to this point and so distort their subject.

11. Compare Wisd 6.17-20 with this Philonic theme. Wisdom's laws are in all probability to be understood as a reference to the laws of the Torah. See Wisd 9.5 - 6, 9. Compare Wisd 2.12 and 6.4.

12. So H.A. Wolfson, "The Philonic God of Revelation and his Latter-day Deniers", HTR 53.101-124 (1960), 105. For further discussion see H.A. Wolf-

son, <u>Philo</u>: <u>Foundations</u> <u>of</u> <u>Religious</u> <u>Philosophy</u> <u>in</u> <u>Judaism</u>, <u>Christianity</u>, <u>and</u> <u>Islam</u>, (Cambridge Mass.: Harvard University, 1962 - 2 vols.), 2.94-164, and H. Braun, <u>Wie</u> <u>Man</u> <u>über</u> <u>Gott</u> <u>nicht</u> <u>denken</u> <u>soll</u>, (Tübingen: J.C.B. Mohr, 1971).

13. See Ebr 49, Cong 72-79, Fug 183-185, Som 1.205, 208, Mos 1.23, QG 1.11, 2.41, 3.23-25. Such preliminary studies Philo often sees symbolozed in the person of Hagar, "whose name means sojourning". See LA 3.244, etc.

14. See Opif 53, 54, Cher 4, Agr 14-16, Ebr 162, Cong 80, Fug 63, Som 2.211, Jos 86, Spec 1.322, 336, Spec 2.165, 230, Spec 3.191, and Praem 74. Philo, however, has no time for those so-called disciples of philosophy who turn their knowledge from its true goal towards the end of worldly gain, the sophists who simply practice "a persuasion which tends to establish a false opinion". See Cher 9, Post 101, Ebr 149, Cong 174, which are representative of a whole host of texts in which sophistry is condemned.

15. See Virt 65, Post 101, 102, Gig 15, Ebr 212, 213, Mig 28, Heres 100-110, 298, Cong 174, Mos 1.4, QG 2.12, 4.140, QE 2.36. Compare Aristobolus as cited by Eusebius in <u>Praeparatio</u> <u>Evangelium</u> 8.10.

16. See Cher 49, Sac 78, 79, Post 18, 78, Immut 4, 92, Heres 182, Cong 37, 127, 174, Fug 137, Som 1.68-70, Spec 3.5, 6, QG 3.42, 43.

17. See Immut 160, Plant 23, 24, 168, Mig 171, Heres 98, Cong 174, Fug 82, Praem 81, QG 3.42, 4.2, 29, 36, but especially QG 4.140 and QE 4.47. S. Sandmel notes that it is precisely at this point that Philo may be distinguished from later rabbinical Judaism; "in rabbinic Judaism the laws are an end in themselves, but in Philo they are a means to what he conceives of as a greater end ... mystic communion with the Godhead", <u>Philo</u> <u>of</u> <u>Alexandria</u>, 83. See also R.A. Baer, <u>Philo's</u> <u>Use</u> <u>of</u> <u>the</u> <u>Categories</u> <u>Male</u> <u>and</u> <u>Female</u>, (Leiden: E.J. Brill, 1970); E. Lohse, <u>The</u> <u>New</u> <u>Testament</u> Environment, 138; E. Starobinski-Safran, "La Lettre et L'Esprit", 49-50.

18. See especially Mig 28, Heres 100, 101, Fug 97, 137, Som 1.69, Mos 1.4, and QG 2.12. The Book of Wisdom also affirms a close relationship between wisdom and the law. See Wisd 6.19 and 9.9. For discussion see D. Winston, Wisdom of Solomon, 33-37, and J. Reider, The Book of Wisdom, loc. cit.

19. On the relationship between λόγος, σοφία, and νόμος see E.R. Goodenough, By Light, Light, 88-93; H.A. Wolfson, Philo, 1.147-150, 183-184, 254-258; and J.D.G. Dunn, Christology, 171.

20. See, for example, Plant 25-27, or Mig 76. Compare Aristobolus as cited by Eusebius in Praeparatio Evangelium 8.10, and Eupolemus as cited by Clement of Alexandria in De Stromata 1.23.

21. So H.A. Wolfson, Philo, 1.115. See also R. Williamson, Philo and the Epistle to the Hebrews, (Leiden: E.J. Brill, 1970), 519: "Philo regarded the Old Testament as having two levels of meaning; the superficial, obvious meaning and a deeper, underlying meaning, to reach which required special skill and help". As both Wolfson and Williamson indicate, Philo was not the inventor of this distinction. Allegorical exegesis had flourished before him on both Greek and Jewish soil. See Aristeas 147-171 and Aristobolus as cited by Eusebius in Praeparatio Evangelium 8.10.

22. See S. Sandmel, Philo of Alexandria, 24. Compare the statement of Eusebius on the two senses of the Torah found in Praeparatio Evangelium 8.10: "the whole Jewish nation is divided into two sections; while the lawgiver meant to lead the multitude on gently by precepts and laws enjoined according to the literal sense, the other class, consisting of those who had acquired a habit of virtue, he meant to exempt from this sense and required them to give attention to a philosphy of a diviner kind, too highly exalted for the multitude, and to the contemplation of the things signified in the meaning of the laws".

23. The critique is explicit in Mig 89-94. For discussion see E.R. Goodenough, By Light, Light,

82-84; H.A. Wolfson, Philo, 1.57-72, 2.227; and H. Chadwick, "Philo", 147.

24. See E.R. goodenough, By Light, Light, 93. "The Torah was then actually to Philo a source of instruction in specific conduct, an inspired formulation of God's purposes for the beginner, and for the vast majority of men who never get beyond the beginner's stage. It was binding upon the man of higher experience in so far as he had still to live among his fellows. But it was no longer as statute Philo's norm and objective. The value of the Torah for the man of higher experience was in its revelation of the experiences of the Patriarchs in becoming νόμοι ἔμψυχοι, an understanding of which could be achieved only by allegorizing the actual words. The aspiration of Philo centered in the hope of reproducing their experiences of God in his own life. The great value of the Torah was then that it gave an exposition of the nature of God and of the mystic way to Him."

25. The extent of the material which Philo finds in the scriptural narrative that is susceptible to being interpreted in this more meaningful way is enormous. His interpretations touch on virtually every strand of the narrative and legal traditions of the Pentateuch down to the smallest details of name, (LA 3.74, 77, 79, 83, 93, 96, 186, 218, 230-232), and place, (LA 3.18, 19, 25, 69, 225, 226 ; to take examples from just one of Philo's treatises).

26. See also below; section 3.3.

27. A fuller discussion and analysis of the semantical range of πνεῦμα in the Philonic literature may be found in A. Laurentin, Le Pneuma dans la Doctrine de Philon, (Paris: Descleé de Brouwer, 1951; G. Verbeke, L'Evolution de la Doctrine du Pneuma du Stoicisme à Saint Augustin, (Paris: Descleé de Brouwer, 1945; M.J. Weaver, Pneuma in Philo of Alexandria, (a doctoral dissertation completed at Notre Dame University in 1973); and M.E. Isaacs, The Concept of Spirit, (London: Heythrop Monographs, 1976).

28. These categories, however, are only adopted for convienence sake. In fact, there is overlap between them fairly frequently in Philo. See below.

29. πνεῦμα, ψυχή, and νοῦς are, therefore not to be artificially separated from one another in Philo's works.

30. Thus the Spirit in Philo is always closely connected with the activity of God and divine power, and not detached from God so as to become a separate, or even a subordinate person or hypostasis. So also J. Drummond, Philo Judaeus, (London: Williams and Norgate, 1888); M.E. Isaacs, The Concept of Spirit, 54-58; H.A. Wolfson, Philo, 2.24-36; and J.D.G. Dunn, Christology, 134.

31. See also E.R.Goodenough, Introduction, 155, E. Muhlenberg, "Das Problem der Offenbarung in Philo von Alexandrien" ZNW 64. 1-18 (1973), 12; F.N. Klein, Die Lichtterminologie bei Philon von Alexandrien und in den Hermetischen Schriften, (Leiden: E.J. Brill, 1962), 31-33; M. Pulver, "Das Erlebnis des Pneuma bei Philon", Eranos Jahrbuch 13.111-132 (1945/46).

32. See H. Chadwick, Philo, 139, 152.

33. Compare Wisd 1.5; 6.9-10, 7.27, 10.4, 9, 13, 15 where personified wisdom is said to restrict her fellowship to the righteous.

34. See Opif 158, LA 3.3, 46, 152, Cher 41, Immut 26, Agr 65, Ebr 212, 213, Heres 98, Som 2.71, Spec 2.-31. See also H.A. Wolfson, Philo, 1.52-54; and P.J. du Plessis, TELEIOS, 116.

35. Compare Wisd 9.9-18.

36. So also Cher 27, Gig 47, Mig 34-35, Som 2.252, and Spec 3.1-6. For further discussion concerning Philo's consciousness of inspiration see H.A.A. Kennedy, Philo's Contribution to Religion, (London: Hodder and Stoughton, 1919), 189; A. Laurentin, Pneuma dans Philo, 31-35; H.A. Wolfson, Philo, 2.24-36; and R.M. Grant, The Letter and the

Spirit, (London: SPCK, 1957), 34.

37. See F.N. Klein, _Die Lichtterminologie,_ 14-70.
    See also M. Pulver, "Das Erlebnis des Pneuma", and
    A. Wlosok, _Laktanz und die Philosophische Gnosis,_
    (Heidelberg: C. Winter, 1960).

38. See, for example, Decal 1, Som 2.252, Spec 3.1-6,
    Immut 2-3, QE 2.7. Compare Wisdom 7.10, 24, 30,
    9.17.

39. See Heres 263-266 and Spec 49. It remains, how-
    ever, an open question as to whether or not Philo
    means in these passages to deny that he believes
    in the cessation of the kind of prophetic ectasy
    that issued in scriptural prophecy. See H.A.
    Wolfson, _Philo,_ 2.52-54. "... the prophecy which
    ceased was a special kind of prophecy, that kind
    of prophecy which inspired the teachings contained
    in scripture. This is exactly the view of Philo.
    The accounts of his experience of prophetic in-
    spiration relate only to the attainment of a know-
    ledge of things by insight when ordinary reasoning
    processes failed him."

40. See Heres 69, Mig 34-35, Cher 9.27.

41. See QG 1.90, 4.1, Gig 31, Som 2.252, Immut 2-4,
    QE 2.7. See also above under n. 38.

42. So F.N. Klein, _Die Lichtterminologie,_ 47. See
    also M. Pulver, "Das Erlebnis des Pneuma", 119.

43. See Gig 47. "Thus may the divine Spirit of wis-
    dom not lightly shift his dwelling and be gone,
    but long, long abide with us, since he did thus
    abide with Moses the wise." So also QG 1.90.

44. For a full discussion see R.A. Horsley, _Paul and
    the Pneumatikoi,_ 43-127.

45. Further discussion is provided in chapter 4.

46. See, for example, Sob 1.9-10, LA 1.45, 108, 3.25,
    Cher 75, Sac 121, Mig 38, Heres 19, 313-314.

47. See, for example, LA 3.100, 131, 140, 144, 147, 159, 207, Sac 7, 8, 43, 65, 111, etc.

48. See, for example, Post 132, Mig 70-85, 168-170, Som 1.102-114, Her 14-21. Compare Wisd 8.12. For further discussion see R.A. Horsley, "Wisdom of Word and Words of Wisdom in Corinth", CBQ 37.224, 239 (1977).

Notes to pages 67-69

1. See W. Wuellner, "Haggadic Homily Genre in 1 Cor-
inthians 1-3" _JBL_ 89.199-204 (1970). See also
Wuellner's, "The Soteriological Implications of 1
Corinthians 1.26-28 Reconsidered:, 666-672 in
Studia Evangelica 6, ed. E.A. Livinstone, (Berlin:
Akademie, 1973), and "Ursprung und Verwendung der
σοφός, δυνατος, εὐγενής Formel in 1 Kor 1.26", 165-
183 in _Donum Gentilicum_, eds. E. Bammel, C.K.
Barrett, and W.D. Davies, (Oxford: Oxford University, 1978).
There had been an attempt prior to Wuellner to relate the form of Paul's presentation in 1 Co 1-3
to Bar 3.9-4.4, a passage usually considered to be
a homily composed for the Jewish fast-day on the
ninth of Ab. See H. St. John Thackeray, _The Septuagint and Jewish Worship_, (London: Oxford University, 1921), 95-100, and, more recently, N.E.
Peterson, "1 Korinther 1.18f. und die Thematik des
Jüdischen Büsstages", _Bib_ 32.97-103 (1951).

2. See P. Borgen, _Bread from Heaven_, (Leiden: E.J.
Brill, 1965), 43-51; or, W. Wuellner, "Haggadic
Homily Genre", 200, whose criteria are virtually
the same. Both authors offer parallel examples of
the use of the genre in other literature.

3. See C.J. Bjerklund, _Parakalo_, (Oslo: Universitat,
1967).

4. See N.A. Dahl, "Paul and the Church at Corinth ac-
cording to 1 Corinthians 1.10-4.21", 313-335 in
Christian History and Interpretation, eds. W.
Farmer, C.F.D. Moule, and R. Niebuhr, (Cambridge:
Cambridge University, 1967).

5. See W. Wuellner, "Haggadic Homily Genre", 199 and
"Soteriological Implications", 671.

6. See J.I.H. MacDonald, _Kerygma and Didache_, (Cambridge: Cambridge University, 1980), 37-68, especially 57f.

7. _Ibid_. 45-47, 55, 57.

8. It is precisely the integrity of the larger structure of 1 Co 1.18-3.20 that is ignored by
K.E. Bailey, "Recovering the Poetic Structure of 1

185

Co 1.17-2.2. A Study in Text and Commentary",
NovT 17.265-296 (1975), who has attempted to argue
that Paul's remarks in 1 Co 1.17-2.2 are a reflection of a previous, separate, poetical composition. On the integrity of the two antithetical
sections of the homily see further below, pp.
99ff.

9. See J.I.H. MacDonald, Kerygma and Didache, 50ff.,
and N.A. Dahl, "Form-Critical Observations on
Early Christian Preaching", 30-36 in Jesus in the
Memory of the Early Church by N.A. Dahl, (Minneapolis: Augsburg, 1976). In the same volume, see
also "Memory and Amanesis in Early Christianity",
11-29, especially 19f.

10. Against U. Wilckens, Weisheit und Torheit, (Tübingen: J.C.B. Mohr, 1959), 11-20, who argues that
the only way that 1 Co 1 and 2 can be treated as a
unity is to suppose a consistently polemical purpose behind these chapters. On this reading Paul
does not intend one to draw any positive estimate
of wisdom whatsoever when he quotes the views of
his opponents in 1 Co 2.6-16. But, as we will
see, there is good reason to believe that Paul may
have had more than a purely polemical purpose in
mind. See below pp. 95ff.

11. See J.I.H. MacDonald, Kerygma and Didache, 55-59.

12. Ibid. 57. Compare N.A. Dahl, "Paul and the Church
at Corinth", 31. "We may therefore suppose that
many passages in the letters of the New Testament
correctly convey preaching."

13. This step seems warranted by the evidence produced, even if a great deal of work remains to be
done in terms of deciding how the homily form
functioned in post-biblical Judaism and the early
church. See J.I.H. MacDonald, Kerygma and Didache, 45,53.

14. So also A.T. Hanson, The New Testament Interpretation of Scripture, (London: SPCK, 1980), 21-96.
The unity of the discourse would also point towards the probability of Pauline authorship for
all of its parts. Against E.E. Ellis, "Exegetical

Patterns in 1 Corinthians and Romans", 213-220 in
Prophecy and Hermeneutic in Early Christianity, by
E.E. Ellis, (Grand Rapids: Eerdmans, 1978), and
H. Conzelmann, "Paulus und die Weisheit", NTS
12.231-244 (1965/66).

15. One should notice particularly how the homily form
is adapted in 1 Co 1-3 through the utilization of
Corinthian terminology. See also below, pp 101-
102. Contrast Rom 1.16-4.25, whose vocabulary is
thoroughly Pauline. This important observation is
overlooked in the recent work of V.P. Branick;
(see further below n. 16).

16. Unfortunately, despite the implications of the evidence which they adduce as to the structure of 1
Co 1.18-3.20, neither Wuellner nor MacDonald have
gone on to provide more than an abbreviated interpretation of the Pauline discourse. Wuellner, for
example, is content to say about the first section
of the homily, that, "in 1.20-2.5, we have the
first treatment of the theme employing a haphtarah
from the prophets", and MacDonald does not go much
beyond this when he says, that, "the first part of
the discourse takes up the question of divine and
human wisdom in a highly rhetorical vein and with
much use of antithesis, reaching a climax in the
gospel statement at 1.23f. which serves to restate
the theme". Both authors are presumably more concerned to establish the existence of the form than
to use it to provide an analysis of the passage.
Since the original composition of this section of
my work, an attempt has been made to provide a
more detailed analysis of Paul's wisdom homily in
1 Co 1.18-3.20. This is to be found in an article
by V.P. Branick entitled, "Source and Redaction
Analysis of 1 Corinthians 1-3", JBL 101.251-269
(1982). In the article, on the basis of themes,
style, and the use of the Old Testament, Branick
seeks to differentiate between an original wisdom
homily composed by Paul prior to and independent
of his correspondence with the Corinthians, and
those sections of 1 Co 1-3, (specifically 2.1-5
and 3.1-4), added by Paul to the original homily
to enable him to include it within 1 Corinthians
and apply it to that context. But, as will be argued in our text at length, to separate off 1 Co

2.1-5 and 3.1-4 from the rest of the homily in
this manner, is artificial. For it begs the question of whether or not, and in what ways 1 Co
1.18-31, 2.6-16, and 3.5-20 may have been adapted
by the apostle to enable him to apply the parts of
an earlier homily on wisdom to the specific contours of the Corinthian situation, and, at the
same time ignores the ways in which 1 Co 2.1-5 and
3.104 provide material integral to the Pauline
homily in its present epistolary context.

17. See Isa 29.14 LXX; and compare σοφός, γραμματεύς,
    and συζητητής in 1 Co 1.20 with Isa 19.12; 33.18,
    and 44.25 respectively.

18. On the meaning and nature of the prophetic cri-
    tique of wisdom, see J.H. Whedbee, Isaiah and Wis-
    dom, (Nashville: Abingdon, 1971).

19. The probability that ἀθετήσω is Pauline is strong-
    ly supported by the fact that no variant text of
    the Septuagint contains this reading, nor does any
    Hebrew text form contain its equivalent. As a
    consequence of this, H. Conzelmann, 42, C.K.
    Barrett, 52, T.C. Edwards, 25, J.B. Lightfoot,
    158, and C. Senft, 38, are all prepared to consid-
    er ἀθετήσω as a Pauline addition, possibly a remi-
    niscence of Ps 33.10 LXX.

20. From the root meaning comes the derivative sense
    in which the verb may be taken to mean, "to nul-
    lify", or, "to declare invalid". See W. Bauer
    - W.F. Arndt -F.W. Gingrich - F.W. Danker, A
    Greek-English Lexicon of the New Testament and
    Other Early Christian Literature, (Chicago:
    Chicago University, 1979 - 2nd edition), 21.

21. Similarly in Luke, the Pharisees are said to have
    'set aside' God's purpose for them. See Lk 7.30.
    Compare Mk 6.26, Lk 10.16, Jn 12.48, Heb 10.28,
    Jude 8.

22. Compare Gal 2.21 and 3.15 which are the only other
    Pauline uses.

23. Thus making 1 Co 1.19 an example of that kind of
    parallelism in which the second half of the verse

seeks to explain further the meaning of the assertion in the first. See G.B. Gray, The Forms of
Hebrew Poetry, (London: Hodder and Stoughton,
1915), 37-86.

24. Compare the Isaianic original which also suggests
that God has done away with the wisdom of the wise
by means of his action. See R.E. Clements, Isaiah
1-39, (London: Marshall, Morgan and Scott, 1980),
239. Comapre Mk 7.6ff where Jesus is reported to
have used the same Isaianic context in his refuta-
tion of the scribes.

25. So H. Conzelmann, 43.

26. See A.J.M. Wedderburn, "ἐν τῇ σοφίᾳ τοῦ θεοῦ- 1
Kor 1.21", ZNW 64.132-134 (1973); and C.K. Barrett, 53-54. The objection that Paul speaks in 1
Co 1.22-23 of "the Greeks" in connection with the
search for wisdom in contrast to "the Jews" is
misguided. In light of the recognition of the
homily genre of the passage as a whole, these
verses may be seen most naturally to comprise a
rhetorical expansion upon Paul's statement in 1 Co
1.21. They describe the universal scope of Paul's
commission to proclaim the gospel in the same
terms and style as Rom 1.14-16. Consequently they
provide us with little evidence as to the nature
and character of the Corinthian situation. However, one should also note how in Philonic literature, σημεῖον is routinely used to denote an ex-
ceptionally compelling line or argument drawn from
an interpretation of scripture; (cf. Fug 204 cp.
Gen 16.11; Congr 92 cp. Gen 14.1ff.). Perhaps,
after all, Paul's point in 1 Co 1.22 is not one of
contrast but of comparison!

27. In a similar way, earlier Jewish sapiential authors had claimed that the wisdom of the Torah had
surpassed, or superseded the wisdom that could be
garnered from creation. See above, pp. 8-15.

28. See J.D.G. Dunn, Jesus and the Spirit, (Philadelphia: Westminister, 1975), 220. "Wisdom then for
Paul is not like the Greek gnosis - an insight into the true reality of what is; sophia is a much
more Jewish concept - the recognition of the ac-

tivity of God, in particular, the recognition that God's salvation-history centers on the crucified messiah. But it is not merely a rational acknowledgement; it includes experiential participation in that salvation-history, the actual experience of God's saving power in the here and now - the 'demonstration of the Spirit and power'; (1 Co 2.-4). It is important that these two elements be held together."

29. So N.A. Dahl, "Paul and the Church at Corinth", 328.

30. Thus σοφός will denote a Jewish teacher; γραμματεύς a scribe, (סופר); and συζητητής an expositor, or interpreter, (דרשן). See K. Grayston, "Not with a Rod", ExpTim 88.13-16 (1976/77), and R.G. Hamerton-Kelly, Pre-Existence, Wisdom, and the Son of Man, (Cambridge: Cambridge University, 1973), 119.

31. See also M. Hengel, The Son of God, (London: SCM, 1976), 74, who believes that 1 Co 1.24 and 1.30 are most naturally understood against a Torah-centric background.

32. Paul's use of scripture is therefore ironic. So also N.A. Dahl, "Paul and the Church at Corinth", 328.

33. See M. Hengel, The Son of God, 58; "the true will of God was no longer embodied in the torah of Sinai, but in the teaching of the messiah Jesus, and his accursed death on a cross, (Deut 21.23), could, and indeed must put in question the law of Moses as an ultimate authority".

34. So J.D.G. Dunn, Christology, 178. Compare 1 Co 1.21, 23, 24.

35. One should notice, as has already been pointed out, that "this kind of specific identity of wisdom with another subject occurs only in relation to the Torah prior to 1 Co 1.24". So M.J. Suggs, "The Word is near you: Romans 10.6-10", 289-312 in Christian History and Interpretation, eds. W. Farmer, C.F.D. Moule, R. Niebuhr; cf. W.D.Davies,

Paul & Rabbinic Judaism, (London: SPCK,   1970
- 2nd edition), 147-196.

36. With C.K.   Barrett, we agree that the   two expressions would "appear to be used synonymously ...
this age, in contrast with the age to come, and
this world, in contrast with the other world;
these are not two completely distinct dualisms".
So C.K. Barrett, 53; compare 70.

37. See F.L. Arrington, Paul's Aeon Theology in First
Corinthians, (a doctoral dissertation completed at
St. Louis University in 1975).   See also A. Ro-
bertson - A. Plummer, 20.

38. The origin of the citation is assured despite the
fact that its form differs, by way of abbrevia-
tion, from both the LXX and the Hebrew text.   See
E.E. Ellis, Paul's Use of the Old Testament, (London: Oliver and Boyd, 1957); 151, 173.

39. The observation that Paul wished to place all of
his stress on the verb καυχάομαι could account for
the abbreviated form of the citation.

40. On the Hebrew usage, see F. Brown - S.R. Driver
- C.H. Briggs, A Hebrew-English Lexicon, (London:
Clarendon, 1953), 259. ' For the Greek usage, see
Bauer-Arndt-Gingrich-Danker, A Greek-English Lexi-
con, 425.

41. See above, pp. 70-71.   See also below, pp. 113ff.

42. See R.A. Horsley, Paul and the Pneumatikoi;
"Pneumatikos versus Psychikos: Distinctions of
Spiritual Status among the Corinthians", HTR
69.269-288 (1976); "'How can some of you say that
there is no resurrection of the dead?': Spiritual
Elitism in Corinth", NT 20.203-231 (1978); "Gnosis
in Corinth: 1 Corinthians 8.1-6", NTS 27.32-51
(1980).   See also B.A. Pearson, The Pneumatikos-
Psychikos Terminology in 1 Corinthians, (Missoula:
Scholars, 1973); "Hellenistic-Jewish Wisdom Specu-
lation and Paul", 43-66 in Aspects of Wisdom in
Judaism and Early Christianity, ed. R.L. Wilken,
(Notre Dame: University, 1975).   Both authors
give numerous examples of Philonic parallels which

show the true provenance of this terminology.

43. For a history of exegesis see W. Wuellner, "Ursprung und Verwendung", 165-166.

44. For an attempt at the isolation of this motif within the comparative literature which is overly amtitious at points, but nevertheless quite useful see J.M. Gibbs, "Wisdom, Power, and Well-Being", 119-155 in Studia Biblica 1978, ed. E.A. Livingstone, (Sheffield: JSOT, 1980).

45. See the parallels cited in the works of Horsley and Pearson listed above in n. 42.

46. See Jer 9.23 LXX. So Paul's use of scripture is once again ironic; compare above, n. 35.

47. κλῆσιν itself is found in 1 Co 1.26, and ἐξελέξατο occurs three times in the space of the next two verses.

48. Our treatment of 1 Co 2.1-5 is therefore to be distinguished from that of W. Wuellner who states that this passage constitutes a digressio; "a stylistic feature familiar also in halakic discussions". See W. Wuellner, "Haggadic Homily Genre", 201. However, the parallel Wuellner adduces in b. Niddah 70b is hardly close to 1 Co 2.1-5. Furthermore, if one follows up his cross reference to S. Sandmel, The First Christian Century in Judaism and Christianity, (New York: Haper and Row, 1969), 75, then it is discovered that Sandmel is concerned to document the rabbinic practice of "interrupting acute halakic discussions with anecdotes about the authorities engaged in these discussions: this probably as a mnemonic device", a procedure only remotely akin, if at all, to 1 Co 2.1-5.

49. For discussion of the textual variants associated with the second of these two expressions see B.M. Metzger, A Textual Commentary on the Greek New Testament, (London: U.B.S., 1975), 546; or, H. Conzelmann, 55. Both authors advance adequate reasons for adopting the text as we have given it.

50. Compare the similar thoughts of L.A. Hartman in his article, "Some Remarks on 1 Corinthians 2.1-5", SEA 34.109-120 (1974).

51. Especially in Sirach and in Philo. See above, pp. 25 and 71. See also R.A. Horsley, "Wisdom of Word", 224-230.

52. N.A. Dahl, in "Paul and the Church at Corinth", 321, has indicated that this same sort of standard was probably used to criticize Paul. "From the statement, 'with me it is a very small thing that I should be judged by you or by any human court', (4.3), we may safely infer that some kind of criticism of Paul had been voiced at Corinth. And it is not too difficult to find out what must have been the main content of this criticism. That becomes evident in phrases like, 'not with eloquent wisdom', (2.1), 'not in persuasiveness of wisdom', (2.4), 'milk not solid food', (3.2). To what extent the phrases, and not merely their content, allude to what was reported to have been said is immaterial. Since the Corinthians evidently understood themselves as wise because they thought themselves inspired pneumatic person, (cf. 3.1), we must conclude that Paul was not merely held to lack the oratorical ability of a Greek rhetor, but also the gift of pneumatic wisdom."

53. T.W. Gillespie has come to a similar conclusion in his article, "A Pattern of Prophetic Speech in First Corinthians", JBL 97.74-95 (1978), 86-89. But Gillespie also goes beyond the bounds of the present study to argue that there is a link between the Corinthian 'word of wisdom', and the "predilection in Corinth for tongues".

54. On the character and importance of this contrast see L. Hartman, "Some remarks on 1 Cor 2.1-5" SEA 34.109-120 (1974), and H.K. Nielsen, "Paulus Verwendung des Begriffes Dunamis. Eine Replik zur Kreuzestheologie", pp 137-158 in Die Paulinische Literatur und Theologie, ed. S. Pedersen, (Arhus: Forlaget Aros, 1980.)

55. See J. Weiss, 50; H. Conzelmann, 55; T.C. Edwards, 48; A. Robertson - A. Plummer, 33.

56. Among Jewish sources see Philo, Leg 37, Agr 13-16, Mos 1.95; Ep Arist 102; and Test Jos 14.5. For Greek and Latin sources see J. Martin, <u>Antike Rhetorik and Poetic</u>, (Gloucester Mass.: Peter Smith, 1957=1924 edition), 65. So also L.A. Hartman, "Some Remarks on 1 Co 2.1-5", 116-117.

57. As J.D.G. Dunn has pointed out, there is a "a widespread recognition in earliest Christianity of the creative power of the word preached ... Paul vividly recalled the experiences of his hearers being convicted and converted by his preaching". so J.D.G. Dunn, <u>Christology</u>, 233. See also above n. 35.

58. As T.W. Gillespie says, "such perjorative evaluations serve to identify the <u>actual</u> over aginst the <u>supposed</u>, source of the wisdom claimed by the Corinthians, and to deny, by definition, its authenticity". So Gillespie, "A Pattern of Prophetic Speech", 89.

1. W. Wuellner is one of only a very few who do not recognize any significant difference between 1 Co 1.18-2.5 and 1 Co 2.6-3.20. According to Wuellner, the theme of the whole homily from 1.18-3.20 is "not that of wisdom as such, but the divine sovereignty and judgement over all wisdom". This theme Wuellner finds continued in 1 Co 2.6ff. See W. Wuellner, "Haggadic Homily Genre", 199-200.

2. Important exceptions to this judgement occur, however, in 1 Co 1.21, 24, and 30.

3. So also J.D.G. Dunn, Unity and Diversity in the New Testament, (Philadelphia: Westminister, 1977), 191. "What we must note here is that Paul claims to have experienced a wisdom deeper than that of his disputants ..."

4. Ibid. See also 289ff.

5. See U. Wilckens, Weisheit und Torheit, 52ff.; M. Winter, Pneumatiker und Psychiker in Korinth, (Marburg: N.G. Elwert, 1975), 21-41; and W. Schmithals, Gnosticism in Corinth, (Nashville: Abingdon, 1971), 151ff. Slightly different are the approaches of R. Bultmann and D. Luhrmann. Bultmann's view is that Paul's pride has induced him to fomulate a wisdom teaching in response to the Corinthians utilizing terms and concepts drawn from his opponents. See R. Bultmann, Glauben und Verstehen, (Tübingen: J.C.B. Mohr, 1954 - 2 volumes), 1.44. D. Lührmann takes 1 Co 2.6ff. to be a Corinthian 'revelation-speech' which Paul has tried to modify by means of additions and alterations. See D. Lührmann, Das Offenbarungsverstandnis bei Paulus und in den Paulinischen Gemeinden, (Neukirchen: Neukirchener, 1965), 114ff. Finally, H. Conzelmann believes that this passage derives essentially neither from Paul nor his Corinthian opponents, but from a Pauline 'wisdom-school'. See H. Conzelmann, "Paulus und die Weisheit", 238ff.

6. See R.W. Funk, Language, Hermeneutic, and the Word of God, (New York: Harper and Row, 1966); 279, 291. On the use of δέ to introduce a qualification, explanation, or parenthetical thought, see

F. Blass - A. DeBrunner - R. Funk, A Greek Grammar
of the New Testament and Other Early Christian
Literature, (Chicago: University of Chicago, 1961
- 10th edition), 231-232; and J.H. Moulton et.
al., A Grammar of New Testament Greek, (Edinburgh:
T&T Clark, 1908, 1929, 1963, and 1976 - 4 vols.),
3.331-332.

7. So R.W. Funk, Language, 279. Note δὲ οὐ, (1 Co
    2.6b), and οὐδέ, (1 Co 2.6c).

8. See U. Wilckens, Weisheit und Torheit, 52 n.1; and
    M. Winter, Pneumatiker und Psychiker, 209. Winter
    contends that this recognition is of little value
    as far as the understanding of the sophia in 1 Co
    2.6ff. is concerned, for Paul says in 1 Co 3.1
    that he has not made known this sophia to the Cor-
    inthians. "Setzt Paulus in 1 Kor 2.6ff. offen-
    sichtlich einen anderer Sophia-Begriff voraus."
    But this solution only multiplies difficulties by
    creating two completely separate kinds of wisdom.

9. A fact recognized by R.W. Funk, Language, 279ff.;
    B.A. Pearson, "Hellenistic-Jewish Wisdom and
    Paul", 50; M.E. Thrall, 24, and C.K. Barrett, 67.

10. So also C.K. Barrett, 79. Of course, to label
    one section of Paul's discourse negative and an-
    other positive is not to argue that these emphases
    are exclusive, as Paul makes positive points in 1
    Co 1.18-2.5, and negative points in 1 Co 2.6-3.17.

11. So U. Wilckens, Weisheit und Torheit; 52, 92; and
    W. Schmithals, Gnosticism in Corinth, 151.

12. This point is arued at length by B.A. Pearson and
    R.A. Horsley in the works cited above under n. 42
    (chapter 4). See also R.W. Funk, Language, 296ff.

13. So J. Reese, "Paul proclaims the Wisdom of the
    Cross: Scandal and Foolishness", BTB 9.147-153
    (1979); especially 149, section 2.

14. This balancing effect has been noticed by many of
    the commentators. See, for example, C.K. Barrett,
    67; A. Robertson - A. Plummer, 34; F.F. Bruce, 37.
    Most, however, have failed to observe that this

effect continues into chapter 3 despite the critical tone of 1 Co 3.1. But see J.I.H. MacDonald,
Kerygma and Didache, 57. The return to a critique
of the Corinthians in 1 Co 3.1-4 should not be allowed to obscure the fact that the tone of 1 Co
3.1ff. is predominantly positive. For, as we have
seen, Paul can also make positive statements about
sophia in the midst of his critique; (cf. 1 Co
1.21, 24, 30). See further below pp. 114, 130.

15. See H. Conzelmann, 57, and A.T. Hanson, New Testament Interpretation, 69. According to Conzelmann, the structural division is between 'wisdom'
in verses 6-9, and ('wisdom') among the mature in
verses 10-16, while Hanson divides the passage according to the emphasis on "what God has revealed"
in verses 6-9, and on the "fact of revelation to
us Christians" in verses 10-16.

16. One should notice how the form of address, restricted in 1 Co 2.6-7 to the first person plural
conforms closely to a similar use of the first
person plural in 1 Co 1.18, 21, and 23. The same
kind of relationship may also be discerned between
1 Co 2.1-6 and 1 Co 3.1 where the form of address
shifts to the first person singular; (cp. κἀγώ
ἐλθών in 1 Co 2.1 with κἀγώ ἠδυνήθην λαλῆσαι in 1
Co 3.1; cp. also 1 Co 2.2-3 and 1 Co 3.2).

17. So R. Scroggs, "Paul: Σοφός and Πνευματικός", NTS
14. 33-55 (1967), 40.

18. See J.H. Moulton et. al., A Grammar of New Testa-
ment Greek, 3.340; F. Blass - A. DeBrunner - R.
Funk, A Greek Grammar of the New Testament, 230-
231; and A.T. Robertson, A Grammar of the Greek
New Testament in Light of Historical Research,
(New York: 1919 - 3rd edition); 1165, 1185.

19. See above n. 36 and 37, (chapter 4). So also A.T.
Lincoln, Paradise Now and Not Yet, (Cambridge University, 1981), 172. Lincoln traces the inter-
changeability between the two terms αἰών and
κόσμος back to a common semitic root, עולם, which
carried a dual reference to both 'age' and
'world'.

20. So M. Hengel, The Son of God, 74. See also B.
Reicke, "The Law and This World According to
Paul", JBL 70. 259-76 (1951); J.D.G. Dunn, Christology; 174, 178, 179; and S. Kim, The Origin of
Paul's Gospel, (Tübingen: J.C.B. Mohr, 1981);
127ff., 258-260. Of course, as A.C. Thiselton has
pointed out, this contrast may not at all have
been evident to the Corinthians who may instead
have thought of their wisdom precisely as eschatological wisdom, the knowledge of the Law intended for the end of the age. See A.C. Thiselton,
"Realized Eschatology at Corinth", NTS 24.510-26
(1978).
It is important also to emphasize that Paul's
phraseology here applies to the law only insofar
as the law continues to be used as the standard
for wisdom apart from reference to Christ. To use
the law in this way is to revert back to the pattern of an era that has been decisively superseded
by the inbreaking of the messianic age. It is in
this sense then that Paul here, as elsewhere, is
content to speak of the law as belonging exclusively to an older age; (cp. Rom 7.4-6, 2 Co 3.7-
11, Gal 3.23-26). The age of the law has been
superseded by the messianic age and the wisdom of
the law has been fulfilled and transcended by the
divine wisdom demonstrated in the life and death
of Jesus.

21. See J.D.G. Dunn, Christology; 39, 179.

22. Proponents of this view include A.W. Carr, "The
Rulers of this Age - 1 Corinthians 2.6-8", NTS
23.20-35 (1977); idem., Angels and Principalities,
(Cambridge: Cambridge University, 1981); M.
Pesce, Paolo à gli arconti à Corinto, (Brescia:
Paideia Editria, 1977); A. Feuillet, "Les Chefs de
ce Siècle et la Sagesse Divine d'après 1 Co 2.6-
9", 25-37 in Le Christ: Sagesse de Dieu, (Paris:
J. Gabalda, 1966); J. Schniewind, "Die Archonten
dieses Aöns. 1 Kor 2.6-8", 104-109 in
Nachgelassene Reden und Aufsatze by J. Schniewind,
(Berlin: Akademie, 1952); G. Miller, "OI APXONTES
TOY AIONOS TOYTOY - A New Look at 1 Corinthians
2.6-8", JBL 91.522-528; J. Munck, Paul and the
Salvation of Mankind, (London: SCM, 1959), 156;
and L.C. Allen, "The Old Testament Background of

(πρό) ορι̅ζειν in the New Testament", <u>NTS</u> 17.104-108 (1970/71).

23. This view is by far the most dominant one in this century, especially since the work of M. Dibelius, <u>Die Geisterwelt im Glauben des Paulus</u>, (Gottingen: Vandenhoeck and Rupprecht); see for example U. Wilckens <u>Weisheit Und Torheit</u>, pp. 61-63.

24. This position has been very influential since it was introduced into the modern discussion by O. Cullmann in <u>Christ and Time</u>, (London: SPCK, 1957); cf. G.B. Caird in <u>Principalities and Powers</u>, (Oxford: Oxford University, 1956), and G.H.C. MacGregor, "Principalities and Powers: The Cosmic Background of Saint Paul's Thought", <u>NTS</u> 1.17-29 (1954/55).

25. On ἀρχόντες as a designation for Jewish rulers see G. Alon, <u>The Jews in Their Land in the Talmudic Age</u>, (Jerusalem: Magnes, 1980), 176-184; S. Safari - M. Stern, <u>The Jewish People in the First Century</u>, (Assen: Van Gorcum and Comp. B.V., 1974 and 1976 - 2 vols.); 1.487, 491-494; and W.A. Meeks - R.L. Wilken, <u>Jews and Christians in Antioch in the First Four Centuries of the Common Era</u>, (Missoula: Scholars, 1978), 7-9.

26. Compare Mt 20.25, Lk 14.1; 23.13, 35; 24.20, Jn 7.26, 48; 22.42, Ac 3.17, 4.5, 8, 26; 13.27, 14.5; 16.19.

27. Moreover, these usages are balanced statistically by cases where ἄρχων is used of a human ruler. See Mt 9.18, 23; Lk 8.41, 12.58, 18.18, Jn 3.1, Ac 7.27, 35; 23.5.

28. See A.W. Carr, "The Rulers of this Age", 24-25. So also J.B. Lightfoot, 174, and T.C. Edwards, 52.

29. So also L.C. Allen, "The Background of (προ) 'ορι̅ζειν", 106. Carr is aware of the difficulties involved in using the Acts speeches as evidence for the views of the early church. See A.W. Carr, "The Rulers of this Age", 25-27.

Notes to pages 91-92

30. So also A. Feuillet, Le Christ: Sagesse de Dieu, 25-37, and R. Scroggs, "Paul: Σοφός and Πνευματικός", 41-42.

31. "There is, therefore, every reason for expecting in the phrase οἱ ἄρχοντες τοῦ αἰῶνος τούτου a reference to Pilate and Caiaphas." So A.W. Carr, Angels and Principalities, 119. So also now G. D. Fee, New Testament Exegesis, Philadelphia: Westminister, 1983, 87-89.

32. This point is brought out strongly in the work of M. Pesce, Paolo à gli arconti à Corinto. So also A. Robertson - A. Plummer, 36-37 who contend that the ἄρχοντες must refer primarily to those who actually took part in the crucifixion that is, to the Jewish rulers; (cf. Lk 23.35).

33. The sense of the genitival participle τῶν καταργουμένων is intended to accord with what Paul has said about Torah-centric wisdom in 1 Co 1.19. Such wisdom has been 'set aside' by God in favor of the wisdom of Christ and the cross. Thus the proponents of this wisdom may also be descibed as 'those who are passing away', or, 'declining into unimportance'. Compare also Ga 3.17 where καταργέω and ἀθετέω are used in parallel. See G.W. Miller, "A New Look at 1 Corinthians 2.6-8", 526, and A.W. Carr, "The Rulers of this Age", 32.

34. So also B.A. Pearson, "Hellenistic-Jewish Wisdom and Paul", 51. "Paul speaks of a wisdom which turns out to be nothing other than the wisdom of God that he had referred to earlier, the wisdom of God's salvific plan centering in the cross of Christ." Compare J.D.G. Dunn, Christology, 174-178; R.G. Hamerton-Kelly, Pre-Existence, Wisdom, and the Son of Man; 115-116, 279-280; A.T. Hanson, New Testament Interpretation, 26-27; R.A. Horsley, Paul and the Pneumatikoi, 128-146; and most of the commentators.

35. The dative has always caused problems for commentators. Is it to be taken with λαλοῦμεν, or with θεοῦ σοφίαν? In either case, it will indicate, "the way in which wisdom manifests itself; its form is one of mystery". So F.W. Grosheide,

200

Notes to pages 92-93

64. See also H. Conzelmann, 62.

36. On the background and use of the word μυστήριον in the Pauline epistles, see especially R.E. Brown, The Semitic Background of the Term "Mystery" in the New Testament; C.C. Cargounis, The Ephesian Mysterion: Meaning and Content, (Lund: Carl Bloms, 1977); G. Bornkamm, "μυστήριον", TDNT 4.802-828; J. Coppens, "'Mystery' in the Theology of St. Paul"; and D. Deden, "Le 'Mystère' Paul- inien", ETL 13.403-432 (1936).

37. So also C.C. Cargounis, The Ephesian Mysterion, 108. "The mysterion is shaped by God's wisdom and is a product of it. At the same time, God's wis- dom is reflected and revealed in the mysterion. There is an interblending of conceptual components between these two terms; (cf. 1 Co 2.7 σοφία ἐν μυστηρίῳ)." This same inter-relationship is also a part of the pre-Christian Jewish background; see R.E. Brown, The Background of the term "Mystery", 41.

38. See J.D.G. Dunn, Jesus and the Spirit, 213. "The most important event of revelation for Paul is the eschatological event of Christ, unveiling the mys- tery of God's final purposes." See also J.D.G. Dunn, Christology, 234-236; G. Bornkamm, "μυστήριον", 819; A.T. Hanson, New Testament In- terpretation, 26-27; A. van Roon, "The Relation between Christ and the Wisdom of God according to Paul", NT 16. 207-239 (1974), 218; and R.A. Horsley, Paul and the Pneumatikoi, 151.

39. Prior to this, as is shown most clearly by the evidence from Qumran, a knowledge of God's mys- teries was to be discerned on the basis of a cor- rect interpretation of the Torah. Thus in 1 QpHab, for example, we find the claim that it is "the Teacher of Righteusness to whom God has made known all of the mysteries of his servants the Prophets"; (7.14). For further comparative mat- erial see above, p. 39. With Paul, however, it is apparent in the light of 1 Co 1.24 and 30 that the Christ-event has surpassed the Torah in terms of its ability to reveal to us θεοῦ σοφίαν ἐν μυστηρίῳ.

40. See 1 Co 2.7, Eph 3.9, Col 1.26, and compare the only other occurrence of the word in Lk 10.21 where it is used in context together with σοφός. The New Testament usage is not, however, distinctive. The close association of ἀποκρύπτω, or κρύπτω with σοφία, or μυστήριον is well attested in pre-Christian sources. See, for instance, Sir 20.30; 41.14, Wisd 6.22, 7.13. See also A. Oepke, "κρύπτω", TDNT 1.957-978, especially 969 and 976.

41. See N.A. Dahl, "Form-Critical Observations on Early Christian Preaching". See also D. Lührmann, Das Offenbarungsverstandnis bei Paulus, 124-126; and G. Bornkamm, "The Risen Lord and the Earthly Jesus", 203-229 in The Future of Our Religious Past, ed. J.M. Robinson, (London: SCM, 1971), 212-214.

42. See J.D.G. Dunn, Christology, 234-236.

43. Ibid. See also P.S. Fiddes, The Hiddenness of Wisdom, passim., who provides much more documentation to support this conclusion.

44. See above, pp. 10ff., 34ff., 50ff.

45. Compare Eph 1.5, 11; Acts 4.28, and Rom 8.29-30.

46. This conclusion is also indicated by the relative pronoun, ἥν which introduces 1 Co 2.8. The accusative case clearly refers back to θεοῦ σοφίαν in 1 Co 2.7 as has been recognized and emphasized by B.A. Pearson, The Pneumatikos-Psychikos Terminology, 33-34, and "Hellenistic-Jewish Wisdom and Paul", 57.

47. Compare the similarly ironic use of scripture as a conclusion in 1 Co 1.31. As C.K. Barrett stresses, the presence of the introductory formula, καθὼς γέγραπται, makes it probable that Paul, at least, believed he was quoting from the Old Testament. See C.K. Barrett, 73. See also E.E. Ellis, Paul's Use of the Old Testament, 34-35.

48. The text in this form fails to appear anywhere in the Septaugint or any of the variant Hebrew text forms, though individual phrases occur in Isa 64.4

and 65.17; (cp. Jer 3.16 and Sir 1.10). Suggestions concerning a source for the composite citation have, therefore, been quite numerous. See P. Prigent, "Ce Que L'Oeil n'à pas vu, 1 Co 2.9. Histoire et Prehistoire d'une Citation", TZ 14.416-429 (1958); M. Philonenko, "Quod Occulus non vidit, 1 Co 2.9", TZ 15.51-52 (1959); A. Feuillet, "L'Enigmé de 1 Co 2.9", RB 70-52-74 (1963); and A.T. Hanson, New Testament Interpretation, 43-66.

49. See A. Schlatter, 26-27; A. Robertson - A. Plummer, 40; J. DuPont, Gnosis, (Paris: J. Gabalda, 1949); 107-108; W.D. Davies, Paul 307; B.A. Pearson, The Pneumatikos-Psychikos Terminology, 34-35; and U. Wilckens, Weisheit und Torheit, 80.

50. So W.D. Davies, Paul, 307. Pearson, following Wilckens, has attempted to bolster the case for an eschatological interpretation of 1 Co 2.9 by attributing the use of the first part of the citation, (1 Co 2.9a and b), to Paul's opponents. According to Pearson, the Corinthians were employing the citation in this abbreviated form to define the contents of their mystical wisdom. 1 Co 2.9c then represents Paul's response; "Paul is saying, in effect, that the heavenly things which eye has not seen, etc., are not a present possession and so do not characterize our life now, as though they could be conjured up in a mystical experience ... they are ὅσα ἡτοίμασεν ὁ θεὸς, for the future possession of those who love him". If, however, Paul's opponents did use 1 Co 2.9a and b to describe their wisdom, it seems much more likely, on the basis of the evidence which Pearson adduces, that the opponents' wisdom was not mystical, but rather was some sort of Torah-centered wisdom. Still, it appears unlikely to me that this citation derives in any part from the Corinthians since 1 Co 2.9a and b fit perfectly well into the context of Paul's argument. Furthermore, all of the other citations in 1 Co 1-3 are uniformly Pauline.

51. This is an objection which must be raised against A.T. Hanson's interpretation of 1 Co 2.9. See

A.T. Hanson, <u>New</u> <u>Testament</u> <u>Interpretation</u>, 43-66.

52. This argument seems strong indeed, for it is hard to understand what reason might have prompted Paul to turn away from the context in such a different direction only then to turn back to the original context of meaning a verse later. See A. Feuillet, <u>Le</u> <u>Christ</u>, <u>Sagesse</u> <u>de</u> <u>Dieu</u>, 39-40.

53. Against B.A. Pearson <u>et</u>. <u>al</u>.; (see n. 49 and n. 50 above). On the other hand, Pearson is certainly right to call into question Wilckens' assertion that the relative pronouns refer to a mythical 'redeemer-figure'.

54. So R.G. Hamerton-Kelly, <u>Pre-Existence</u>, <u>Wisdom</u>, <u>and</u> <u>the</u> <u>Son</u> <u>of</u> <u>Man</u>, 115-116. See also 117; "Paul is using synedoche, and, taking the title of the whole plan, namely, 'wisdom', he speaks of the contents of that plan". Compare A. van Roon, "The Relation between Christ and the Wisdom of God", 216.

55. See Rom 11.33 and compare Job 11.8 LXX. See also J. Blunck, "βάθος", <u>NIDNTT</u> 3.197-198; H. Schlier, "βάθος", <u>TDNT</u> 1.517-518; and F.F. Bruce, 39.

56. So A. Oepke, "κρύπτω", 976 and A. Feuillet, "L'Enigme de 1 Co 2.9".

57. Reading ἃ instead of ὅσα in 1 Co 2.9c with p 46 and Sinaiticus. The second ἃ is then resumptive, though the grammatical structure is irregular as is noted by H. Conzelmann, 56 n. 64. See also A. Robertson - A. Plummer, 40. It may not be impossible to read 1 Co 2.6c as a Pauline comment rather than as a part of the citation. This, however, would strengthen and not weaken the case which sees in 1 Co 2.6c an applicational significance. 1 Co 2.6a and b apply to Christians because God has prepared these 'things' for them. In his most recent article, "Das Kreuz Christi als der Tiefe der Weisheit Gottes zu 1 Kor 2.1-16", 43-81 in <u>Paolo</u> <u>a</u> <u>Una</u> <u>Chiesa</u> <u>Divisa</u>, ed. L. de Lorenzi, (Rome: Abbazia di S. Paolo Fuori le Mura, 1980), U. Wilckens comes quite close to this conclusion. "Kein menschliches Auge, kein Ohr,

kein Herz hat die Inhalte der Göttlichen Weisheit je erfasst - ausser den Geliebten Gottes, denen er sie bereitet hat." So p. 53.

58.   This helps to explain why Paul lays such stress in 1 Co 1.17ff. on the event of the crucifixion and its interpretation in the kerygma. For preaching is itself a part of God's plan, designed to reveal to humanity the wisdom of God's action in the cross. Such revelation, however, can only be accomplished in relationship to the plan of God as a whole, (cf. 1 Co 1.21), in relation to God's hidden plan for the salvation of all persons and the redemption of creation. Hence Paul understands the crucifixion of Christ to be the defining center of God's wise plan.

59.   Reading δέ and not γάρ for the reasons outlined by B.M. Metzger in A Textual Commentary on the Greek New Testament, 546. However, the connection is just as close if the latter reading is adopted. See G.T. Montague, The Holy Spirit: Growth of a Biblical Tradition, (New York: Paulist, 1976), 136.

60.   While the object is missing from 1 Co 2.10, it is clearly to be inferred as at least closely related to the ἅ of 1 Co 2.9c, given the identity of subject, and the similarity of action between the two verses. So also F.F. Bruce, 39; A Robertson - A. Plummer, 43; and K. Maly, Mündige Gemeinde, (Stuttgart: Katholisches Bibelwerk, 1967),40.

61.   See above p. 85.

62.   See R.A. Humphries, Paul's Rhetoric of Argumentation in 1 Corinthians 1-4, (an unpublished doctoral dissertation completed at the Graduate Theological Union in 1979), 74ff. The outline reproduced in our text is slightly modified from that of Humphries.

63.   So R.A. Humphries, Paul's Rhetoric of Argumentation, 75.

64.   For discussion, see above pp. 78-82.

65. The following argument was dependent for its initial impetus, though not for its final form, on P.L. Watkins, The Holy Spirit in 1 Corinthians, (an unpublished Masters thesis completed at Durham University in 1972). See p. 78.

66. Most commentators take the expression in this way. See, for example, C.K. Barrett, 75; F.F. Bruce, 39; A. Robertson - A. Plummer, 43; J. Hering, 18; W. Orr - J.A. Walther, 165; C. Senft, 51; and E.B. Allo, 45.

67. This position is argued strongly by B.A. Pearson, The Pneumatikos-Psychikos Terminology, 103 n. 22 and 26; and "Hellenistic-Jewish Wisdom and Paul", 51.

68. The difficulty for the interpretation which refers the plural expressions to all Christians is the formally parallel, and closely linked λαλοῦμεν in 1 Co 2.13. The difficulty for the alternative is that it turns 1 Co 2.12 into an affirmation about the reception of the Spirit that is limited to Paul alone. Thus, the proposal combining the two alternatives is made by R.A. Humphries, Paul's Rhetoric of Argumentation, 74.

69. Compare H. Conzelmann, 65.

70. While this solution may look like a simple variant of the 'all Christians' position, the contention of R. Funk is to be kept in mind. "Given the polemical context, it is obvious that Paul does not propose to embrace his opponents in this 'we' without qualification." See R.W. Funk, Language, 293 n. 73. See also J.D.G. Dunn, Unity and Diversity, 289-290.

71. See above section 5.2.

72. See above section 5.1.

73. This issue has already been treated in general terms above, in section 5.1. It is raised again here only because this section is so often put forward as one of the hardest bits of evidence for the contention that 1 Co 2.6ff. represents the

theology of Paul's opponents and not that of Paul himself.

74. See, for example, U. Wilckens' comment that τα βάθη is "typisch gnostisch"; Weisheit und Torheit, 82; or M. Winter, Pneumatiker und Psychiker, 208.

75. See B.E. Gartner, "The Pauline and Johannine Idea of 'To Know God' against the Hellenistic Background", NTS 14.209-231 (1967/68); R.G. Hamerton-Kelly, Pre-Existence, Wisdom, and the Son of Man, 120-125; M.E. Isaacs, The Concept of Spirit; 77, 78, 80, 97, 105; and B.A. Pearson, The Pneumatikos-Psychikos Terminology, 39. All of these scholars accept that Paul's use of the 'like-by-like' idea is derivative. However, as most of them admit, if this is so then it is certain, nonetheless, that 1 Co 2.11 in its present form represents Paul's own view and not those of the Corinthians.

76. There are only three other uses of βάθος in the undisputed Pauline epistles, (in Rom 8.39, 11.33, and 2 Co 8.2), and of these only Rom 11.33 is similar in thought to 1 Co 2.10b. ἐραυνάω is even more scarce, occurring only on one other occasion in Paul's correspondence; (in Rom 8.27).

77. So U. Wilckens, Weisheit und Torheit, 82; M. Winter, Pneumatikos und Psychikos, 208; B.A. Pearson, The Pneumatikos-Psychikos Terminology, 39.

78. So G. Delling, "ἐρεύναω", TDNT 2.655-657. The quotation is taken from p. 656. (ἐραύναω is, of course, the later form of ἐρεύναω.)

79. This is the sense in 11 of the 32 cases listed by G. Mayer in Index Philonaeus, (Berlin: Walter de Gruyter, 1974), 120. The references are in Sac 52, 89; Det 57, Post 40, Conf 183, Mig 176, Cong 45, Mut 236, Som 1.41, 167; and Abr 147.

80. See A.A. Anderson, The Book of Psalms, (London: Marshall, Morgan, and Scott, 1972 - 2 vols.), 2.806. An especially enthusiastic appraisal of the wisdom character of this psalm may be found in G. von Rad, The Problem of the Hexateuch and Other

Essays, (Edinburgh: Oliver and Boyd, 1966), 248.

81. So G. Delling "ἐρεύναω", 657. Compare I Pet 1.11.

82. The latest edition of the Bauer-Arndt-Gingrich
     -Danker lexicon notes that πάντα in this sense can
     be used with a demonstrative force to refer to
     "all the things of a whole that is implied from
     the context". See A Greek-English Lexicon, 632
     (2,a,δ).   See also B. Reicke, "πᾶς, ἁπᾶς", TDNT
     5.888-896, who notes, on p. 889, (2, b), that the
     "extent and content (of πάντα) is to be decided by
     the context". An especially striking example of a
     limited πάντα may be found in Lk 9.43, (cp. Lk
     1.3, 2.39, 10.22, and Acts 24.8), though further
     instances may also be found throughout the New
     Testament literature.

83. This seems, for example, to be the clear inference
     behind the 'blessing' of Psalm 118.2 LXX, and the
     same kind of thinking also seems to lie beneath
     the surface of the Philonic references cited above
     in n. 79.

84. This interpretation of Paul's thought is reinforc-
     ed if the καί which connects the two clauses of 1
     Co 2.10b is translated epexegetically, for then it
     serves to extrapolate the search of the Spirit to
     the furthest possible limits, 'even to the depths
     of God's thoughts'.

85. One finds instructive instances of the use of
     βάθος, or a close cognate, in Job 11.8 LXX, in
     Prov. 18.4 LXX, and in Ecc 7.24 LXX what is called
     βαθὺ βάθος   is probably sophia; (cp. vs.   23).
     Philo also links βάθος with sophia and ἐπιστήμη in
     Ebr 112 and Som 2.271. A third instance from
     Philo in Virt 12 is of special significance in the
     light of its parallel to the plurals of 1 Co 2.9
     and 10. "The mind penetrates through the depths
     of material things accurately, observing their
     whole contents and their several parts." τὰ βάθη
     seems to function similarly in 1 Co 2.10 with
     reference to the wisdom of God as a whole and the
     ἃ of its parts. The attempt that is often made,
     therefore, to link βάθος closely, if not solely to
     Gnosticism is surely misguided, as has been shown
     by B.A. Pearson, The Pneumatikos-Psychikos Termin-

ology, 108 n. 77. Against H. Conzelmann, 66; W.F. Orr - J.A. Walther, 151; etc. As Pearson argues, it is much more probable that the gnostic and the New Testament usage developed independently and simultaneously from common roots. See also R. Scroggs, "Paul: Σοφός and Πνευματικός", 51, and A.T. Hanson, New Testament Interpretation, 70ff.

86. The latter passage is important because it connects βάθος with an idea of inscrutability, or hiddenness; (cp. 1 Co 2.8 and 9). The former is meaningful because it may indicate that Philo used , like , in connection with his allegorical search for the wisdom of the scriptures; "the wisdom which lies deep below the surface".

87. A conceptual similarity between Rom 11.33 and 1 Co 2. 10-16 is suggested a) by the use of vocabulary distinctive to the earlier situation in Corinth, and b) by the fact that Paul goes on to an Old Testament citation in Romans that also figures prominently in 1 Corinthians; (i.e. Isa 40.13). Thus it seems fair to argue that Rom 11.33 can provide us with a parallel that might shed some light on 1 Co 2.10b.

88. See C.E. B. Cranfield, A Critical and Exegetical Commentary on the Epistle to the Romans, (Edinburgh: T&T Clark, 1975 and 1979 - 2 vols.), 2.588-590; and E. Kasemann, A Commentary on Romans, (Grand Rapids: Eerdmans, 1980), 318-321.

89. See H. Conzelmann, 66. "This verse proves the thesis by means of the analogy between human and divine spirit." See also C. Senft, 52; E.B. Allo, 46; and A. Robertson - A. Plummer, 44: "this verse, taken as a whole, confirms the second clause of verse 10, and thereby further explains the words διὰ τοῦ πνεύματος".

90. Though, at the same time, it is necessary to add that this analogy, in one form or another, seems to have enjoyed a very wide currency in Hellenistic times generally. See H. Conzelmann, 66, and others cited in n. 91 below.

Notes to pages 105-108

91. See B.A. Pearson, "Hellenistic-Jewish Wisdom and Paul", 55; and The Pneumatikos-Psychikos Terminology, 39. See also B.E. Gartner, "'To Know God'", passim.; R.G. Hamerton-Kelly, Pre-Existence, Wisdom, and the Son of Man, 121-123; and M.E. Isaacs, The Concept of Spirit, 80.

92. So, according to Pearson et. al., (see n. 91), Paul is opposing one 'like-by-like' principle, (God's Spirit is like man's spirit, and so God's thoughts are discoverable), with another, (God's Spirit is unlike man's spirit and so God's thoughts remain unknown to created man).

93. It is hard to know how to take the δέ of 1 Co 2.12, but the most viable option seems to be to understand it as adversative, or contrastive, indicating a change in perspective between verse 11 and verse 12.

94. Compare Judith 8.14. So also E.B. Allo, 46; C. Senft, 52; K. Maly, Mündige Gemeinde, 40; A. Robertson - A. Plummer, 44; R.A. Humphries, Paul's Rhetoric of Argumentation, 76f.; and R.B. Hoyle, The Holy Spirit in St. Paul, (London: Hodder and Stoughton, 1927), 48.

95. Compare Rom 5.17-19. The use of the Qal Vahomer form is a well known feature of rabbincial debates. See E.P. Sanders, Paul; 112, 168, 193. See also H. Muller "Der Rabbinische Qal-Wahomer-Schluss in Paulinischer Typologie", ZNW 58.73-92 (1967).

96. Our text is largely based upon the presentation of A. Robertson - A. Plummer, 44.

97. See F.F. Bruce, 39, who is one of the commentators who takes ἡμεῖς in this way.

98. This is the conclusion recognized in the grammars. See, for example, Blass-DeBrunner-Funk, A Greek Grammer of the New Testament, 196-199, especially sections 388 and 391; A.T. Robertson, A Grammer of the Greek New Testament, 997-999; and C.F.D. Moule, An Idiom-Book of New Testament Greek, (Cambridge: Cambridge University, 1953).

210

5

99. We are far from the first to suggest this alternative. See J. Weiss, 64; A. Robertson - A. Plummer, 46; C.K. Barrett, 75; and U. Wilckens, "Das Kreuz Christi", 54.

100. See above section 5.23.

101. See especially C. Senft, 53. In light of this, it may be that there should be no major break in punctuation between 1 Co 2.12 and 13. If there is none, then verse 13 is simply the conclusion of the whole thought, and the neuter plural pronoun which begins verse 13 should be read as an accusative and not a nominative.

102. See Blass-DeBrunner-Funk, A Greek Grammar of the New Testament, section 369 (3).

103. We have been unable to find any writer who cites a convincing terminological parallel to this expression, though a conceptual link is proposed by M.E. Isaacs, The Concept of Spirit; 97, 105 between the 'spirit of the world' and the anima mundi concept of Stoicism.

104. This factor serves to eliminate the view that sees in this expression a reference to a personal demonic power. The view is discussed, but not affirmed in A. Robertson - A. Plummer, 45. See also H. Conzelman, 67 n. 107.

105. See H. Conzelmann, 66-67, who suggests, but does not defend this possibility.

106. See B.E. Gartner, "'To Know God'", 218-220; B.A. Pearson, "Hellenistic-Jewish Wisdom and Paul", 40; and C. Senft, 52.

107. See C.K. Barrett, 74; F.F. Bruce, 40; and R. Scroggs, "Paul: Σοφός and Πνευματικός", 51.

108. See above pp. 105ff.

109. See B.A. Pearson, The Pneumatikos-Psychikos Terminology, 39, and "Hellenistic-Jewish Wisdom and Paul", 54. See also M.E. Isaacs, The Concept of

Spirit, 77-78; B.E. Gartner, "'To Know God'",
218-220; and C. Senft, 56.

110. The genitive expressions, as is noted by M.E.
Isaacs, The Concept of Spirit, 98, seem to point
in the same direction.   As the prepostion ἐκ appears to indicate, they are both genitives of
source, or origin.   The 'spirit of the world'
comes to belong to us in view of our origin as a
part of the created cosmos.   The Spirit that we
have received, however, has come from God.

111. See also H. Conzelman, 67 n. 111.

112. In 1 Co 2.4, the antithesis is set up between
speech ἐν πειθοῖς σοφίας λόγοις, and speech ἐν
ἀποδείξει πνεύματος. In 1 Co 2.12, a corresponding antithesis is set up between speech ἐν
διδακτοῖς ἀνθρωπίνης σοφίας λόγοις, and speech ἐν
διδακτοῖς πνεύματος. It is worthwhile noting
that in both cases λογοῖς is dropped in the second half of the antithesis, and in both πνεῦμα is
anarthrous.

113. See above section 4.4.

114. As the parallel with 1 Co 2.4 shows, ἀνθρωπίνης
is Paul's perjorative addition to the normal Corinthian expression, λόγοι σοφίας.

115. Other, alternatives are possible if one chooses
to render συγκρίνοντες as 'comparing' rather than
'interpreting'.   See A. Robertson - A. Plummer,
47, who present a complete range of options.   See
also J.D.G. Dunn, Jesus and the Spirit, 235-236,
who presents an interesting and quite unique interpretation of the phrase.

116. Compare 1 Co 12.6 where the 'word of wisdom' is a
'spiritual gift'.

117. Both Paul and the Corinthians are apparently
agreed, however, that the deeper wisdom of God is
a product of the Spirit's illumination.   The disagreement lay, as we have seen so far:
    1. In the nature of wisdom; (the Corinthians
       sought an enlightened interpretation of the

> Torah and an experience of spiritual communion with God; Paul found the result of the Spirit's working to be a knowledge of the new christological wisdom of God).
>
> 2. In the nature of spiritual illumination; (the Corinthians thought of an enlightenment of the human spirit coming as the culmination of a life ordered by the study and practice of wisdom; Paul saw a continual growth in wisdom based upon the believer's receipt of God's Spirit).
>
> 3. In the authenticating criteria of spiritual illumination; (the Corinthians saw such criteria in eloquent, learned words; Paul, however, rejects this).

118. See A.T. Lincoln, _Paradise Now and Not Yet_, 40. In addition to statistical considerations, Lincoln adds the fact that "the apostle employs these terms with no explanation, evidently expecting his readers to be familiar with them".

119. Compare the τέλειος-νήπιος contrast of 1 Co 2.6 and 3.1ff., or the σοφός-μορός contrast of 1 Co 3.18 with the πνευματικός-ψυχικός distinction.

120. See N.A. Dahl, "Paul and the Church at Corinth", 321; J.D.G. Dunn, _Unity and Diversity_, 277; R.G. Hamerton-Kelly, _Pre-Existence, Wisdom, and the Son of Man_, 120. This link between wisdom and spirit serves as a most decisive indication that the Corinthian controversy is to be connected with a Jewish background. For the link between wisdom and the Spirit is distinctive to the traditions of later Jewish wisdom literature. See above pp. 16ff., 40ff., and 54:f.

121. See U. Wilckens, _Weisheit und Torheit_; M. Winter, _Pneumatiker und Psychiker_, and W. Schmithals, _Gnosticism in Corinth_.

122. The first view seems to have been restricted to Valentinian Gnosticism, the second to be characteristic of other gnostic groups. See B.A. Pearson, _The Pneumatikos-Psychikos Terminology_, 76-81; and E.M. Yamauchi, _Pre-Christian Gnosticism_, (London: Tyndale, 1973), 14ff.

123. Undoubted parallels exist, for example, as between 1 Co 2.14ff. and Hyp Arch 138.13-15.

124. See also above pp. 1-3.

125. This proposal has been associated most recently with the works of B.A. Pearson, but it appears to have originated with J. DuPont in his work, Gnosis, (Paris: J. Gabalda, 1949), cf. 172-180.

126. Loosely quoted from B.A. Pearson, The Pneumatikos-Psychikos Terminology, 37.

127. Though, as R.A. Horsley has pointed out, the methodology of this proposal is formally the same as that of the gnostic hypothesis. See R.A. Horsley, "Pneumatikos versus Psychikos", 271 n. 7.

128. However, each of the individual terms may be found. See R.A. Horsley, "Pneumatikos versus Psychikos", 271.

129. This unsubstantiated premise lies at the center of Pearson's work. See B.A. Pearson, The Pneumatikos-Psychikos Terminology, 11-12.

130. Examples of this distinction in the Philonic corpus occur in Opif 135, LA 1.42, Det 79, 83; Heres 55, Som 1.34, Spec 4.123, and QG 2.59.

131. See R.A. Horsley, "Pneumatikos versus Psychikos", 272ff.

132. As we have seen, however, Philo was not without precedent in terms of his notion of a pattern of sapiential achievement. See above pp. 20 and 41.

133. The following summary is based upon our earlier analysis. See above pp. 52f.

134. Pearson speaks about this stage of the pattern in only two places. See The Pneumatikos-Psychikos Terminology, 39, and "Hellenistic-Jewish Wisdom and Paul", 54.

135. Ibid.

136. See above pp. 61-62.

137. This explains why none of the terms which are used in Philo to designate the position of inferior status within the contrasts are terms which are ordinarily viewed by him as negative outside the boundaries of the contrasts. The terms only become prejorative within the context of the antitheses, by virtue of a competing claim to superior status.

138. See above pp. 105ff.

139. See R.A. Horsley, "Pneumatikos versus Psychikos", and Paul and the Pneumatikoi. Horsley's other articles also seek to explain various facets of the Corinthian situation against the background of his overall thesis. These are cited above in n. 42, (chapter 4), and in the bibliography.

140. See above n. 127, 128, and 132.

141. See R.A. Horsley, "Pneumatikos versus Psychikos", 274ff.

142. Ibid. 277, 280. "It would appear, then, that the Corinthians used pneumatikos-psychikos along with the rest of these terms to make the same basic contrast between people of different levels of spiritual ability and attainment ..."

143. Horsley has made these suggestions in his unpublished doctoral dissertation, Paul and the Pneumatikoi. See pp. 78-79.

144. Ibid. 78.

145. Ibid. 79. Compare A.T. Lincoln, Paradise Now and Not Yet, 40-41. Lincoln thinks it likely that the contrast arose within Christian circles which were influenced by "Jewish-Christian wisdom speculation". See Jude 19 and James 3.15.

146. So R.A. Horsley, Paul and the Pneumatikoi, 76.

147. See above pp. 16ff., 40ff., and 54ff.

148. See above pp. 50ff.

149. So S. Safari, "Education and the Study of the Torah", 2. 945-970 in S. Safari - M. Stern, The Jewish People in the First Century, 2.945. So also m. Sota 9.15. "The Torah leads to watchfulness, watchfulness to strictness, strictness to sinlessness, sinlessness to holiness, holiness to the Holy Spirit, and this last to the resurrection of the dead."

150. So also E.P. Sanders, who argues that Hellenistic Judaism falls firmly within the sphere of Jewish convenantal nomism. See Paul, 552-557, and "The Covenant as a Soteriological Category and the Nature of Salvation in Palestinian and Hellenistic Judaism", 11-44 in Jews, Greeks, and Christians, eds. R.G. Hamerton-Kelly and R. Scroggs, (Leiden: E.J. Brill, 1976).

151. Against E.R. Goodenough, By Light, Light, passim.

152. See above pp. 119 and 120.

153. See above pp. 54f.

154. See D. Lührmann, Das Offenbarungsverstandnis bei Paulus, 135; and M. Winter, Pneumatiker und Psychiker, 212-214.

155. Accordingly, 1 Corinthians is full of practical and ethical questions, questions that betray a concern for wisdom. 1 Corinthians, however, is unlike Galations, which also seems to be written against the background of ethical and practical questions, in that the Corinthians do not appear, like their Galatian counterparts, to have emphasized the issue of circumcision and excluded the uncircumcised from the sphere of salvation. The issue was therefore not one of salvation through the law, but one of perfection through the spiritual study of the law, and this seems to account satisfactorily for the difference in Paul's tone in the two letters. 2 Corinthians, however, would indicate that the Judaizers were later able to exploit the Jewish faction within the Corinthian congregation.

156. A claim to this kind of exalted spiritual experience may also be reflected, as W.D. Davies indicates, in 2 Co 12.11 where Paul is 'forced' to recount his own experiences in this vein apparently in order to refute his opponents. See W.D. Davies, Paul, 197.

157. The whole pattern, therefore, together with the terminology might indicate a Jewish-Gentile division at Corinth. The Jewish believers saw their gentile counterparts as admitted into God's new covenant, but still distinguished themselves, as those of a higher religious experience and understanding, from others. The existence and character of the Jewish faction might explain the ascetic tendencies in 1 Corinthians, while the gentiles who rejected the law could account for the libertarian strains within the letter.

158. See H. Conzelmann, 67-68.

159. Ibid. Conzelmann, however, has not seen how the form of this question derives directly from the context of the Corinthians' belief-structure.

160. See J.D.G. Dunn, Jesus and the Spirit, 219.

161. See J.B. Lightfoot, 182; H. Wendland, 26; H. Lietzmann, 14-15.

162. So C.K. Barrett, 78.

163. Ibid. See also F.F. Bruce, 41; and W.F. Orr – J.A. Walther,, 167.

164. See 1 Co 2.14, 15; 4.3, 4; 9.3; 10.25, 27; 14.24.

165. See Bauer-Arndt-Gingrich-Danker, A Greek-English Lexicon, 56.

166. See Lk 23.14, Acts 4.9; 12.19, 24.8; 28.18, 1 Co 9.3; 14.24.

167. See, for example, Acts 17.11.

168. So J.D.G. Dunn, Jesus and the Spirit, 235.

169. On the link between wisdom and eloquence, see above section 4.4.

170. As A.T. Hanson has shown, κύριος here must be meant in reference to God, and not to Christ. See A.T. Hanson, New Testament Interpretation, 77.

171. Paul's conclusion depends, therefore, upon ἀνακρίνω and συμβίβαζω being understood as synonyms. See C.K. Barrett, 78.

172. See J.D.G. Dunn, Unity and Diversity, 52; and A. Robertson - A. Plummer, 51.

173. "'Spiritual' and 'fleshly' mark older and younger, mature and immature brothers within the same family ..." So C.K. Barrett, 79.

174. So also J.D.G. Dunn, Unity and Diversity, 208.

175. Ibid. 192-193, 293-295.

176. See J.D.G. Dunn, Jesus and the Spirit, 293-299.

177. We may note, for example, how Paul's mind moves over from one image to another in the space of a single verse in 1 Co 3.9. See P.S. Minear, The Church in the New Testament, (London: Lutterworth, 1961), 49.

178. The peculiar interrogative τί οὖν may be adduced as grammatical evidence in support of this conclusion, especially if, as C.K. Barrett believes, it is not "fully argumentative", but rather "resumptive". So C.K. Barrett, 83. R.J. McKelvey, The New Temple, (London: Oxford University, 1969); C.J. Roetzel Judgement in the Community, (Leiden: E.J. Brill, 1972); and F. Schnider - W. Stenger, "The Church as a Building and the Building up of the Church", Concilium 10.21-34 (1972) who are also in agreement with our analysis.

179. See Ex 15.17, 2 Sam 7.10, Ps 80.8, 15; Isa 5.2, 7; 60.21; 61.3, Jer 2.21, 11.17; 32.41, Ezek 17.5, 10; 19.10, 13, Hos 9.13, Amos 9.15, 2 Esd 5.23, 2 Macc 1.29. For discussion, see M.A.

Chevalier, Esprit de Dieu, Parole d'Hommes, (Neuchatel: Delachaux and Niestle, 1966), 26-31; B. Gartner, The Temple and the Community in Qumran and the New Testament, (Cambridge: Cambridge University, 1973), 124-125 F. Schnider - W. Stenger, "The Church as a Building", 22. On the question of the proper translation for γεώργιον see H. Riesenfield, The Gospel Tradition, (Philadelphia: Fortress, 1970), 197-199.

180. On the meaning of συνεργοί in 1 Co 3.9 see V.P. Furnish, "Fellow-Workers in God's Service", JBL 80.364-370 (1961).

181. See F.F. Bruce, "Apollos in the New Testament", EkkPhar 57.354-365 (1975).

182. See H. Conzelmann, 74; C. Senft, 58.

183. See C.K. Barrett, 85; W.F. Orr - J.A. Walther, 171-172; P.S. Minear, Images, 49.

184. See J. Weiss, Earliest Christianity, (New York: Harper and Row, 1959=1939 edition - 2 vols.), 1.334-336; C.K. Barrett, 85; H. Conzelmann, 73 n. 44. So also M.A. Chevalier, "La Construction de la Communauté sur le Fondement du Christ", 109-129 in Paolo a Una Chiesa Divisa, ed. L. de Lorenzi, (Rome: Abbazie di S. Paolo Fuori le Mura, 1980), 121-123.

185. So especially C.K. Barrett, 85.

186. In Old Testament literature a connection between the two metaphors is a repeated feature in Jeremiah; (cf. 1.10; 18.9; 24.6; 31.28, and 45.4). The connection is made elsewhere in pre-Christian Judaism in the literature associated with the Qumran community, in some apocalyptic material, and in the writings of Philo. It is also evidenced in Greek sources. For references and discussion see A. Fridrichsen, "Ackerbau und Hausbau", TSK 94.135-136 (1922); B. Gartner, Temple and Community, 28-29; R.G. Hamerton-Kelly, Pre-Existence, Wisdom, and the Son of Man, 124-125; and P. Vielhauer, Oikodome, (Karlsrühe: Tron, 1940), 79.

187. To try and separate the kerygma from the Christ-event is impossible. Paul's reference in 1 Co 3.11 is neither exclusively impersonal, as is suggested by the parallel between 1 Co 3.10 and 11a, nor exclusively personal per 1 Co 3.11b. It is both. The foundation of the cummunity lies in the Christ-event of which Paul's proclamation is itself a part; (cf. 1 Co 2.5).

188. In this connection, Paul makes use of a self-designation of his own. As an evangelist who brings the message of the Christ-event, Paul calls, himself σοφός ἀρχιτέκτων. As R.G. Hamerton-Kelly has shown, the term against its most probable background, (i.e. Exod 28.3; 31.3; 35.31), anticipates the identification between God's building and God's temple that becomes explicit in 1 Co 3.16-17. See R.G. Hamerton-Kelly, Pre-Existence, Wisdom, and the Son of Man, 125. n. 3. Against J.M. Ford, "'You are God's Sukkah' (1 Co 3.10-17)", JBL 21.139-142.

189. Helpful backgrounds to Paul's thought at this point appear in the Testament of Abraham. See C.W. Fishburne, "1 Corinthians 3.10-15 and the Testament of Abraham", NTS 17.109-115 (1970/71). In a baraitha from the early tannaitic period reflecting debate between the school of Hillel and the school of Shammai one finds further parallel material. See J.T. Townsend, "1 Corinthians 3.10-15 and the School of Shammai", HTR 61.500-504 (1968).

190. The thought of purgatory in relation to 1 Co 3.15 is clearly mistaken. The fire is testing, not purifying. So H. Conzelmann, 77, following J. Gnilka, Ist 1 Corinthians 3.10-15 ein Schriftszeugnis für das Fegfeuer, (Düsseldorf: Trultsch, 1955). See also P. Vielhauer, Oikodome, 78-86, and J. Pfammater, Die Kirche als Bau, (Rome: Liberia Editrice Dell' Universita Gregoriana, 1960), 19-44.

191. See J.D.G. Dunn, Jesus and the Spirit, 295.

192. Despite the fact that there is a very real concentration upon the doctrinal, or didactic aspect

of the Corinthian situation in 1 Co 3.10-15, it
is important to notice that the personal dimension is still present; (cp. 1 Co 3.5-9). This is
evident, for example, in 1 Co 3.10a when Paul
speaks about 'another' who is currently at work,
(ἐποικοδομεῖ), among the Corinthians. Moreover,
it appears as if this is the person who has
called forth the warnings of 1 Co 3.10b and 11,
at least in the first instance; (even if the ad-
monitions are also meant to have a more general
currency as well). But who was this individual?
He is evidently not Apollos, for Apollos' work at
Corinth is repeatedly referred to in the past
tense in 1 Co 3.5-9 and no exception is taken to
his efforts. What little evidence there is seems
to point us in the direction of a relation between the ἀλλός of 1 Co 3.10 and Cephas, or a
person claiming to operate with his authority.
See C.K. Barrett; 87-88, 90-91; "Christianity at
Corinth","", 290-297; "Cephas and Corinth", 28-39
in Essays on Paul, by C.K. Barrett, (London:
SPCK, 1982); F.F. Bruce, 43; T.W. Manson, Studies
in the Gospels and Epistles, (Manchester:
Manchester University, 1962), 190-224; and M.A.
Chevalier, "La Construction de la Communate",
125-128. If this identification is correct, it
would add further weight to the connection between wisdom at Corinth and Judaism.

193. The parallels within the Qumran literature are
very close here, as has been shown by B. Gartner,
The Temple and the Community, 56-60. But they
should be set within a wider context, as has been
argued forcefully by R.J. McKelvey. McKelvey
points to three streams of thought in Judaism in
connection with the temple; (i.e. one can find
discussion in the sources about a 'new temple', a
'heavenly temple', and a 'spiritual temple').
See R.J. McKelvey, The New Temple, 9-57.

194. A reference to Paul's oral instruction while in
Corinth is probably signified, but J.C. Hurd has
proposed that 1 Co 3.16 be interpreted in the
light of Paul's 'previous' letter to the Corinthians; (cf. 1 Co 5.9-13), the contents of which
Hurd finds in 2 Co 6.16-7.1. See J.C. Hurd, The

Origin of 1 Corinthians, 235-237.   See also R.J.
McKelvey, The New Temple, 100.

195.   So M. Fraeyman, "La Spiritualisation de L'Ideé du
Temple   dans   les   Epitrès   Pauliniennes",   ETL
23.378-412 (1947),   387-388.   See also K. Maly,
Mundige Gemeinde,   70; H.   Conzelmann,   75;   C.K.
Barrett, 90.   Compare 1 Co 6.19-20.   "The conception of the body of the individual Christian be-
liever as the temple of God in this text is best
explained as a particularlization of the conception of the church as the temple."   So R.J.
McKelvey, The New Temple, 102.

196.   It is interesting, however, to consider for a
moment the likelihood of a further Corinthian
background to Paul's temple metaphor in 1 Co
3.16-17.   For within the Philonic literature, in
contrast to the Pauline emphasis, one finds a
conception of the individual soul as the temple
of God.   In Cher 99-101, for example, one finds
this thought expressed in language closely ap-
poximating 1 Co 3.16-17, and in Som 1.149, there
is a clear reference to the soul as God's temple.
With reference to these passages, and to the general similarity between Corinthian thought and
Philonic thought, it seems possible to suggest
that the Corinthians could have been influenced
by such an individualistic belief.

197.   So R.J. McKelvey, The New Temple, 101.   See also
M. Fraeyman, "La Spiritualisation de L'Ideé du
Temple",   388; F.F. Bruce, 45; A.   Robertson - A.
Plummer, 66.

198.   On the form of 1 Co 3.17 see E. Kasemann, "Sen-
tences of Holy Law in the New Testament", 66-81
in New Testament Questions of Today by E.
Kasemann, (London: SCM, 1969), 66-88.   See also
A.   Robertson - A. Plummer, 67, and B. Gartner,
The Temple and the Community, 59.

199.   The reason for this distinction is advanced in 1
Co 3.17b: "the temple of God is holy", and so to
divide the community into distinct groups is, in
Paul's view, to desecrate the sanctity of God's

dwelling place.   See R.J. McKelvey, <u>The</u> <u>New</u> Temple, 101.

200.   See above pp. 67, 71ff., and 88.   So also H. Conzelmann, 79, C.K. Barrett, 93; C. Senft, 62; and J. Weiss, 86.

1. See F.C. Baur, "Die Christuspartie in der korinthi-
schen Gemeinde. Der Gegensatz des paulinichen und
petrinischen Christentums in der altesten Kirche.
Der Apostel Petrus in Rom.", TZTH 4.61-206 (1831).

2. For a useful discussion of this view see J.C. Hurd,
The Origin of 1 Corinthians, 99-101. See also the
presentation of C.K. Barrett in "Christianity at
Corinth"; 273, 286-297. According to Barrett, the
Jewish group at Corinth, "adopted a Jewish-
Christian 'nomistic' attitude, not extreme enough
to divide the church, (as a demand for circumcision
would have done), or to disenfranchise Paul from
the apostolic body, but awkward enough to raise
difficulties and to cast a certain amount of doubt
on Paul's status"; (273).

A SELECTED BIBLIOGRAPHY

The following bibliography contains, with
several exceptions, only those books and
articles that have been cited within the
body or the footnotes of this book.   The
absence of any particular work does not
necessarily indicate that it has not been
consulted.

Articles appearing in works of standard
reference, such as lexica, grammars, and
encyclopedias, have everywhere been omit-
ted.

Abbreviations follow the forms established in the footnotes.

Allen, L.C. "The Old Testament Background
of (προ)'ορίζειν in the New
Testament". <u>NTS</u> 17.104-108
(1970/71).

Allo, E.B. <u>Saint Paul, Première Épître aux
Corinthiens.</u>
Paris: J. Gabalda, 1956.

Alon, G. <u>The Jews in Their Land in the
Talmudic Age.</u>
Jerusalem: Magnes, 1980.

Anderson, A.A. "The Use of 'Ruah' in 1 QS, 1
QH, and 1 QM". <u>JSS</u> 7.293-303
(1962).

<u>The Book of Psalms.</u>
London: Marshall, Morgan, and
Scott, 1972 - 2 volumes.

Arrington, F.L. <u>Paul's Aeon Theology in First
Corinthians.</u> (Washington, DC:
University Press of America,
1978).

Baer, R.A. <u>Philo's Use of the Categories
Male and Female.</u>
Leiden: E.J. Brill, 1970.

Baird, W. "Among the Mature - The Idea of
Wisdom in 1 Corinthians 2.6".
<u>Int</u> 13.425-432 (1959).

Baldwin, C.S. <u>Ancient Rhetoric and Poetic.</u>
Gloucester Massachusettes:
Peter Smith, 1959=1924 edition.

Barrett, C.K. "Christianity at Corinth".
<u>BJRL</u> 46.269-297 (1964).

<u>A Commentary on the First
Epistle to the Corinthians.</u>
London: A&C Black, 1971 - 2nd
edition.

Essays on Paul.
London: S.P.C.K., 1982.

Bauckmann, E.G.   "Die Proverbien und die Spruche
                         des Jesus Sirach".
                         ZAW 72.33-63 (1960).

Baumann, R.   Mitte und Norm des
                         Christlichen, Eine Auslegung
                         von 1 Kor. 1.1-3.4.
                         Münster: Aschendorff, 1968.

Beavin, E.L.   Ruah Hakodesh in Some Early
                         Jewish Literature.
                         An unpublished doctoral
                         dissertation completed at
                         Vanderbilt University in 1961.

Belkin, S.   Philo and the Oral Law. The
                         Philonic Interpretation of
                         Biblical Law in relation to the
                         Palestinian Halakah.
                         Cambridge Massachusettes:
                         Harvard University, 1940.

Berwick, W.P.   The Way of Salvation in the
                         Wisdom of Solomon.
                         An unpublished doctoral
                         dissertation completed at
                         Boston University Graduate
                         School in 1957.

Betz, O.   Offenbarung und
                         Schriftforschung in der
                         Qumransekte.
                         Tübingen: J.C.B. Mohr, 1960.

Bjerklund, C.J.   PARAKALO.
                         Oslo: Universität, 1967.

Black, M.   The Scrolls and Christian
                         Origins.
                         London: Thomas Nelson, 1961.

Black, M.   The History of the Jewish
Millar, F.   People in the Age of Jesus
Vermes, G.   Christ, (175BC - AD 135).
                         A New English Version.
                         Edinburgh: T&T Clark, 1973 and
                         1979 - 2 volumes.

Bonnard, P.E.

La Sagesse En Personne Annoncée
et Venue: Jesus Christ.
Paris: Les Editions du Cerf,
1966.

Borgen, P.

Bread from Heaven.
Leiden: E.J. Brill, 1965.

Braun, H.

Qumran und das Neue Testament.
Tubingen: J.C.B. Mohr, 1966 - 2
volumes.

Wie Man Über Gott Nicht Denken
soll.
Tubingen: J.C.B. Mohr, 1971.

Brehier, E.

Les Ideés Philosophiques et
Religieuses de Philon
D'Alexandrie.
Paris: J. Vrin, 1925 - 2nd
edition.

Brown, R.E.

The Semitic Background of the
Term "Mystery" in the New
Testament.
Philadelphia: Fortress, 1968.

Bruce, F.F.

The Teacher of Righteousness in
the Qumran Texts.
London: Tyndale, 1957.

"The Dead Sea Habakkuk Scroll"
ALUOS 1.5-25 (1958/59).

Biblical Exegesis in the Qumran
Texts.
London: Tyndale, 1960.

"Holy Spirit in the Qumran
Texts".
ALUOS 6.49-55 (1969).

I & II Corinthians.
London: Marshall, Morgan, and
Scott, 1971.

"Apollos in the New Testament".
EkkPhar 57.354-365 (1975).

231

Bultmann, R.   Glauben und Verstehen.
                    Tübingen: J.C.B. Mohr, 1954 - 2
                    volumes.

Cadbury, H.J.   "The Grandson of Ben Sira".
                    HTR 48.219-225 (1955).

Caevel, J. de   "La Connaissance Religieuse
                    dans les Hymnes D'Action de
                    Grâces de Qumran".
                    ETL 38.435-460 (1962).

Caird, G.B.   Principalities and Powers. A
                    Study in Pauline Theology.
                    Oxford: Oxford University,
                    1956.

Cargounis, C.C.   The Ephesian Mysterion.
                    Lund: Carl Bloms, 1977.

Carmignac, J.   "Les Rapports entre
                    L'Ecclesiastiqué et Qumran".
                    RevQ 3.209-218 (1961/62).

Carr, A.W.   "The Rulers of this Age - 1
                    Corinthians 2.6-8".
                    NTS 23.20-35 (1977).

                    Angels and Principalities. The
                    Background, Meaning, and
                    Development of the Pauline
                    Phrase Hai Archai kai hai
                    Exousai.
                    Cambridge: Cambridge
                    University, 1981.

Chadwick, H.   "Philo and the Beginnings of
                    Christian Thought".
                    137-157 in The Cambridge
                    History of Later Greek and
                    Early Medieval Philosophy, ed.
                    A.H. Armstong.
                    Cambridge: Cambridge
                    University, 1970.

Charlesworth, J.H.   "The Origin and Subsequent
                            History of the Authors of the
                            Dean Sea Scrolls: Four
                            Transitional Phases among the
                            Qumran Essenes"
                            RevQ 10.203-213 (1980).

Chevalier, M.A.   Esprit de Dieu, Parole
                            d'Hommes.
                            Neuchatel: Delachaux & Niestle,
                            1966.

                            "La Construction de la
                            Communauté sur le Fondement du
                            Christ".
                            109-129 in Paolo a Una Chiesa
                            Divisa, ed. L. de Lorenzi.
                            Rome: Abbazia di S. Paolo Fuori
                            le Mura, 1980.

Christ, F.   Jesus Sophia. Die Sophia-
                            Christologie bei den
                            Synoptikern.
                            Zurich: Zwingli, 1970.

Clements, R.E.   Isaiah 1-39.
                            London: Marshall, Morgan, and
                            Scott, 1980.

Colson, F.H.   Philo.
Whittaker, G.H.   Cambridge, Mass: Harvard
                            University, 1929 - 1962; 10
                            volumes.

Conzelmann, H.   "Paulus und die Weisheit"
                            NTS 12.231-244 (1965/66).

                            1 Corinthians.
                            Philadelphia: Fortress, 1975.

Coppens, J.L.   "Le Don de L'Esprit D'Apres les
                            Textes de Qumran et le
                            Quatrième Évangile" 209-223 in
                            L'Evangile de Jean, ed. M.E.
                            Boismard.
                            Louvain: Desclée de Brouwer,
                            1958.

Coppens, J.L.   "'Mystery' in the Theology of
Saint Paul and its Parallels at
Qumran"
132-158 in Paul and Qumran, ed.
J. Murphy O'Connor.
London: G. Chapman, 1968.

Cranfield, C.E.B.   A Critical and Exegetical
Commentary on the Epistle to
the Romans.
Edinburgh: T&T Clark, 1975 and
1979 - 2 volumes.

Crenshaw, J.L.   Old Testament Wisdom.
London: S.C.M., 1982.

Cross, F.M., Jr.   The Ancient Library of Qumran
and Modern Biblical Studies.
London: Duckworth, 1958.

Cullmann, O.   Christ and Time.
London: S.P.C.K., 1957.

Dahl, N.A.   "Paul and the Church at Corinth
according to 1 Corinthians
1.10-4.21".
313-335 in Christian History
and Interpretation, eds. W.
Farmer, C.F.D. Moule, and R.
Niebuhr.
Cambridge: Cambridge
University, 1967.

Jesus in the Memory of the
Early Church.
Minneapolis: Augsburg, 1976.

Davies, W.D.   "Paul and the Dead Sea Scrolls:
Flesh and Spirit".
157-183 in The Scrolls and the
New Testament, ed. K. Stendahl.
London: S.C.M., 1958.

Christian Origins and Judaism.
Philadelphia: Westminister,
1962.

Paul and Rabbinic Judaism.
London: S.P.C.K., 1970 - 2nd
edition.

234

Deden, D.   "Le 'Mystère' Paulinien".
                             ETL 13.403-432 (1936).

Denis, A.M.   _Les Thèmes de Connaissance_ dans
                             le Document de Damas.
                             Louvain: Desclée du Brouwer,
                             1967.

Dibelius, M.   _Die Geisterwelt im Glauben des_
                             Paulus.
                             Göttingen: Vandenhoeck &
                             Rupprecht, 1909.

DiLella, A.   "Conservative and Progressive
                             Theology: Sirach and Wisdom".
                             401-416 in _Studies in Ancient_
                             Israelite Wisdom, ed. J.L.
                             Crenshaw.
                             New York: KTAV, 1976.

                             The Hebrew Text of Sirach.
                             The Hague: Mouton & Co., 1966.

Drummond, J.   _Philo Judaeus._
                             London: Williams & Norgate,
                             1888.

Duesberg, H.   _Les Scribes Inspirés._
Fransen, I.   Bruges: Éditions de Maredsous,
                             1966.

Dunn, J.D.G.   _Baptism in the Holy Spirit._
                             London: S.C.M., 1970.

                             Jesus and the Spirit.
                             Philadelphia: Westminister,
                             1975.

                             Unity and Diversity in the New
                             Testament.
                             Philadelphia: Westminister,
                             1977.

                             Christology in the Making.
                             London: S.C.M., 1980.

Dupont, J.   Gnosis. La Connaissance
                          Religieuse dans les Épîtres de
                          Saint Paul.
                          Paris: J. Gabalda, 1949.

Dupont-Sommer, A.   The Essene Writings from
                          Qumran.
                          Oxford: Blackwell, 1961.

Edwards, T.C.   A Commentary on the First
                          Epistle to the Corinthians.
                          London: Hodder and Stoughton,
                          1903.

Eichrodt, W.   A Theology of the Old
                          Testament.
                          London: S.C.M., 1972 - 2
                          volumes.

Ellis, E.E.   Paul's Use of the Old
                          Testament.
                          London: Oliver and Boyd, 1957.

                          Prophecy and Hermeneutic in
                          Early Christianity.
                          Grand Rapids: Eerdmans, 1978.

Ellis, P.F.   "Salvation through the Wisdom
                          of the Cross".
                          324-333 in Sin, Salvation, and
                          the Spirit, ed. D. Durken.
                          Collegeville: Liturgical, 1979.

Feuillet, A.   "L'Enigmé de 1 Corinthians
                          2.9".
                          RB 70.52-74 (1963).

                          Le Christ: Sagesse de Dieu.
                          Paris: J. Gabalda, 1966.

Feuillet, R.   "Témoine du Christ Crucife. 1
                          Co 2.1-5".
                          ASeign 36.11-16 (1974).

Fichtner, J.

Die Altorientalische Weisheit
in ihrer Israelitisch-Jüdischen
Auspragung. Eine Studie zur
Nationalisierung der Weisheit
in Israel.
Giessen: Alfred Töpelmann,
1933.

Fiddes, P.S.

The Hiddenness of Wisdom in the
Old Testament and later
Judaism.
An unpublished doctoral thesis
completed at Oxford University
in 1976.

Fishburne, C.W.

"1 Co 3.10-15 and the Testament
of Abraham".
NTS 17.109-115 (1970/71).

Flusser, D.

"The Dead Sea Sect and
pre-Pauline Christianity".
217-246 in Scripta
Hierosolymitana 4: Aspects of
the Dead Sea Scrolls, eds.
C. Rabin and Y. Yadin.
Jerusalem: Magnes, 1958.

Foerster, W.

"Der Heilige Geist im
Spätjüdentum".
NTS 8.117-134 (1962).

Ford, J.M.

"'You are God's Sukkah' (1 Co
3.10-17)".
JBL 21.139-142.

Fraeymann, M.

"La Spiritualisation de L'Idée
du Temple dans les Épîtres
Pauliniennes".
ETL 23.378-412.

Fridrichsen, A.

"Ackerbau und Hausbau"
TSK 94.135-136 (1927).

Funk, R.

Language, Hermeneutic, and the
Word of God.
New York: Harper and Row, 1966.

Furnish, V.P.

"Fellow-workers in God's
Service".
JBL 80.364-370 (1961).

Garnet, P.   Salvation and Atonement in the
                            Qumran Scrolls.
                            Tubingen: J.C.B. Mohr, 1977.

Gartner, B.   The Temple and the Community in
                            Qumran and the New Testament.
                            Cambridge: Cambridge
                            University, 1973.

Gartner, B.E.   "The Pauline and Johannine Idea
                            of 'To Know God' against the
                            Hellenistic Background".
                            NTS 14.209-231 (1967/68).

Gaster, T.H.   The Scriptures of the Dead Sea
                            Sect.
                            London: Secker and Warburg,
                            1957.

Germann, H.   "Jesus ben Siras Dankgebet und
                            die Hodajoth".
                            TZ 19.81-87 (1963).

Gibbs, J.M.   "Wisdom, Power, and Well-Being"
                            119-155 in Studia Biblica 1978,
                            ed. E.A. Livingstone.
                            Sheffield: J.S.O.T., 1980 - 3
                            volumes.

Gillespie, T.W.   "A Pattern of Prophetic Speech
                            in First Corinthians".
                            JBL 97.74-95 (1978).

Gnilka, J.   Ist 1 Corinthians 3.10-15 ein
                            Schriftszeugnis für das
                            Fegfeuer?
                            Düsseldorf: Trultsch, 1955.

Goodenough, E.R.   By Light, Light. The Mystic
                            Gospel of Hellenistic Judaism.
                            Amsterdam: Philo Press,
                            1969=1935 edition.

                            An Introduction to Philo
                            Judaeus.
                            New Haven: Yale University,
                            1940.

Grant, R.M.   The Letter and the Spirit.
                     London: S.P.C.K., 1957.

Gray, G.B.   The Forms of Hebrew Poetry.
                     London: Hodder and Stoughton,
                     1915.

Grayston, K.   "Not with a Rod".
                     ExpTim 88.13-16 (1976/77).

Grosheide, F.W.   A Commentary on the First
                     Epistle to the Corinthians.
                     London: Marshall, Morgan, and
                     Scott, 1954.

Grundmann, W.   "Die νήπιοι in der Christlichen
                     Paranese".
                     NTS 5.188-205 (1958/59).

Hadot, J.   Penchant Mauvais et Volonté
                     Libre dans la Sagesse de Ben
                     Sira.
                     Brussels: Universitaires,
                     1970.

Hamerton-Kelly, R.G. Pre-Existence, Wisdom, and the
                     Son of Man.
                     Cambridge: Cambridge
                     University, 1973.

Hanson, A.T.   The New Testament
                     Interpretation of Scripture.
                     London: S.P.C.K., 1980.

Hartman, L.A.   "Some Remarks on 1 Corinthians
                     2.1-5".
                     SEA 34.109-120 (1974).

Haspecker, J.   Gottesfurcht bei Jesus Sirach.
                     Ihre Religiose Struktür und
                     ihre Literarische und
                     Doktrinare Bedeutung.
                     Rome: Päplisches Bibelinstitüt,
                     1967.

Heinemann, I.   "Philons Lehre vom Heiligen
                     Geist und der Intüitiven
                     Erkenntnis".
                     MGWJ 64.8-29; 101-122 (1920).

239

Hengel, M.

Judaism and Hellenism. Studies in their Encounter in Palestine during the early Hellenistic Period.
London: S.C.M., 1974 - 2 volumes.

"Besprechung von Th. Middendorp, Die Stellung Jesu ben Siras zwischen Jüdentum und Hellenismus".
JSJ 5.83-87 (1974).

The Son of God. The Origins of Christology and the History of Jewish Hellenistic Religion.
London: S.C.M., 1976.

Jews, Greeks, and Barbarians.
London: S.C.M., 1980.

Hering, J.

La Première Épître de Saint Paul aux Corinthiens.
London: Epworth, 1962 - 2nd edition.

Holmes, S.

"The Wisdom of Solomon" 1.518-568 in The Apocrypha and Pseudipigrapha of the Old Testament, ed. R.H. Charles.
Oxford: Clarendon, 1913 - 2 volumes.

Holm-Nielsen, S.

Hodayot. Psalms from Qumran.
Aarhus: Universitets, 1960.

Hooker, M.D.

"'Beyond the things which are written': An Examination of 1 Corinthians 4.6".
NTS 10.127-132 (1963/64).

"Hard Sayings - 1 Corinthians 3.2"
Theol 69.19-22 (1966).

Pauline Pieces.
London: Epworth, 1979.

Horgan, M.P.P.	Pesharim: Qumran Interpretations of Biblical Books. Washington D.C.: Catholic Biblical Association, 1979.
Horsley, R.A.	Paul and the Pneumatikoi. First Corinthians Investigated in Terms of the Conflict between Two different Religious Mentalities. An unpublished doctoral dissertation completed at Harvard University in 1970.
	"Pneumatikos versus Psychikos: Distinctions of Status among the Corinthians". HTR 69.269-288 (1976).
	"Wisdom of Word and Words of Wisdom in Corinth". CBQ 39.224-239 (1977).
	"'How can some of you say that there is no resurrection of the dead?': Spiritual Elitism in Corinth". NT 20.203-231 (1978).
	"Spiritual Marriage with Sophia". VigChr 33.30-54 (1979).
	"Gnosis in Corinth: 1 Corinthians 8.1-6". NTS 27.32-51 (1980).
Hoyle, R.B.	The Holy Spirit in Saint Paul. London: Hodder and Stoughton, 1927.
Humphries, R.A.	Paul's Rhetoric of Argumentation in 1 Corinthians 1-4. An unpublished doctoral dissertation completed at The Graduate Theological Union in 1979.

Hurd, J.C., Jr.   The Origin of 1 Corinthians.
                  London: S.P.C.K., 1965.

Imschoot, P. van "Sagesse et Ésprit dans
                  L'Ancien Testament".
                  RB 47.23-53 (1938).

Isaacs, M.E.   The Concept of Spirit. A Study
                  of Pneuma in Hellentistic
                  Judaism and its bearing upon
                  the New Testament.
                  London: Heythrop, 1976.

Jacob, E.   "Wisdom and Religion in
                  Sirach".
                  247-260 in Israelite Wisdom,
                  eds. J.G. Gammie, W.A.
                  Brugemann, W.L. Humphrys and
                  J.M. Ward.
                  Missoula: Scholars, 1978.

Johnston, G.   "'Spirit' and 'Holy Spirit' in
                  the Qumran Literature".
                  27-42 in New Testament
                  Sidelights, ed. H.K. McArthur.
                  Hartford: Hartford, 1960.

Kasemann, E.   New Testament Questions of
                  Today.
                  London: S.C.M., 1969.

                  A Commentary on Romans.
                  Grand Rapids: Eerdmans, 1980.

Kennedy, H.A.A.   Philo's Contribution to
                  Religion.
                  New York: Hodder and Stoughton,
                  1919.

Kigne, J.J.   "'We', 'Us', and 'Our' in 1 and
                  2 Corinthians".
                  NT 8.171-179 (1966).

Kim, S.   The Origin of Paul's Gospel.
                  Tübingen: J.C.B. Mohr, 1981.

242

Klein, F.N.   Die Lichtterminologie bei
                       Philon von Alexandrien und in
                       den Hermetischen Schriften.
                       Leiden: E.J. Brill, 1962.

Knox, J.L.   "The Divine Wisdom".
                       JTS 230-237 (1937).

Koole, J.L.   "Die Bibel des Ben Sira".
                       OTS 14.374-396 (1965).

Küchler, M.   Fruhjüdische
                       Weisheitstraditionen. Zum
                       Fortgang Weisheitlichen Denkens
                       im Bereich des Frühjüdischen
                       Jahweglaubens.
                       Fribourg: Universitats, 1979.

Kuhn, H.W.   Enderwartung und Gegenwartiges
                       Heil. Untersuchungen zu den
                       Gemeindeliedern von Qumran.
                       Göttingen: Vandenhoeck &
                       Rupprecht, 1966.

Larcher, C.   Études sur le Livre de la
                       Sagesse.
                       Paris: J. Gabalda, 1969.

Laurentin, A.   Le Pneuma dans la Doctrine de
                       Philon.
                       Paris: Desclée de Brouwer,
                       1951.

Leaney, A.R.C.   The Rule of Qumran and its
                       Meaning.
                       London: S.C.M., 1966.

                       "The Experience of God in
                       Qumran and in Paul".
                       BJRL 51.431-452 (1968/69).

Lehmann, M.R.   "Ben Sira and the Qumran
                       Literature".
                       REVQ 3.103-116 (1961/62).

Lewy, H.   Philo. Selections from the
                       Philosphical Writings.
                       Oxford: Phaidon, 1946.

Licht, J.   "The Doctrine of the
                             Thanksgiving Scroll".
                             IEJ 6.1-13; 89-101 (1956).

Lietzmann, H.   An die Korinther I/II.
Kummel, W.G.   Tübingen: J.C.B. Mohr, 1949
                             - 4th edition.

Lightfoot, J.B.   Notes on the Epistles of Saint
                             Paul.
                             Grand Rapids: Zondervan, 1957.

Lincoln, A.T.   Paradise Now and Not Yet.
                             Cambridge: Cambridge
                             University, 1981.

Lipscomb, W.L.   "Wisdom at Qumran".
Sanders, J.A.   277-285 in Israelite Wisdom,
                             eds. J.G. Gammie, W.A.
                             Bruggeman, W.L. Humphrys, and
                             J.M. Ward.
                             Missoula: Scholars, 1978.

Lohse, E.   The New Testament Environment.
                             London: S.C.M., 1976.

                             Die Texte aus Qumran.
                             München: Kosel, 1971.

Lührmann, D.   Das Offenbarungsverstandnis bei
                             Paulus und in den Paulinischen
                             Gemeinden.
                             Neukirchen: Neukirchener, 1965.

MacDonald, J.I.H.   Kerygma and Didache. The
                             Articulation and Structure of
                             the Earliest Christian Message.
                             Cambridge: Cambridge
                             University, 1980.

MacGregor, G.H.C.   "Principalities and Powers: The
                             Cosmic Background of Saint
                             Paul's Thought".
                             NTS 1.17-29 (1954/55).

244

Mack, B.L.   Logos und Sophia.
Untersuchungen zur
Weisheitstheologie im
Hellenistischen Jüdentum.
Göttingen: Vandenhoeck &
Rupprecht, 1973.

MacKelvey, R.J.   The New Temple.
London: Oxford University,
1969.

Maier, G.   Mensch und Freier Wille. Nach
den Jüdischen Religionsparteien
zwischen Ben Sira und Paulus.
Tübingen: J.C.B. Mohr, 1971.

Maly, K.   Mündige Gemeinde.
Untersuchungen zur Pastoralen
Führung des Apostels Paulus im
1 Korintherbrief.
Stuttgart: Katholisches
Bibelwerk, 1967.

Manson, T.W.   Studies in the Gospels and
Epistles.
Manchester: Manchester
University, 1962.

Mansoor, M.   The Thanksgiving Hymns.
Leiden: E.J. Brill, 1961.

Marböck, J.   Weisheit im Wandel.
Untersuchungen zur
Weisheitstheologie bei Ben
Sira.
Bonn: Peter Hanstein, 1971.

"Gesetz und Weisheit. Zum
Verstandnis das Gesetzes bei
Jesus Sira".
BZ 20.1-21 (1976).

"Sir 38.24-39.11: Der
Schriftgelehrte Weise".
293-316 in La Sagesse de
L'Ancien Testament, ed. M.
Gilbert.
Leuven: Université, 1979.

Marcus, R.	Philo. Quaestiones et Solutiones in Genesim et Exodum. Cambridge, Mass: Harvard University Press, 1969 and 1970 - 2 volumes.
Martin, J.	Antike Rhetorik: Technik und Method. München: Beck, 1974.
Masson, C.	"L'Évangile et la Sagesse selon 1 Co 1.17-3.23". RThPh 6.95-110 (1957).
Meeks, W.A. Wilken, R.L.	Jews and Christians in Antioch in the First Four Centuries of the Common Era. Missoula: Scholars, 1978.
Metzger, B.M.	A Textual Commentary on the Greek New Testament. London: U.B.S., 1975.
	The Oxford Annotated Apocrypha. Revised Standard Version. New York: Oxford University, 1977 - 2nd edition.
Middendorp, Th.	Die Stellung Jesu ben Siras zwischen Jüdentum und Hellenismus. Leiden: E.J. Brill, 1973.
Miller, G.W.	"ΟΙ ΑΡΧΟΝΤΕΣ ΤΟΥ ΑΙΩΝΟΣ ΤΟΥΤΟΥ - A New Look at 1 Corinthians 2.6-8". JBL 91.522-528 (1972).
Minear, P.S.	The Church in the New Testament. London: Lutterworth, 1961.
Montague, G.T.	The Holy Spirit. Growth of a Biblical Tradition. New York: Paulist, 1976.
Montgomery, J.W.	"Wisdom as a Gift". Int 16.43-64 (1962).

Moore, G.F.   Judaism in the First Centuries
of the Christian Era. The Age
of the Tannaim.
Cambridge Massachusettes:
Harvard University, 1927.

Mühlenberg, E.   "Das Probleme der Offenbarung
in Philo von Alexandrien".
ZNW 64.1-18 (1973).

Müller, H.P.   "Der Rabbinsche
Qal-Wahomer-Schlüss in
Paulinischer Typologie".
ZNW 58.73-92 (1967).

Munck, J.   Paul and the Salvation of
Mankind.
London: S.P.C.K., 1959.

Nickelsburg, B.W.E.   Jewish Literature between the
Bible and the Mishnah. A
Historical and Literary
Introduction.
London: S.C.M., 1981.

Nikiprowetzky, V.   "L'Exegèse de Philon
D'Alexandrie".
RHPR 53.309-329 (1973).

Le Commentaire de L'Écriture
chèz Philon D'Alexandrie.
Leiden: E.J. Brill, 1977.

Nötscher, F.   Zur Theologischen Terminologie
der Qumran-Texte.
Bonn: Peter Hanstein, 1956.

"Heligkeit in den
Qumranschriften".
RevQ 2.315-344 (1959/60).

Von Alten zum Neuen Testament.
Bonn: Peter Hanstein, 1962.

Orr, W.F.   1 Corinthians.
Walther, J.A.   New York: Doubleday, 1976.

Päscher, J.   Der Königsweg zu wieder gebürt
                            und Vergottung bei Philon von
                            Alexandreia.
                            Paderborn: Publisher Unknown,
                            1931.

Pautrel, R.   "Ben Sira et le Stoicisme".
                            RSR 51.535-549 (1963).

Pearson, B.A.   The Pneumatikos-Psychikos
                            Terminology in 1 Corinthians.
                            Missoula: Scholars, 1973.

                            "Hellenistic-Jewish Wisdom
                            Speculation and Paul".
                            43-66 in Aspects of Wisdom in
                            Judaism and Early Christianity,
                            ed. R.L. Wilken.
                            Notre Dame: Notre Dame
                            University, 1975.

Pesce, M.   Paolo a gli arconti a Corinto.
                            Brescia: Paideia Editria, 1977.

Peterson, N.E.   "1 Korinther 1.18f. und die
                            Thematik des Jüdischen
                            Busstages".
                            Bib 32.97-103 (1951).

Pfammater, J.   Die Kirche als Bau.
                            Rome: Liberia Editrice Dell'
                            Universita Gregoriana, 1960.

Pfeiffer, G.   Ursprung und Wesen der
                            Hypostasenvorstellungen im
                            Jüdentum.
                            Stüttgart: Calwer, 1967.

Pfeiffer, R.H.   A History of New Testament
                            Times with an Introduction to
                            the Apocrypha.
                            New York: Harper Brothers,
                            1949.

Philonenko, M.   "Quod Occulus non vidit, 1 Co
                            2.9".
                            TZ 15.51-52 (1959).

Plessis, P.J. du ΤΕΛΕΙΟΣ. The Idea of
                 Perfection in the New
                 Testament.
                 Uitgave: J.H. Kok N.V. Kampen,
                 1959.

Priest, J.   "Ben Sir 45.25 in light of the
                 Qumran Literature".
                 RevQ 17.111-118 (1964).

Prigent, P.   "Ce Que L'Oeil n'à pas vú, 1 Co
                 2.9. Histoire et Prehistoire
                 d'une Citation".
                 TZ 14.416-429 (1958).

Prumm, K.   "Zur Neutestamentlichen
                 Gnosis-Problematik.
                 Gnostischer Hintergrund und
                 Lehreinschlag in den beiden
                 Eingangskapiteln von 1
                 Korinthians?"
                 ZKTh 87.339-442 and 88.1-50
                 (1965 and 1966).

Pryke, J.   "'Spirit' and 'Flesh' in the
                 Qumran Documents and some New
                 Testament Texts".
                 RevQ 5.345-360 (1964-66).

Pulver, M.   "Das Ergebnis des Penuma bei
                 Philon".
                 ErJb 13.111-132 (1945).

Rad, G. von   Wisdom in Israel.
                 London: S.C.M., 1972.

Rankin, O.S.   Israel's Wisdom Literature.
                 Its Bearing on Theology and the
                 History of Religion.
                 Edinburgh: T&T Clark, 1936.

Reese, J.A.   "Paul proclaims the Wisdom of
                 the Cross: Scandal and
                 Foolishness".
                 BTB 9.147-153 (1979).

Reicke, B.   "The Law and This World
                 according to Paul".
                 JBL 70.259-76 (1951).

Reider, J.   The Book of Wisdom.
                           New York: Harper & Brothers,
                           1957.

Reister, W.   "Die Sophia im Denken
                           Philonis".
                           161-164 in Frau Weisheit, ed.
                           B. Lang.
                           Düsseldorf: Patmos, 1975.

Rickenbacker, O.   Weisheitsperikopen bei Ben
                           Sira.
                           Freiburg: Universitats, 1973.

Rigaux, B.   "Révélation des Mystères et
                           Perfection à Qumran et dans le
                           Nouveau Testament".
                           NTS 4.237-262 (1957/58).

Ringgren, H.   The Faith of Qumran.
                           Philadelphia: Fortress, 1963.

Robertson, A.   A Critical and Exegetical
Plummer, A.   Commentary on the First Epistle
                           of Saint Paul to the
                           Corinthians.
                           Edinburgh: T&T Clark, 1911.

Romaniuk, C.   "Le Thème de la Sagesse dans
                           les Documents de Qumran".
                           RevQ 9.429-435 (1978).

Roon, A. van   "The Relation between Christ
                           and the Wisdom of God according
                           to Paul".
                           NT 16.207-239 (1974).

Rost, L.   Judaism Outside the Hebrew
                           Canon.
                           Nashville: Abingdon, 1976.

Roth, W.   "On the Gnomic-Discursive
                           Wisdom of Jesus Ben Sirach".
                           Semeia 17.59-79 (1980).

Rylaarsdam, J.C.   Revelation in Jewish Wisdom
                           Literature.
                           Chicago: University of Chicago,
                           1974=1946 edition.

Safari, S.
Stern, M.

The Jewish People in the First Century.
Assen: Van Gorcum and Comp. B.V., 1974 and 1976 - 2 volumes.

Sanders, E.P.

"The Covenant as a Soteriological Category and the Nature of Salvation in Palestinian and Hellenistic Judaism".
11-44 in Jews, Greeks, and Christians, eds. R.G. Hamerton-Kelly, and R. Scroggs.
(Leiden: E.J. Brill, 1976).

Paul and Palestinian Judaism.
Philadelphia: Fortress, 1977.

Sanders, J.A.

The Psalms Scroll of Qumran Cave 11.
Oxford: Clarendon, 1965.

Sandmel, S.

The First Christian Century in Judaism and Christianity.
New York: Harper & Row, 1969.

Philo's Place in Judaism. A Study of the Conceptions of Abraham in Jewish Literature.
New York: KTAV, 1971 - 2nd edition.

Judaism and Christian Beginnings.
New York: Oxford University, 1978.

Philo of Alexandria.
Oxford: Oxford University, 1979.

Sauer, A.

"Wisdom and Law in Old Testament Wisdom Literature".
CTM 43.600-609 (1972).

Scharlemann, M.H.

Qumran and Corinth.
New York: Bookman Associates, 1962.

Schlatter, A.   Der Korintherbrief.
                       Stuttgart: Calwer, 1950.

Schmithals, W.   Gnosticism in Corinth.
                       Nashville: Abingdon, 1971.

Schnackenburg, R.   "Christian Adulthood according
                       to the apostle Paul".
                       CBQ 25.354-370 (1963).

Schnider, F.   "The Church as a Building and
Stenger, W.   the Building-up of the Church".
                       Conc 10.21-34 (1972).

Schniewind, J.   Nachgelassene Reden und
                       Aufsatze.
                       Berlin: Akademie, 1952.

Schreiner, J.   "Geistbegabung in der Gemeinde
                       von Qumran".
                       BZ 9.161-180 (1965).

Scroggs, R.   "Paul: Σοφος and Πνευματικος".
                       NTS 14.33-55 (1967/68).

Senft, C.   La Première Épître de Saint
                       Paul aux Corinthiens.
                       Paris: Delachaux & Niestle,
                       1979.

Sheppard, G.T.   "Wisdom and Torah: The
                       Interpretation of Deuteronomy
                       underlying Sirach 24.23".
                       166-176 in Biblical and Near
                       Eastern Studies, ed. G.A.
                       Tuttle.
                       Grand Rapids: Eerdmans, 1978.

                       Wisdom as a Hermeneutical
                       Construct. A Study in the
                       Sapientializing of the Old
                       Testament.
                       Berlin: Walter de Gruyter,
                       1980.

Smend, R.   Die Weisheit des Jesus Sirach
                       Erklart.
                       Berlin: George Reiner, 1906.

Snaith, J.G.
"The Importance of Ecclesiasticus (The Wisdom of Ben Sira)".
ExpTim 75.66-69 (1963/64).

Ecclesiasticus or the Wisdom of Jesus son of Sirach.
Cambridge: Cambridge University, 1974.

Stadelmann, H.
Ben Sira als Schriftgelehrter. Eine Untersuchung zum Berüfsbild des vor-Makkaischen soper unter Berücksichtigung seines Verhaltnisses zu Priester, Prophten, und Weisheitslerertum.
Tübingen: J.C.B. Mohr, 1980.

Starobinski-Safran, E.
"La Lettrè et L'Esprit chêz Philon D'Alexandrie".
RCJ 10.43-51 (1976).

Suggs, M.J.
"The Lord is Near You: Romans 10.6-10".
289-316 in Christian History and Interpretation, eds. W. Farmer, C.F.D. Moule, and R. Niebuhr.
Cambridge: Cambridge University, 1967.

Tcherikover, V
Hellenistic civilization and the Jews.
New York: Atheneum, 1979=1959 edition.

Thackeray, H. St. John
The Septuagint and Jewish Worship.
London: Oxford University, 1921.

Thiselton, A.C.
"Realized Eschatology at Corinth".
NTS 24.510-26 (1978).

Thrall, M.E. The First and Second Letters of Paul to the Corinthians. Cambridge: Cambridge University, 1965.

Townsend, J.T. "1 Corinthians 3.10-15 and the School of Shammai". HTR 61.500-504 (1968).

Vaux, R. de Archaeology and the Dead Sea Scrolls. London: Oxford University, 1973.

Verbèke, G. L'Évolution de la Doctrine du Pneuma du Stoicisme à Saint Augustin. Paris: Desclée de Brouwer, 1945.

Vermes, G. "The Qumran Interpretation of Scripture in its Historical Setting". ALUOS 6.85-97 (1966-68).

The Dead Sea Scrolls in English. Harmondsworth: Penguin, 1975 - 2nd edition.

The Dead Sea Scrolls. Qumran in Perspective. London: Collins, 1977.

Vielhauer, P. Oikodome. Karlsrühe: Tron, 1940.

Weaver, M.J. Pneuma in Philo of Alexandria. An unpublished doctoral dissertation completed at Notre Dame University in 1973.

Wedderburn, A.J.M. "ἐν τῇ σοφίᾳ τοῦ θεοῦ - 1 Kor 1.21". ZNW 64.132-132 (1973).

Weiss, J. Der Erste Korintherbrief. Göttingen: Vandenhoeck & Rupprecht, 1970=1910 edition.

Weiss, J.   Earliest Christianity.
                             New York: Harper and Row,
                             1959=1939 edition - 2 volumes.

Wendland, H.   Die Briefe an die Korinther.
                             Göttingen: Vandenhoeck &
                             Rupprecht, 1965 - 11th edition.

Wernberg-Møller, P.   The Manual of Discipline.
                             Leiden: E.J. Brill, 1957.

                             "The Two Spirits in 1 QS
                             3.13-4.26".
                             RevQ 3.413-441 (1961).

Whedbee, J.H.   Isaiah and Wisdom.
                             Nashville: Abingdon, 1971.

Wieder, N.   "The 'Law-Interpreter' of the
                             sect of the Dead Sea Scrolls:
                             The Second Moses".
                             JJS 4.158-175 (1953).

Wilckens, U.   Weisheit und Torheit.
                             Tübingen: J.C.B. Mohr, 1959.

                             "Das Kreuz Christi als die
                             Tiefe der Weisheit Gottes zu 1
                             Kor 2.1-16".
                             43-81 in Paolo a Una Chiesa
                             Divisa, ed. L de Lorenzi.
                             Rome: Abbazia di S. Paolo Fuori
                             le Mura, 1980.

Wilson, R. McL.   Gnosis and the New Testament.
                             Oxford: Blackwell, 1968.

Winston, D.   The Wisdom of Solomon.
                             New York: Doubleday, 1979.

Winter, M.   Pneumatiker und Psychiker in
                             Korinth.
                             Marburg: N.G. Elwert, 1975.

Winter, P.   "Ben Sira and the Teaching of
                             the Two Ways".
                             VT 5.315-318 (1955).

255

Wolfson, H.A.   "The Philonic God of Revelation
                       and His Latter-day Deniers".
                       HTR 53.101-124 (1960).

                       Philo. Foundations of
                       Religious Philosophy in
                       Judaism, Christianity, and
                       Islam.
                       Cambridge Massachusettes:
                       Harvard University, 1962 - 2
                       volumes.

Worrell, J.E.   Concepts of Wisdom in the Dead
                       Sea Scrolls.
                       An unpublished doctoral
                       dissertation completed at
                       Claremont Graduate School in
                       1968.

Wuellner, W.   "Haggadic Homily Genre in 1
                       Corinthians 1-3".
                       JBL 89.199-204 (1970).

                       "The Soteriological
                       Implications of 1 Corinthians
                       1.26-28 Reconsidered".
                       666-672 in Studia Evangelica 6,
                       ed. E.A. Livingstone.
                       Berlin: Akademie, 1973.

                       "Ursprung und Verwendung der
                       σοφός, δυνάτος, εὐγενής Formel
                       in 1 Kor 1.26".
                       165-183 in Donum Gentilicum,
                       eds. E. Bammel, C.K. Barrett,
                       and W.D. Davies.
                       Oxford: Oxford University,
                       1978.

Yamauchi, E.M.   Pre-Christian Gnosticism.
                       London: Tyndale, 1973.

Zenger, E.   "Die Späte Weisheit und das
                       Gesetz".
                       43-56 in Literatür und Religion
                       des Frühjüdentums: Eine
                       Einführung, eds. J. Maier and
                       J. Schreiner.
                       Wurzburg: Echter, 1973.

Ziegler, J.   Sapientia <u>Salomonis</u>.
                       Gottingen: Vandenhoeck &
                       Rupprecht, 1962.

                       <u>Sapientia</u> <u>Iesu</u> <u>Filii</u> <u>Sirach</u>.
                       Gottingen: Vandenhoeck &
                       Rupprecht, 1965.

James A. Davis is presently Assistant Professor
of Biblical Studies at Trinity Episcopal School
for Ministry in Ambridge, Pennsylvania, having
been previously a Visiting Assistant Professor
in the Department of Philosophy and Religion at
Western Kentucky University. A graduate of the
College of Wooster   and   Trinity Evangelical
Divinity School, he is an ordained minister in
the Presbyterian Church (U.S.A.).   From 1979-82
he was engaged in research under the direction
of Dr. James D.G. Dunn at the University   of
Nottingham. The present book is a revised form
of the thesis for which he was awarded a Ph.D.
in 1982.